# THE RETURN OF CURIOSITY

## WHAT MUSEUMS ARE GOOD FOR IN THE 21ST CENTURY

*Nicholas Thomas*

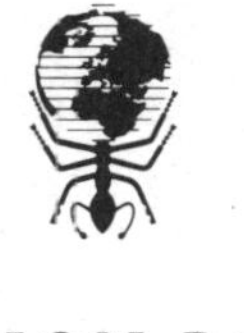

REAKTION BOOKS

*For Annie Coombes*

Published by Reaktion Books Ltd
Unit 32, Waterside
44–48 Wharf Road
London N1 7UX, UK
www.reaktionbooks.co.uk

First published 2016, reprinted 2017



Printed and bound in Great Britain by Bell & Bain, Glasgow

A catalogue record for this book is available from the British Library

ISBN 978 1 78023 656 8

‘Timely and rewarding . . . Thomas’s substantial track record and the wisdom he has garnered along the way enables Thomas to make a compelling and uplifting case for the power that museums have as a force for good in the twenty-first century.’ – *Science Museum Journal*

‘Nicholas Thomas’s *The Return of Curiosity* is a fresh and critical look at museums as sites of knowledge and wonder. He calls on museums to reveal the complexity of their collections as things with histories as things. This is not, he argues, “because everyone needs a lesson in the history of collection, but because the strange gathering of related stuff that constitutes the collection has a certain magic; it amounts to a realm of exploration that people ought to have the opportunity to enter and enjoy as well as understand.” Museum visitors have agency. And Thomas persuasively argues that museums should do everything in their power to encourage their visitors to follow their curiosities. For “this curiosity, this questioning is a skill . . . [And] that is what, for all of their faults, museums are good for in the twenty-first century.” I couldn’t agree more.’ – James Cuno, President and CEO, The J. Paul Getty Trust

‘An intelligent, balanced and reflective overview of what it is, exactly, that matters about museums at the moment – a broad question that should concern all present or would-be museum professionals, and any general reader who cares about the place of material culture in contemporary life.’ – Stephen Deuchar, Director, The Art Fund

‘I breathe a sigh of relief that so fine a scholar should have written such a sober and well-informed account of the positive role of museums of all kinds. Let us hope that critics, trustees, bureaucrats, and patrons pay attention.’ – Ivan Gaskell, Professor of Cultural History and Museum Studies and Head of the Focus Project, Bard Graduate Center

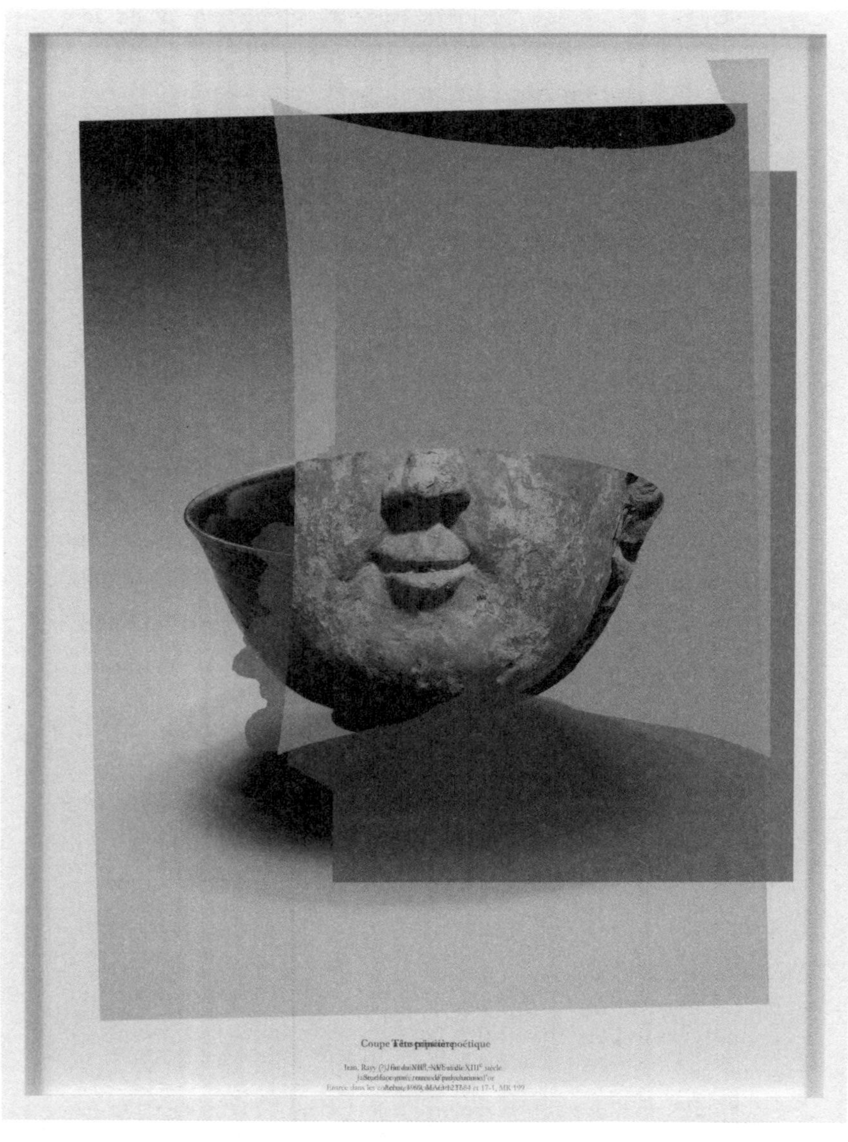

Walid Raad, *Preface to the Third Edition (Édition française), Plate III*, 2012, archival colour inkjet print.

# CONTENTS

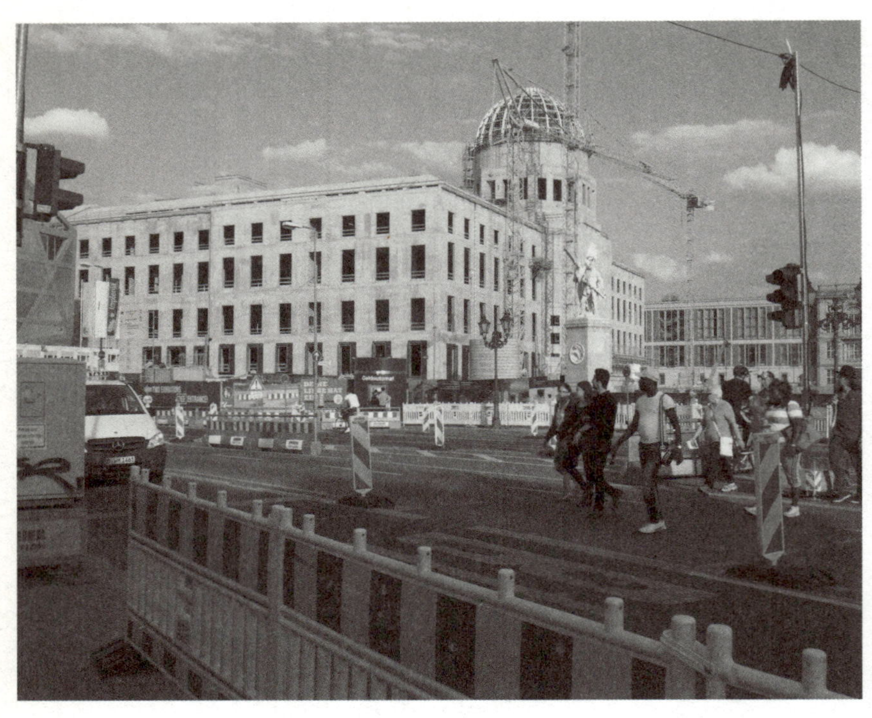

Mark Adams, 2015. *Schlossplatz, Berlin. The Humboldt-Forum under Construction*, digital file.

# INTRODUCTION

Since the turn of the millennium, the world we inhabit has changed: as is commonly observed, the war on terror, the actuality of climate change and the emergence of social media have had profound and diverse impacts on the lives of people globally. Among many other changes, one is striking and it motivates this book, even though, if asked to list the big social or cultural shifts of our time, few people would be likely to mention museums. But these institutions, which started out as expressions of Renaissance erudition, have undergone a kind of belated adolescence, growing suddenly in fits and starts, assuming new attitudes and responsibilities, demanding and obtaining attention and money. Museums, in the twenty-first century, loom larger than they ever have before. They are more socially and economically vital, they seek to offer their publics more and they arguably succeed in doing so in those countries in which they have long been established. And new museums are being founded, on both a humble and a grand scale, and finding supporters and audiences in many communities and nations in which they were not previously significant.

It is symptomatic of this rapid growth and change that museums are much noticed and discussed: in the news media, in practitioners' conferences and journals and by way of wider critical and scholarly commentary.[1] Yet the voluminous writings and various genres seem not to address or account for the formidable importance that museums have assumed – almost unexpectedly, given how commonly it was thought, until just recently, that the efflorescence of digital culture would render physical collections and museum visits redundant. Professionals write about advances in conservation, cataloguing systems and museum education; those in museum studies are preoccupied with the politics of exhibitions and community representation; commentators on the 'creative industries' remark on the scale of investment in culture and the growth of tourism and tax revenues; architectural critics appraise buildings and precincts, among them some of the most adventurous and spectacular presences in new cityscapes. Much of this literature is illuminating, about the histories of collections, the outcomes of negotiations with indigenous people, the promise and possibilities of online outreach and many other issues. But we seem not to be asking what it is about museums that enables them to appeal to millions of new visitors, and that empowers ambitious claims, not just to educate and entertain people, but to tell all our stories, foster social cohesion, further international diplomacy, empower advanced research and deliver a diverse range of other social and economic benefits.[2] There is something about material culture in the distinctively assembled form of the collection that now enlivens the museum, I suggest, rendering it, at best, surprisingly fertile and socially progressive – even if effective in less instrumental terms than museum advocates sometimes claim.

This book draws together issues and contexts that have mostly been discussed separately. It is interested in the larger social and economic drivers of museum renewal, but also in the qualities of collections and the particular oddities of museum artefacts, such as their cataloguing and labelling. I try to get to grips with the ways museums may foster civil society and reflect on the much-rehashed issue of repatriation, but also address questions that may be less familiar, questioning assumptions around what I call – by way of deliberate oxymoron – the 'natural artefact'. I treat the museum as something like an archaeological site, a manifold set of deposits that offer lenses upon human creativity, human history and environmental change, but am concerned also to think prospectively about the potential of collections, arguing that they represent a creative technology, a means of making new things.

A good deal of the museum studies literature has focused on renowned national institutions and so-called universal survey museums, such as the Louvre and the British Museum. Curators of art have theorized contemporary practice and exhibition-making extensively. And many commentators have joined the argument about ethnographic and archaeological collections such as those of the Pitt Rivers, the American Museum of Natural History and the Pergamon, undeniably products of the imperial age, presumed now to be targets of the world's repatriation claims.[3] This book may be unusual for ranging over art, anthropology, science and history museums, and the spectrum from great metropolitan institutions to local collections in out-of-the-way places. While this means that what I have to say may suffer the weakness of all generalization, and is certainly more apt for some cases than others, my gamble is that affinities between science and art collections, among others, may be unexpected and revealing. Mixing things up helps deepen our sense of what museums per se, as opposed to specific kinds of institutions, are good for in the twenty-first century.

If cross-disciplinary enquiry has its hazards, I am also well aware that there are profound differences from nation to nation in how museums operate. In Britain, national and local governments, among other public agencies, are interested in museums' effectiveness in fostering social inclusion. In the United States, campaigns to win and sustain the support of private donors influence activities across the board. Yet rather than consider every setting singular, I hope to acknowledge the varied expressions of wider trends – affinities being notable, despite differing national settings, not least because curators, designers, directors, architects and culture ministers travel, meet each other, share ideas and draw on each other's languages, framing problems and approaching solutions in terms that borrow internationally. This book is inevitably weighted towards examples I know best, from Britain; it also reflects the crossovers of my working life, between art and anthropology, between museums of art and those often now called 'world cultures' museums, once those of ethnology or *für Völkerkunde*. Yet it draws also on wider experience I have been fortunate to have in a variety of curatorial, research and advisory roles, in relation to history, maritime and science collections, as well as those of art and anthropology, in various parts of Asia, Europe, the Pacific and North America. It draws too on the time I have spent in many museums, as a parent and rank-and-file visitor.

Moreover, if the old anthropology and natural history museums appear the poor cousins of the great art institutions – in most countries, the most prominent and most visited of all museums – the former have been paradoxically influential. Decades ago, the curators of ethnographic collections felt themselves challenged. The sense that they had to engage with so-called source communities – the descendants of people from whom collections were obtained – led not just to dialogue but to new ways of undertaking curatorial work, conservation and public programming. Though inevitably complex and sometimes frustrating for both communities and curators, this has proved a deeply rewarding process of sharing knowledge (more than just an expression of moralistic correctness). What started out as experiments arising from painful and contentious histories of dispossession, and from the present significance of collections made in the past, has become business as usual. Public engagement and responsiveness to community are now, in diverse respects, vital to the orientation and work of museums of all kinds.

My title, *The Return of Curiosity*, may perplex some. Isn't curiosity, they might ask, more a personal trait, or an attribute of humanity in general, that has neither gone nor come back? The suggestion that avid interest in novel things, experiences and situations may be a human propensity in a deep sense is an intriguing one. Those interested in the evolution of our species' behaviour might take the view that our capacity to venture into and indeed to dominate many environments, to find not only diverse ways of subsisting but a capacity to generate surpluses, enabling the extraordinary elaboration of society that has unfolded (for better or worse) over human history, has all been made possible by curiosity. If we had never wanted to try eating something different, test a novel technique or see a new place, it is hard to see how or why experiments in agriculture and technology, travel or cross-cultural trade should ever have taken place.[4]

In any case, curiosity has also been conceived and valued differently over time, especially over the period marked by the ascendancy of mercantile capitalism, when the moral implications of people's seemingly insatiable appetite for new things assumed greater, and evidently problematic, economic and political significance. Edmund Burke's classic treatise of 1757, *A Philosophical Enquiry into the Origin of Our Ideas of the Sublime and Beautiful*, began by dismissing curiosity as a skittish attitude of children – arousal by mere novelty – to be juxtaposed with the mature and masculine exercise of reason and judgement. 'The most superficial of all the affections . . . an appetite which is very sharp, but very easily satisfied . . . it has always an appearance of giddiness, restlessness, and anxiety,' he wrote.[5] There is also a long history to the idea, familiar to anyone who has read the Curious George stories to children, that curiosity gets you into trouble. If it would be entertaining to trace the bad reputation that this propensity has had, awkwardly balanced by the celebration of inquisitiveness in Samuel Johnson's *Dictionary*, and otherwise in science, over the centuries, that would be tangential to the purposes of this book.

Most recently, it is specifically cross-cultural curiosity that has been disparaged. It has been stigmatized, as a more or less unintended consequence of the ascendancy of postcolonial studies and the politics of identity, which have dismissed travellers', Orientalists' and anthropologists' accounts of non-European cultures as ideological constructions directly or indirectly intended to affirm the dynamic and progressive qualities of the West, relative to traditional orders elsewhere. While critical consideration of the intellectual and cultural expressions of colonialism was certainly overdue, and much so-called scholarship concerned with the non-European world was indeed woefully prone to rehash stereotypes, the arguments led to a surprisingly widespread sense that interest in cultures beyond the West was in itself improper, as if not just tainted by colonial attitudes, but inherently an appropriation. Advocates of the 'decolonization' of knowledge argued that indigenous scholars were equipped to articulate valid understandings of history and culture, based in customary concepts that were often profoundly different to those of European thought; anthropologists, it was suggested, ought to stay at home and study their own cultures, and indeed many did so.

This was far from just a set of squabbles among scholars and activists. More generally, affirmations of ethnicity and renewed interest in national identity fostered a sense that people needed to know their own cultures and histories. Hence in contexts ranging from those of national independence in Africa, liberation following the collapse of the Soviet Union, national reimagining in settler societies such as New Zealand and Australia and growing interests in independence in Scotland, a possessiveness and an introversion came to be explicitly or implicitly upheld. A 'national museum' was no longer just the major state-supported museum in the particular country; it was also a museum *of* the nation, one dedicated to its own story and identity. From Australia to Estonia there are such museums that actually hold significant international collections but do not exhibit them, considering material from outside the nation to be outside the remit of the nation's museum. If this trend implied a narrowing of focus and imagination, the picture was always contradictory, as the art world became more inclusive and cosmopolitan, even if it tended to celebrate internationally intelligible contemporary styles, rather than a wider range of global cultural expressions, some of which were less easily converted into biennale and art-fair currencies.

Twenty years ago, the great British cultural theorist Stuart Hall asked, 'Who needs identity?' If, in some milieux, languages of national heritage and belonging remain persuasive, Hall provocatively suggested that identities were both 'necessary' and 'impossible'.[6]

In history and related fields, many scholars have drawn attention to the formative character of travel, trade and migration in the constitution of societies. Some places are more obviously cosmopolitan than others, but I cannot think of a modern human community not shaped by histories of interaction and movement. It is a truism that the present is a time of globalization, and it is true that economies around the world are interconnected as never before, that various forms of online communication connect us to an unprecedented degree and that international corporations and cross-border, quasi-governmental institutions are more constraining of and otherwise salient to our daily lives than formerly. Yet in other senses, trans-oceanic and transcontinental trading systems, pilgrimages, migrations, diasporas and mixed populations, exotic objects and ideas have been the stuff of human history for millennia. 'Ethnic identity' and 'national heritage' may be very much alive today, but in their purer expressions they are the cultural counterparts of a political and economic axiom consigned to the past – Stalin's 'socialism in one country' – and are about as valid and sustainable.

If economic recessions typically render governments unpopular, the fallout during the second decade of the twenty-first century has been unusually harsh. In many countries the cycle of disenchantment has accelerated, as oppositions have been elected and rejected in succession, and fringe parties with no identity other than hostility to immigrants, such as the Front National in France, have made dramatic advances into the mainstream. Whether they can hold onto or build on that support in the future remains to be seen, but the current climate fosters the myth of rupture that has been a defining characteristic of modern culture for centuries: people are highly invested in the notion that we inhabit a world that has suffered unprecedented change, that formerly stable and coherent societies are now unstable, dynamic and heterogeneous. While great changes have indeed taken place since 2000, most generations of recent centuries could feel the same way, and there is nothing new about immigration. What is not novel, but nevertheless urgent, is the challenge of fostering understandings of community, identity, history and nation that reflect the interconnected, migratory and entangled qualities of our histories. Multiculturalism may be a political project that has been more or less controversial at various times, but it is also an inescapable and irreversible condition of many past and present societies – now the overwhelming majority of societies – that needs to be fully acknowledged rather than denied, its inevitable conflicts and difficulties, as well as its fertility and richness, understood. Curiosity may be, as Burke suggested, an unstable attitude, but it is marked by an eagerness to encounter what is new or unfamiliar, an openness to difference and perhaps a willingness to suspend judgement.

People often go to museums to see works and objects that are already canonized, such as the paintings that we are all supposed to see before we die; in practice, what's often more rewarding about visits to exhibitions and collections are unexpected discoveries of pieces that may be minor in art-historical terms or otherwise supposedly of secondary interest but that appeal to you nevertheless, that enable you to know something new or that take you somewhere you have not previously been. Being curious enables us to travel in this fashion, but it surely also equips us better to acquire an awareness of the societies we all now inhabit, and to act and live within them.

This book argues that the revitalization of museums reflects not only planners' and politicians' ambitions and interests, among other social and economic trends, but a return to curiosity. Many historians have discussed museums' emergence from cabinets of curiosity, as if arbitrary accumulations on the part of acquisitive dilettantes were succeeded by reputably systematic art and science collections. The narrative points to the vital association between the artefacts and the attitude – curiosities provoked curiosity and vice versa, we suppose – but overlooks an intriguing qualification to Burke's diatribe, that for all its faults, curiosity was inescapable, it 'blends itself more or less with all our passions'.[7] This is a consequential admission, and implies that this eager, suspect desire never could quite have been expurgated from the constitution of the museum. In any case, my claim is that what is good about museums in the present responds to and sustains curiosity of all kinds, and that curiosity is moreover fertile and necessary, not only for people in general, but specifically for those of us alive in the twenty-first century.

The first of this book's three main chapters reviews the reinvigoration of museums that is at once astonishing, yet difficult to track, because it has involved many more or less related strands, some of which date back to the 1970s and even the 1960s, but which gained greater momentum only from the 1990s onwards. While it is important to touch on this renewal's various aspects, ranging from interests in museums as drivers of urban regeneration to the new, mass appeal of contemporary art, I hope not to lapse into the journalistic register of 'trendspotting'. I ask what it is about entering collections, and what it is about museums as civic spaces of a singular sort, that gives them the potential they appear now to have.

In the second chapter I turn to the constitution of collections, which I argue are not just masses of works and things, but stranger and more surprising assemblages than we have appreciated. In place of what I suggest are three misleading naturalisms, of heritage, the collection and the artefact, which imply essentially fixed physical identities and forms of belonging, I try to bring into view the sense in which collections are made up, above all, of relations – with identifications in the form of labels and catalogue entries, with other artefacts and images, with histories, with people. These manifold relations amount to shape-shifting networks, but the word 'network' is unhelpfully diagrammatic and diminishes the substance of the issue here. The things that connect are not merely geometric points, but more or less remarkable works and objects that have their own telling qualities.

Third, none of this would matter so much if collections were above all resources for the understanding of the present and the past – even if they are peculiarly rich ones, revelations of natural and human histories, cultural diversity, human creativity and extraordinary personal stories. If they were only those things, they could still be of special importance – if, that is, they are not locked away, but accessible to those interested in them, those who might explore the past through them. But collections do not merely enrich our senses of where we have come from, of the constitution of the cultures we inhabit; they are also resources for the future, creative technologies that people can use to create new things.

The conclusion returns to the wider social question of what, in our time, museums have to offer. Since this book could be seen to be at odds with mainstream museum studies – a critical literature that has seen museums above all as challenged, flawed and in retreat – it should be stressed at the outset that the discussion is not intended to be triumphalist. Often in museums I am, no doubt like many other visitors, disappointed by displays that seem facile, unimaginative or inadequately representative. The creative potential that I celebrate depends on institutions' openness, and especially on the accessibility of collections, which too often is constrained by poor facilities, a lack of resources and unfortunately just a lack of will. Well-intentioned projects can anyway lapse into traps of various kinds, familiar to curators, designers and other practitioners. And the 'success' of exhibitions and such projects as new museum developments is relative, many-faceted and, to state the obvious, a matter of opinion. Some institutions may 'succeed' for the wrong reasons, or in terms that appear partial, not least because, if one quality is inevitable in museum work, it is compromise. Curators and museum-makers must contend with masses of special and fragile physical stuff, with constraints upon money, space and time, as well as, equally importantly, belief in whatever it is that they aim to accomplish. To a greater degree than scholarly theorization, museum work is emphatically 'in the world' – it negotiates between what may be desirable, acceptable and feasible. And the task has become no easier: what is possible has diminished and continues to contract, as we endure a lengthening period of austerity. All that said, this book is written out of tentative optimism. For all their faults and compromises, museums have a new vitality; they have more to offer than we used to think and may even be places in which the most intractable antagonisms and inequities of our time are addressed and redressed.

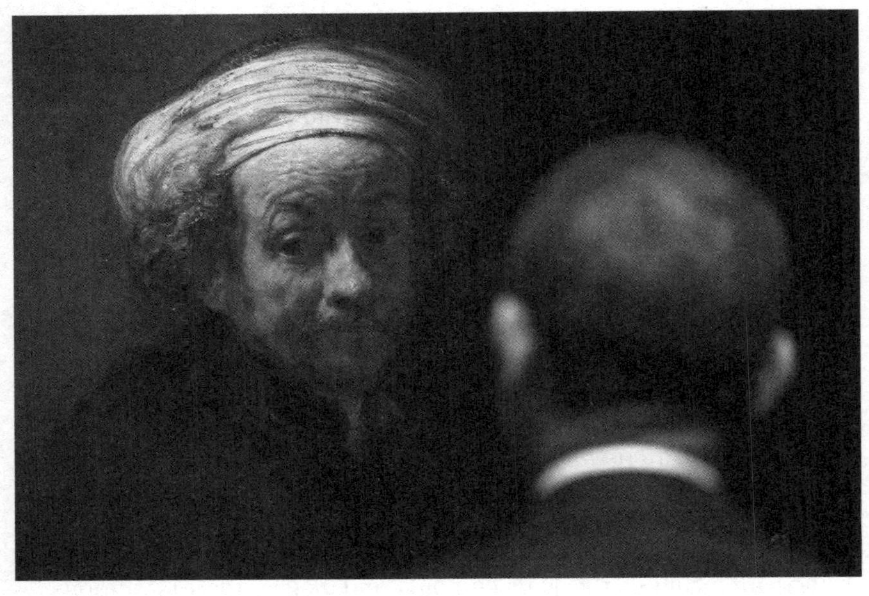

Barack Obama at the Rijksmuseum, Amsterdam, 24 March 2014.

I

# THE ASCENDANCY OF THE MUSEUM

Museums make grand claims: to represent the natural world, to narrate civilization, to survey the arts. Even on a more local scale, there may be much at stake in a promise to tell the story of a district or a town. So it is not surprising that, for as long as they have been around, museums have been controversial and have had both advocates and detractors. Over the last decades of the twentieth century, the detractors were most vocal. It was a period marked by mounting criticism of museums by commentators and scholars from many disciplines, as well as by a succession of often damaging public controversies. Museums were lambasted variously as temples of elite culture, warehouses of colonial loot and hegemonic institutions – instruments of the state created to inculcate ideologies and hierarchies. This was part and parcel of the late twentieth-century sea change in the humanities, marked by political and philosophical challenges to traditional methods, disciplines and the cultural canon. But there were also broader shifts that eroded the status of the museum: in the field of art, for example, the vital new practices from the 1970s onwards had been site-specific, on the body, performative and public. If art museums have since found ways of representing and canonizing the corporeal and ephemeral, it seemed for a time that these practices neither needed nor wanted the traditional institutions.[1] And as digital and online media emerged in the 1990s, museums appeared just too static, just too physical, to be vital presences within the emerging environment.

Many people had, in any case, long thought of museums as places for dead things. In the 1960s, the Frankfurt School philosopher Theodor Adorno referred to the 'unpleasant overtones' of the German adjective *museal* (museum-like) that referred to objects 'in the process of dying'. Chris Marker and Alain Resnais' film essay *Les Statues meurent aussi* (1953), about African works in Western museums, had already rendered the proposition anti-colonial.[2] From an opposed political position, Margaret Thatcher said much the same thing in the 1980s, by which time museums were thought to be dying themselves.[3] Books with titles such as *On the Museum's Ruins* appeared.[4] When the historian and theorist Gyan Prakash wrote in 1996 that 'A sense prevails today that museums have become history – finished, exhausted, lifeless,' this was surely correct as an evocation of the commentary of the period.[5] The museum might be where you took your child to see a dinosaur, but at worst it seemed a dinosaur itself, a bulky and cumbersome creature, devoid of vitality, if not actually extinct. And indeed, in the 1980s, if museums of natural history and anthropology were often dusty, art museums tended to be staid; what they had in common was that they were uninviting.

Yet, in hindsight, it is hard to think of another context in which scholars and cultural critics have been so badly wrong-footed. The last twenty to thirty years have not witnessed the obsolescence, the redundancy or the decline of the museum. To the contrary, the period has been remarkable for renewal, and the process was already well and truly under way when Prakash diagnosed exhaustion. It is unhelpful to argue that there was any single moment or turning point when museums came to be seen, or seen again, as vital and fertile places – the history has been too uneven to be narrated in these terms. Yet among landmark events must be counted the inauguration of the Centre Georges Pompidou in Paris in 1977. The combination of the building's radicalism and the simplicity of its architectural concept – its instantly famous revelation of pipework, of services and infrastructure – exemplified the claim of democratization. The pitch for a new audience was moreover facilitated by the openness of the Place Beaubourg, the museum's situation in the midst of a café quartier. An eighteen-year-old Australian in Paris for the first time, I happened to visit the Pompidou within a year of its opening, in the spring of 1978. Some combination of Henri Michaux's esoteric inscriptions (one of the centre's first temporary shows), a light-headed mood the morning after a long party, my impressionable nature at the time, made the place seem not just cool, but a point of entry into a new world. I was certainly unsophisticated, but I suspect far from alone among young people at that time, who found the Pompidou far more enticing than the aloof facades we associated with the standard art gallery. The 'new museum' was an architectural event, an architectural movement, to which museology itself would in fits and starts play catch-up.[5]

Over the period since, governments, foundations and sponsors of all kinds have spent an unprecedented amount of time, money and energy on museums. The closing decades of the nineteenth century and those of the early twentieth saw the establishment of many great city, university and state collections in Europe, North America and elsewhere, but the proliferation of new, extended, renovated and rehoused institutions over the last twenty or so years has amounted to something else again. The sheer number of art galleries, science, history, archaeology and world cultures museums has increased dramatically, as has that of local heritage, single-artist, special interest and other often quirky smaller museums.[7] So, moreover, has the scale of activity – blockbusters, biennales and busy events programmes are business as usual, and even smaller institutions mount changing displays, offer concerts and talks in galleries, run programmes for schools and friends' evenings, make collections accessible online and try to build constituencies through social media. The phenomenon of museum growth has been energized from the bottom up as well as from the top down.[8]

Among instances of this wave of development that might be cited: Canada, New Zealand and Australia are some of the countries in which new museums of the nation have been created, opening in 1989, 1998 and 2001 respectively. Each of these societies had been (as they still are) engaged in a protracted and painful reassessment of dealings between settlers and indigenous peoples, and the new museums' many tasks included the reimagining of national histories.[9] All have had moments of controversy but proved considerably more popular than forecast. In Paris, new art museums with specific remits such as the Musée d'Orsay (primarily nineteenth-century French art) and the Musée du quai Branly (world art) have been successfully established in Paris, bringing the number of museums in the city to around 150. Seven hundred journalists attended the press preview of the reopening in 2013, following a decade of reconstruction, of the Rijksmuseum in Amsterdam.[10] During his visit in March 2014, Barack Obama was photographed contemplating Rembrandt's *Self-portrait as the Apostle Paul* of 1661, as if carefully advertising the precious moment of reflection that the art museum offers those leading the most demanding of possible lives. In Berlin, a series of relocations and renovations have reconstituted the Museumsinsel in the Spree; one of Europe's largest current museum development projects involves the creation of the Humboldt-Forum, a world cultures institution, in the reconstructed palace, the Stadtschloss, on an adjacent site.[11] The foundation of a 'museum island' on the Berlin model has become an aspiration of city leaders, even where they do not have a literal island for the purpose. In London, the Tate evolved from a single-site institution to a consortium in which Tate Modern looms largest. So vital has this vibrant institution become to the cultural life of the capital that it is hard to believe that the Herzog & de Meuron conversion of the Bankside power station opened to the public just fifteen years ago. It is now one of the three most visited tourist attractions in the country and has recently undergone substantial expansion.

In the nineteenth century, the business of museum-making was largely the province of the West and its settler colonies, though the establishment of national art and natural history museums from 1818 onwards in (what were at the time) the prosperous creole nations of Argentina, Brazil and Chile should not be overlooked. The Indian Museum in Kolkata recently celebrated its bicentenary; institutions were established in Egypt from 1835 on, and in Japan in the 1870s. Today the geographic distribution of projects of museum-making is very uneven, but there are hotspots scattered around the globe. In the Emirates, collaborations with the Louvre and the British Museum promise the creation of museums of art and civilization on the grandest scale. These partnerships have proved lucrative for the European partners: Abu Dhabi paid U.S.$520 million merely for the association with the Louvre brand, while fees for curatorial advice and loans bring the overall value of the deal to around a billion euros. The British Museum's collaboration with the Zayed National Museum is more limited in scope, but is believed nevertheless to be worth some U.S.$10 million a year.[12] The conditions of employment of the primarily South Asian labour force have made these projects controversial; they have also attracted the scrutiny of the Lebanese artist Walid Raad, whose playful but serious works around the theme include evocations of strangely vacant, hyper-monumental spaces and prints of superimposed artefacts (see frontispiece), such that their qualities are confused and their captions illegible.[13]

A recent five-year plan by the Chinese government sought to bring the number of museums in the country to 3,500, a target said to have been achieved several years ahead of schedule; a further 451 museums were opened in 2012.[14] As astonishing as the capital commitment is the implication that a vastly expanded cohort of curators, conservators, museum educators and administrators have been trained, in turn implying an efflorescence of museum studies programmes in the country's universities – though it is also reported that many of the new institutions have struggled both to recruit staff and to assemble collections. But if there is something unrealistic about the pace of this museum-making campaign, it is fully consistent with the Chinese state's longstanding effort to present itself as the inheritor of a four-thousand-year-old civilization and its engagement with UNESCO's World Heritage project. China has some 45 designated sites, more than any country other than Italy.

While hybrid war memorials and museums have existed for many years, a new form of memorial museum, most influentially conceived by Daniel Libeskind, commemorates and interprets historic atrocities, the approach to the Holocaust being adapted to

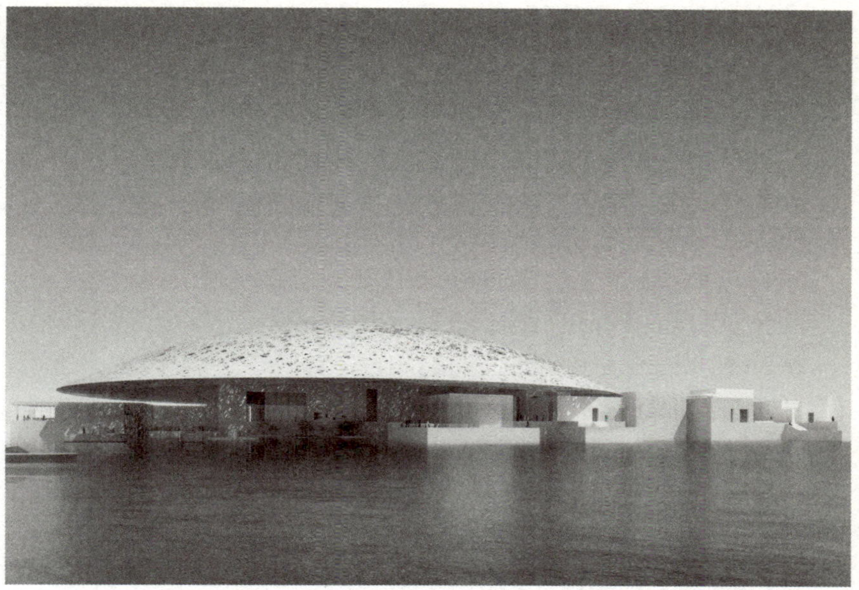

The Louvre Abu Dhabi: the architect's visualization.

deal with other histories of genocide, slavery, repression and political violence. While museums have represented history in various ways for as long as they have existed, they have increasingly become places in which difficult histories are revealed and reassessed – they are, or are in part, 'sites of conscience'.[15] The tasks that museums are asked to perform have become larger and more consequential as well as merely more diverse.

In and around major institutions in many countries, ambitious extensions and renovations, often involving new civic spaces, have almost become the norm. Regional and local museums are similarly being refurbished on relatively smaller but still significant scales. Given widespread antipathy toward most kinds of major public investment, it is surprising that so few of these developments have been dismissed as white elephants. Few indeed have failed to substantially increase visitor numbers. The British Museum and the Metropolitan Museum of Art have in recent years received 6.7 and 6.8 million visitors per annum, while the Louvre brings in more than 10 million, of whom about two-thirds are international tourists.[16] Even a university collection such as that of the Pitt Rivers in Oxford, which was once quiet and quaint, has been transformed into a vigorous public museum with hundreds of thousands of visitors annually and busy outreach and education programmes.

New museums, grand developments and more visitors are not aspects of a single trend, but of related trends, manifested differently and unevenly in different countries and in different museum environments. Nor does success, however judged, necessarily indicate that all the varied critiques of museums were simply 'wrong' or unjustified. To be sure, some claims were overstated, even absurd. Douglas Crimp proposed in 1980 that alongside the asylum, clinic and prison, the museum was an 'institution of confinement' awaiting Foucault-inspired analysis. Whether the public, the curators or the artworks themselves were considered its unhappy inmates remained unspecified.[17]

Yet, among other provocations, Pierre Bourdieu and Alain Darbel's *L'Amour de l'art* – an influential earlier account of the propensity of art museums to reinforce the confidence and status of the privileged while conversely disempowering others – was arguably valid at the time the surveys upon which it was based were undertaken, in the early to mid-1960s, and for a good many years afterwards.[18] If its thesis is less obviously so today, that is precisely because such arguments motivated change. Many governments have pressed museums to be more inclusive, and gone as far as making some funding dependent on 'widening participation', in UK government jargon – that is, increasing engagement on the part of less affluent social groups. At a more individual level, in many museums the person who leads education or public programmes probably read Bourdieu and Darbel while undertaking a museum studies degree, or at any rate is familiar with the issues of exclusion that the book raised. In England, by 2012–13 public participation in the cultural sector passed a symbolic mark in the sense that over half of all adults visited a museum or gallery during the year. Even the figure for lower socio-economic groups increased to just under 40 per cent.[19] These, like most statistics, are no more than uncontextualized indicators. (They also reflect the fact that, since 2000, free general admission has become the norm for public institutions in the United Kingdom; this is also the case in Australia and New Zealand, but is relatively uncommon otherwise.) However, the numbers do suggest that the exclusion identified and censured in *L'Amour de l'art* has been partially ameliorated. While – in societies seemingly marked not merely by persistent, but growing, inequality – there can be no complacency about the challenges of increasing access, we have nevertheless witnessed a sea change.

In a different political domain, contention around the question of repatriation has in no sense diminished. The issues tend to be misconstrued in the media; it is assumed that people in any and every former colony want historic objects brought back, whereas interests in expatriate artefacts are in fact very heterogeneous. Antiquities and artefacts are not invariably or necessarily perceived as cultural property or heritage. Those with fundamentalist Christian or Islamic commitments, for example, often disown images associated with earlier traditions or animist ancestors. Others who seek fervently to participate more fully in modernity and the world of consumption may just be indifferent, while those who do care may be sceptical regarding the commitment and the capacity of weak postcolonial states to look after great and fragile ancestral work, or positively supportive of their arts' presence in prestigious metropolitan museums. A discourse of the 'object as ambassador' has emerged – an argument of some indigenous artists and leaders, notably from the Pacific, that artworks help champion their cultures and causes and may be appropriately and proudly displayed in the Louvre, the Metropolitan or the museums belonging to prestigious universities.[20] On the other hand, wherever the issue arises, communities tend to agree that human remains should be repatriated. Notwithstanding the opposition of biological anthropologists, there is increasing preparedness on the part of governments and museums to do so. At the same time, the traffic in looted antiquities – which has escalated in recent years with conflict in Iraq and Syria – has come under sustained scrutiny. Leading museums, ranging from the Getty to the National Gallery of Australia, have been caught out disregarding international protocols, or otherwise woefully failing to exercise due diligence, in establishing that important classical and Asian works were legitimately available to them.[21]

From the 1980s onwards, heritage and museum studies were increasingly widely taught and a scholarly literature burgeoned, which embraced on the one hand technical guidance in fields such as museum education, cataloguing and conservation, and on the other critical theory focused on issues of representation and politics. Museums were taken to be suffering an ongoing crisis of legitimacy, and their claims to represent cultures and histories were considered questionable. The engagements with cultural critique and the politics of difference were, needless to say, part of the zeitgeist, but ironically the oppositional stance was more or less officially embraced: the two must-read anthologies, *Exhibiting Cultures* (1991) and *Museums and Communities* (1992), were published by the Smithsonian 'in cooperation with' the American Association of Museums, the main U.S. organization representing the sector, and with the support of the Rockefeller Foundation. 'The inherent contestability of museum exhibitions is bound to open the choices made in those exhibitions to heated debate,' the first of these collections announced. 'Groups attempting . . . to assert their social, political and economic claims in the larger world challenge the right of established institutions to control the presentation of their cultures.'[22] Though there was much of value in the two books, and though the essays were inevitably eclectic, this notion that representation was everywhere contested, and such contestation the dominant issue of our time, was the sound bite – the issue that the books put in the spotlight. The debate was undoubtedly important but soon became repetitive, and it is striking that journal articles, conferences and collections of essays that rehash the same themes continue to appear.

Given that commentators and students were preoccupied with questions of 'representation' and the politics of identity that underpinned the rhetoric of the period, the response – almost necessarily, but in any case constructively – took the form of dialogue and collaboration between museums and communities: people would have a say in how they and their cultures and traditions were represented. This in turn raised (and continues to raise) the question of whether the museum was typically a place that marginalized or formerly colonized people could enter comfortably. Less adequately examined has been the more general question of who or what constituted 'community'. If this notion was too anodyne or no longer fit for purpose in disciplines such as sociology, it was powerfully reinvigorated in the museum context, essentially as shorthand for prospectively interested people beyond the institution itself. In any event, a commitment to engage became increasingly central to curatorial practice, especially but not exclusively among those charged with the care of ethnographic collections.[23]

Consultative protocols and processes emerged early in the former settler colonies where museums were located among, or in close proximity to, aboriginal groups, and in the United States, where from 1990 the Native American Graves Protection and Repatriation Act (NAGPRA) required that federally funded museums return human remains and funerary and sacred objects to native descendants. Until the 1990s there was something of a gulf between the expectations and approaches to work in Auckland, Denver, Sydney and Vancouver, on the one hand, and on the other those in European museums, far away from native peoples and less subject to immediate pressure from them. If there continue to be clear differences of orientation, the ground has shifted, and it is notable that (for example) senior curators of the Pacific at major museums in London, Paris and New York include (at the time of writing) individuals of indigenous descent. More generally, as air travel became cheaper, not only curators but community activists and artists travelled more frequently, and in due course online conversation became routine. It became practically possible, as well as desirable on moral and other grounds, to initiate and sustain dialogue. No big exhibition on Benin, on the Maori or on the Inuit would today be conceived without consultation, though people often approach dialogue with different aims and hopes, and the process has sometimes been engaged in to forestall criticism rather than with real preparedness to acknowledge and accommodate local or indigenous interests. Behind the scenes, many rewarding projects have focused on collections, documentation, archives, digitization and conservation. Artefacts that for decades, in some cases for centuries, had languished in storage came, together with associated images and archives, to be accessible and available again to interested community members. The move towards collaboration, the emergence of the museum as a 'contact zone' and the scope for a new traffic in information and images has amounted to a sea change hardly imaginable a generation ago, and one that has been both positive and of fundamental importance.[24]

Repatriation is, to borrow the language of consumer electronics, 'pre-loaded' with potent assumptions about cultural property, identity, collectivity and belonging. It is also an issue that carries a rhetorical charge. When former Scottish National Party leader Alex Salmond advocated the 'return' of the Lewis chess pieces from the British Museum (thought to have been made in Norway, but excavated in Scotland's Outer Hebrides) he used an iconic set of artefacts to convey that charge, to empower claims about heritage and sovereignty.[25] This sort of argument, in which the pieces themselves and their ownership and location give concreteness to the more encompassing nationalist proposition, is quite different to the kinds of negotiations taking place between curators and members of so-called source communities, the descendants of peoples who made the objects that now form collections. One takes place via the media, in the political sphere; the other is no less political but works itself out through tribal and museum diplomacy, and most importantly through personal contact, both within the community and museum, and between the two. Repatriation appears, in the world of public politics, to be a zero-sum contest, but engagement over time, in the oddly intimate settings of museum stores and workrooms, has tended to result in an interest in sustaining relationships. Certain forms of curatorial authority, or comprehensive sets of digital images, may be 'repatriated'; a language of 'custodianship' may be adopted; objects are shared through long-term loan; metropolitan museums may fund training, internships or other programmes for members of the indigenous communities in question, and otherwise seek to build skills and be seen to contribute.[26]

These engagements are ideally, and in practice often, continuing: an exhibition loan is followed up by a collections study trip, by an artist's residency, by some online initiative, by a project with young people, a diplomat's visit or a catalogue. Not all such contacts are necessarily equally rewarding or successful; some will inevitably be marked by misgivings or dissent, and some aboriginal people will refuse what they regard as attempts to co-opt them. But such relationships are nevertheless widely sustained and are necessarily incomplete: for as long as potent artefacts from (for example) the Torres Strait remain in (for example) Cambridge, Islanders will make claims on the museum that houses them, and those claims will be responded to, more or less effectively, with collaborative projects of one sort or another. If, on the other hand, an object or a collection is simply and definitively given back, that's that: whatever relationships it has given rise to will come to an end.

The eagerness, or anxiety, of curators to go down the path of dialogue and collaboration exemplifies a sense in which poachers have become gamekeepers. Some among the students of the 1970s, '80s and '90s, who were fired up by debates around racism, indigenous rights, multiculturalism and empire, are now curators and museum directors, while others are senior policymakers or managers of funding agencies. Most importantly, the sense that museums had to engage communities ceased to be confined to the specific sphere of ethnography and world cultures collections, and was generalized across not only museum milieux but the wider heritage and cultural sectors. In the United Kingdom, the Heritage Lottery Fund, which directs the proceeds of state-sponsored gambling to projects such as museum redevelopment, understands community empowerment as central to its mission. 'We want more people and a broader range of people to take an active part in heritage,' is how a recent document puts it.[27] Similarly, Arts Council England's core strategy statement is entitled 'Great art and culture for everyone'. What had been an oppositional argument is now firmly enshrined in the sector's governance and planning.

All this is to say that the image of the museum in the museum studies literature and in wider commentary, which is still that of a more or less illegitimate institution struggling to respond to challenges to its authority, has not caught up with the ways museums have moved on. Institutions have changed for the reasons just cited, because so many of those who have worked within them over the last twenty years were engaged by – indeed were sometimes the authors of – what became classic critiques, which at first informed innovation and then shaped standards. But museums have changed for a host of different and deeper reasons too.

The central concern of this book is with apparently simple questions which debates in museology have largely (and oddly) overlooked, such as, what do museums contain? I argue that a deeper sense of the constitution and potential of collections partly explains the ascendancy of the museum; or, in any case, that such a sense may inform and empower what is positive around museums in the present. But, before, as it were, going inside the museum and addressing the challenges and arguments that its masses of artworks, specimens and artefacts raise, it is important to consider, a little more deeply, what is behind the new, almost supercharged dynamism of the sector. Rather than stand in awe before the advances of the behemoths of the cultural industries, it is worth asking what exactly have been, and still are, the drivers of the varied but related developments that seem so energetic just now.

These consist of both external social and economic trends and developments internal to museum organization and practice. Some are in the nature of longer-term trajectories; others reflect more recent shifts. At the broadest level, economic change has been fundamental. In Europe and America, over the second half of the twentieth century, the middle classes grew, participation in higher education expanded and hence more people entered the social groups typically engaged by the arts and by what museums have to offer. More recently, there has been much discussion (especially on the part of business think tanks, keen to cash in) of the global growth of the middle class, which is now said to amount to more than 50 per cent of the world's population.[28]

After the end of the Second World War tourism, quite literally, took off. In 1950, people undertook just over 25 million international trips. By 1980, this figure had increased to 278 million, and by 2000, to 687 million. Most consequentially for the cultural sector today is that, following a slowdown in the aftermath of the 9/11 attacks, growth recovered its momentum and has tended in recent years to exceed forecasts – in 2013, trips grew by 5 per cent, reaching 1.087 billion globally.[29] Behind the gross statistics are many more particular trends, such as the emergence and rapid expansion of low-cost air travel in Europe (and within other regions) from the end of the 1990s onwards, and the associated popularization of the 'city break'. It is banal, but nevertheless significant, that a quick international shopping, museum-going and eating-out trip, which not so long ago was the habit only of those who were genuinely rich, has become a routine form of mass tourism for Europeans now accustomed to the ease of the single currency and more or less borderless travel. Elsewhere in the world – everywhere else with any money – airports are more crowded and are extended and rebuilt almost as often as museums.

Profound as these changes are, their expression in new understandings among policymakers and others has been still more vital. During the 1990s, governments became increasingly interested in the capacity of culture and what came to be called the creative industries to stimulate, indeed to drive, economic growth. These concerns were certainly not new – as the long history of approaches to film finance and tax breaks makes clear – but the potential was accorded new importance and was underwritten variously through EU cultural funds, through city money in North America, by New Labour in Britain and by new investments in culture in the emerging economies of Asia.

If museums were not initially central to these concerns, they were soon effectively positioned in the debate, not least because of what has become the textbook instance of a new museum, understood essentially as a tourist attraction, and therefore as a factor of potentially decisive importance in urban regeneration and regional development. An initiative of the autonomous Basque administration, the success of the Guggenheim Bilbao turned less on access to the 'parent' museum's modern art collections, essential as they were to the new institution's credibility and programming, than the Centre Pompidou model – that is, the commissioning of a celebrity architect to create a distinctive and spectacular precinct. The story has been often rehearsed: following the internationally publicized opening of the Frank Gehry building in 1997, the city became, at a stroke, a major destination, and within a few years received some four million visitors. It has been claimed that the economic benefit during this initial period was of the order of €500 million, and that the associated increase in tax revenue more than covered the museum's capital cost of €86 million.[30]

Such calculations are complex, and no development that actually took place can be weighed up against other, hypothetical uses of the same money. But the important issue is not so much whether the economic gains have been at the level claimed; it is rather that a compelling narrative emerged, which has appealed to both national leaders and those in regional and city administrations – the latter now often those who make plans and spend money, in an age of devolved and decentralized government. The Louvre Abu Dhabi partnership, cited above, was essentially modelled on the Bilbao project, and as it happens, the Guggenheim Abu Dhabi is in development on the same 'museum island'. More important than extravagant projects of this order, though, are hundreds of new or repackaged art galleries, centres and museums in smaller cities and towns in many countries. In Britain, the BALTIC Centre for Contemporary Art in Gateshead is a Tate equivalent for the north, the region that lost out over the decades of deindustrialization. Turner Contemporary in Margate is comparatively smaller, but both brought innovative architecture to areas in need of regeneration, created new public precincts as well as engaging gallery spaces, and were constructed with a view to the transformation of the quality of life in their environs.[31] Harbourside sites, in Antwerp and Marseilles among other places, were formerly rough and sleazy areas but now afford evocative locations for museums addressing maritime history, trade, cultural exchange and world cultures, alongside waterfront cafés and stylish apartments in converted warehouses.

The success of these particular institutions and others like them has been underpinned by another shift of quite a different order. Within a generation, contemporary art has become a form of popular culture. It was once the case that historic painting had a substantial following among an educated audience, while 'modern art' was mocked for its incomprehensibility and dubious merit in scores of *New Yorker* cartoons and otherwise by a sceptical media. As late as the 1980s, genuinely avant-garde installation and performance practices had fans mainly around art schools and in art milieux themselves, though Pop art, among other movements, anticipated the much-touted if only ever partial breakdown of the distinction between high and low culture diagnosed and advocated in postmodern theory, which itself exemplified the emergence of academic discourse as a form of fashion, and fashionability as a force to be reckoned with in scholarship and theory. By the early 1990s the cultural landscape had changed beyond recognition, particularly in Britain, where the then-Young British Artists, energetically promoted by the London listings magazine *Time Out*, had become celebrities.[32] The Saatchi Collection, and the 'Sensation' exhibition that showcased it in 1997, not only gave many artists individual prominence, but drew the kind of work they produced into the mainstream. Contemporary art was suddenly just cool – as accessible to middle-class urban youth as music, design and cinema.

Contemporary art, moreover, was nothing if not an international language. The curators of biennales (which were themselves proliferating) drew on work from around the world, but rarely selected customary or grass-roots art forms that, as it were, spoke only local languages. Their spaces were open only to those artists articulate in the international idioms of mixed-media installation, video and conceptualism. The contemporary art market and the postcolonial theory that was influential in the humanities over the 1980s and '90s celebrated both boundary-crossing and global culture, privileging the diaspora and artists working from it. Hence contemporary art could promise access to diversity and cosmopolitanism, even if Asia and Africa were more often represented by artists resident in Europe or North America than in their countries of origin. If the contemporary art world has too often failed to go the distance, to broadly and meaningfully represent arts that belong to the present from a fuller and truly global range of milieux, communities and nations, it has nevertheless appeared to be progressive, to be moving beyond established traditions, embracing the world and representing it. Certainly, new hierarchies are replacing old.

This is not the place for a more wide-ranging critique of the art market's effective monetization of the principles of diversity and inclusion, though the growth and internationalization of the art market has itself, in various direct and less direct ways, fostered museum development as well. But more importantly, from the point of view of audiences rather than buyers, contemporary art's growing appeal and overt internationalism have done much to empower the museum sector. The practice of staging artists' residencies and interventions in non-art museums has also meant that the accessibility of contemporary practice has brought new audiences into history, anthropology and science museums. Indeed, the dialogue of art and science, famously considered a lost cause by C. P. Snow, has undergone efflorescence. If, for a few years, SciArt was a self-conscious project, deliberately promoted by agencies, such as the Wellcome Trust, that sought to orchestrate exchange, it was not long before collaborations and experiments ranging across astronomy, medicine, zoology, botany, palaeontology and other disciplines became mainstream; they are now routinely presented across natural history and science museums as well as art spaces.[33]

Steadily growing numbers of museum visits are the upshot of all these factors, as well as of the longer history of the professionalization of various areas of museum work, extending back to the 1960s. Institutions such as the British Museum had mounted temporary exhibitions to a limited extent even during the nineteenth century, but it was not until after the Second World War that shows began to be designed and promoted professionally; in New York, the Museum of Modern Art found inspiration in the innovative display techniques and aesthetics of the Fifth Avenue department stores. At the British Museum, lecture tours of the galleries had long been offered, but the first education officer was not appointed until 1972, which happened to be the same year the Museum mounted what is considered its first 'blockbuster' – 'Treasures of Tutankhamun' – which drew nearly 1.7 million visitors over nine months in the same year.[34] Though many nineteenth-century exhibitions, including those of the World's Fair genre, attracted astonishing numbers of paying visitors, the blockbuster in the museum context is considered an innovation of the late 1960s, associated particularly with Thomas Hoving's directorship of the Metropolitan Museum of Art in New York.[35]

In due course, all major museums entered the game, running costly advertising campaigns to promote temporary shows as one-off opportunities to encounter and experience great art, archaeological finds, heroic histories or otherwise marketable subjects. Though often censured for leading to a neglect of permanent collections, as well as for fostering curatorial sensationalism, these shows not only and obviously popularized the exhibition experience; at best they also stimulated and showcased new scholarship. They certainly helped to sustain museums financially, through the proliferation of sponsorship opportunities and the generation of revenue through sales of merchandise and catalogues. Indeed, the handsomely designed and richly illustrated exhibition catalogue, perhaps ideally a souvenir of a memorable, even affecting, museum visit, may sell in the tens of thousands, and has proven one of the most resilient of publishing genres over the last half-century, qualifying the often-made announcement of the print book's impending death. Blockbusters, incidentally, have also helped drive the development of friends' and members' schemes: tens of thousands of people are now commonly signed up for the groups associated with major museums. The subscription fees generally include not only entry into big temporary exhibitions, but unrestricted access, at a time when capacity crowds and timed-ticket visits are becoming more routine.

If there is thus a widespread sense among politicians and cultural professionals that museums do whatever they do much better than they used to, it is substantiated by the support of both local communities and wider publics, including international tourists. It is sustained, in some cases, by dauntingly effective revenue-generating operations, or at any rate by success in making the argument for funding in a way that convinces many public and private administrations and agencies. Of course, over the years of austerity, institutions in many European countries as well as elsewhere have suffered cutbacks, and have commonly had to reduce staff through redundancies, and otherwise curtail programmes. Recent developments have been nothing if not uneven, and there have undoubtedly been losers as well as winners. It is in the nature of museums that funding is almost invariably insufficient, that opportunities and new investments in one area highlight crisis in another. Technical advances in many fields, ranging from conservation to online cataloguing, may create new and exciting possibilities but also inflate expectations, exacerbating the financial and logistical difficulties of looking after, and maintaining access to, collections that in some cases consist of millions of artefacts and specimens. Although museum management is always challenging, and while some institutions are not just constrained but in real financial trouble, neither the momentum of the sector nor an unexpected resilience are in doubt. Most likely because many who work in museums care deeply about them, about the collections and their presence in the community, staff and volunteers tend to find ways of reinventing institutions and sustaining their activities, even in a constrained fashion and under the most adverse of circumstances.

All these developments raise the question of what museums actually offer, not for policymakers, city planners and economists, but for the diverse range of people who spend time in them. The remainder of this book is a roundabout answer to this question, an answer inspired by what museums contain – that is, collections. But it makes sense to start with what may be more familiar responses, which should be acknowledged here. The chair of a leading British arts charity recently stated that museums offered their visitors enjoyment, education and importantly also 'spiritual uplift', the sense of wonder and even elation that a person may feel encountering a work of art that is beautiful or otherwise profoundly impressive or moving.[36] Notwithstanding the critique of aesthetics that had been the departure point for so much theory over the last half-century, broad claims of this sort embrace important truths: images and artefacts may be powerfully affecting; they can indeed palpably lift people's spirits; visitors may be entranced or intrigued or struck or otherwise stimulated, not only by artworks, but by relics, specimens and artefacts of many kinds. Museums are said also to express the character of places and the identities of communities, and provide a sense of history, of deeper cultural roots. Yet if these sorts of claims deserve consideration, they are unspecific: it could equally be said that theatre or music, reading a novel, even participation in a religious service, are all enjoyable and educational – they may all provide 'spiritual uplift' and may all connect their audiences with history or local identity. What is distinctive about museums and the experience of visiting them?

It is ironic that museums are now said, as if interchangeably, to be engaging with visitors or audiences and concerned with 'audience development'. The word's etymology relates, needless to say, to hearing: an audience with a pope or monarch was an opportunity to be heard, and even if the word is commonly used now to refer to any target constituency or market, we still associate an audience first and foremost with a play, a concert or a lecture. Utterly obvious as it may be that performances of this sort are very different in nature to exhibitions or museums, it is worth reflecting upon precisely how a museum visit is singular, relative to other kinds of participation in cultural activities. Although the guided tour stands as a significant exception, the museum visitor is not typically part of a constituted group that gathers to hear or witness a coherent programme or performance that occupies a specific time. The point is not that the one implies passivity and the other activity: play- and concert-goers may watch and listen actively and sometimes assertively. But they hear or witness the same show, which presupposes a focus of attention – the action, dialogue or performance on the stage – and has not only a given duration but a conventional temporal order within that: a series of movements and pieces, scenes and acts, an interval, applause and possibly an encore, a series that is at once anticipated and respected by the audience as well as the performers, whose engagement and mood is modulated as the programme progresses.

The museum visit neither falls within a specific part of the day, nor does it have a defined duration. If, to be sure, galleries can be seen as theatres for the study of usually static objects, and museum architecture, lighting, display furniture and scenography encourage particular ways of seeing, and otherwise enable or constrain the visitor, there is nothing in the museum visit that is quite like theatre seating, that orients the audience, as if to facilitate its absolute attention for the duration of the defined performance event. A museum visit is, in contrast, more like a walk through a building and often through its courtyards or outdoor precincts; admittedly a special sort of walk through a building of a singular kind, punctuated by encounters with objects, yet with no fixed focus or any single centre of attention. Most importantly, and within whatever happens to be the scope of the particular museum, its content is weakly scripted and is determined only in the broadest terms. While classic essays have illuminated the ideological work of great institutions such as the Louvre – which presented the citizen with the nation state as successor to, and bearer of, the history of civilization – the diverse publics that patronize such museums today take away at once much more and rather less than this message.[37] Indeed, a good many visitors are well aware of the role that universal museums formerly played in affirming the greatness of imperial nations, and express ambivalence (through social media, for example): it's wonderful to encounter great antiquities, they say, but disturbing to reflect on how they reached the museum in question.[38] The ideological framing of great historic museums may give the experience of visiting them a partly anachronistic character: one encounters not only the foreignness or the historic distance of what they contain (the Metropolitan's thirteenth-century *Madonna and Child* by Berlinghiero, for example) but also the expression of museum-makers' ambitions, which may be intelligible, if dated – the civic pride of the city fathers – or less familiar, in the case of anatomical collections, which may be perceived as eccentric, creepy, even seemingly perverted. The heterogeneity of audiences now makes these responses genuinely unpredictable, since while I encounter the icon as an expression of a medieval culture remote from my own, adherents of Orthodox churches presumably see an earlier instance of very similar works made today, intimately associated with their faith and their daily lives.

The visitor cannot look at anything that the museum does not hold or display, but he or she is likely to look at only part of what is shown, and may spend a long time in one room, or before one work or group of specimens, and may pass by other works, displays and rooms altogether. While visitors to a smaller museum such as Kettle's Yard in Cambridge – the house and collection of former Tate curator Jim Ede – probably look over the whole house, the mutability of a visit is amplified by leaps with the size of the building and the extent of its galleries. A knowing visitor may proceed quickly to a favourite work or a section of particular interest, while others wander and stop simply at what catches their eye. Some may be engaged as much by a museum's architectural aspects as by the works it contains. An international tourist making the most of a one-off visit may allocate the better part of a full day to a famous museum; someone who works nearby may drop in for half an hour during a lunch break.

If temporary exhibitions generally have a linear structure (if only because people have to produce tickets at a specific entry point, or because their layout aims to facilitate 'people flow'), the opposite is true of most permanent galleries. The planetarium, birds, Asia, Margaret Mead, the native cultures of the northwest coast and dioramas of the fauna of the tundra or the savanna may be encountered in more or less that order, the reverse, or various others in the American Museum of Natural History. In short, the museum visit is in the broadest terms an encounter with works or specimens representative of world civilizations, art, natural history or whatever the institution contains, as well as with whatever the institution itself represents, but, given that, *it is defined by lack of definition*. It may moreover be solitary, it may be the occasion for time with an old friend, it may be a family outing, it may form part of a community project, such as a group visit during Black History Month. In each of these cases, what is anticipated differs and will be articulated through different thoughts, commentaries and conversations, perhaps with strangers, other visitors who happen to be looking at the same thing, perhaps with museum docents or staff, as well as with the family members or friends with whom one is visiting the location.

These points are painfully obvious, but they are obvious in a consequential way. In practice, the route through a museum and its duration may be hurried or contracted by the need to find a bathroom or café for an elderly parent or impatient child. But, in principle, one can *take one's time* in a museum. Even when you are short of time, you can choose to linger in front of one object, or swiftly take in the paintings in a room. If, from one angle, a museum visit differs from going to a play in the same way that dipping into an encyclopaedia differs from reading a novel properly, from start to finish – the one entailing eclectic sampling, the other obedience to a narrative – it is again obvious, but again consequential, that exhibitions differ from both encyclopaedias and novels, from books of all kinds, not only in this relationship to temporality but in that their vital elements are physical things: specimens, paintings, installations, artefacts. An exhibition can, of course, consist of books, in which case we are reminded that books are not just texts but a form of material culture, with distinctive binding, paper, typography and design that speak of their period, aspirations and intended circulation, among the affluent or the masses, or maybe a highly singular story of ownership, reading, use. The collected Shakespeare shown at the end of the British Museum's 2012 exhibition 'Shakespeare: Staging the World' was shared among fellow prisoners on Robben Island, some of whom identified and signed their favourite passages. 'Cowards die many times before their deaths; / The valiant never taste of death but once . . . Seeing that death, a necessary end / will come when it will come', lines from *Julius Caesar*, Act II, Scene 2, were marked by Nelson Mandela, as if to prompt recollection of the last resonant words of his own treason trial speech. This object is remarkable for bringing unexpected connections – between Shakespeare and one of the twentieth century's great liberation struggles – into view.[39] This is why it matters that exhibitions are made up of things, rather than texts or utterances: suggesting unexpected connections *is what they do*.

In the Western humanities and social sciences, last century's inter- and post-war decades were distinguished by the sovereignty of language. Following Saussure and Lévi-Strauss, intellectuals across many disciplines and in the wider spheres of culture were preoccupied with semiotics, with meaning, with translation and with the media, understood as discourse, ideology or 'text'. It was only during and after the 1980s that scholars and theorists began to return to and reflect upon other dimensions of human experience, society and history – those to do with the body, with place and space and with material culture. The material things that surround us, that we may accumulate, value and discard, and that fill the world's museums, have a double character, a contradictory nature, a lack of fixity. On the one hand, things possess particular humility, in that they are mutable and they submit as if willingly to recontextualization. In Arjun Appadurai's deservedly celebrated account of 'the social life of things', something such as a hat may start out in a shop, may be worn, inherited and sold or discarded; this passage may see it shift from being a commodity to a gift, to a useful item of personal property, to a poignant family heirloom, to a commodity again in the form of an article of antique apparel, even a museum piece, or just a piece of rubbish, in the end destroyed.[40] More notoriously, a Melanesian ritual assemblage may cross oceans and continents, be in succession a colonial trophy, an ethnologist's curiosity, a tribal art masterpiece owned by a connoisseur and a new museum's expression of 'world culture'. Curators have felt these seemingly brutal recontextualizations like the open wounds of artefacts, though there is greater awareness now that objects were often traded, redefined and appropriated within and across indigenous milieux before reaching any European collection: contexts of different sorts may 'do justice to them', in the sense of respecting their creation.

Equally essential to materiality is a certain intractability on the part of the artefact. A sword, a pot, a blanket, a ring or a mask all bear material properties that do not change, are recognizable across cultures and epochs, and that manifest human interests and needs that are intelligible if not actually shared. This may be evident enough in the case of a water container or a fabric that might warm a body or bodies, but even an arresting hybrid spirit mask may be recognized and appreciated as such, cross-culturally, even if the particular beliefs that motivate its character and form are grasped superficially, or not at all. These enduring and recognizable qualities remain in tension with any particular use or reuse: they may make recontextualization plain and poignant. Which is to say that almost any historic artefact, almost anything likely to be encountered in a museum, bears a particular uncertainty: it is both what it was and what it is. If this is most glaring with respect to ethnographic objects that were once given meaning in a flow of life and ritual, this is only because their travels are, as it were, overtly unsettling. Many works in mainstream art museums – once situated in churches, in the country houses of aristocrats or in private or domestic settings – have been no less radically decontextualized, and hence speak of other and past lives, of 'then' as well as 'now', 'there' as well as 'here'. The doubleness of the artefact – which is equally a doubleness of the natural specimen, the pressed plant or fossil – is thus also the paradox of physical immediacy and nebulous identity.

Museums are commonly understood as partly educational institutions, but materiality's combination of real presence and ambiguity makes them bearers of knowledge of both a powerful and an oblique kind. Much more could be said about the 'telling' capacities of museum artefacts and collections, but I am concerned at this point simply to pin down the plausible and potentially important but also vague claim that they offer something like 'spiritual uplift', or at any rate potent and enlivening effect. They do so precisely because material culture has these qualities – it *is* the conjuncture of intimate actuality and significant ambiguity. By intimate actuality is meant what is remarkable about the physical presence of an object, which may be extraordinary in any way, or in any one of a number of perhaps incommensurable ways. Despite the rhetoric and indeed the real value of digital access, there is nothing like actually seeing a work: no substitute for the sense of minute detail, intricate composition, texture, fabric and scale, and for the presence of the object in the round or in time, 'in the flesh', in light that changes as one adjusts one's view, steps back from, walks closer to or past something.

It is a commonplace that major artworks should be seen in person, but the vital issue is not that of aesthetics or artistic appreciation in a narrow sense. It is, rather, that of effect: artworks and many other sorts of things, including ordinary, nondescript or discarded objects, may be captivating in their presence and intricacy, in signs of age or damage that they bear, or en masse. This is to get 'up close and personal'; it brings a knowledge of a thing that is sensory and sensual, not always and never fully susceptible to articulation, even if visceral, as in the case of Henry Tonks's studies of war injuries and the human pathology exhibits at the Royal College of Surgeons. But if this knowledge is unconventional – it isn't put into words – it is also a knowledge of possibilities that may remain unresolved. This is the 'significant ambiguity' of the object. Something such as a pebble

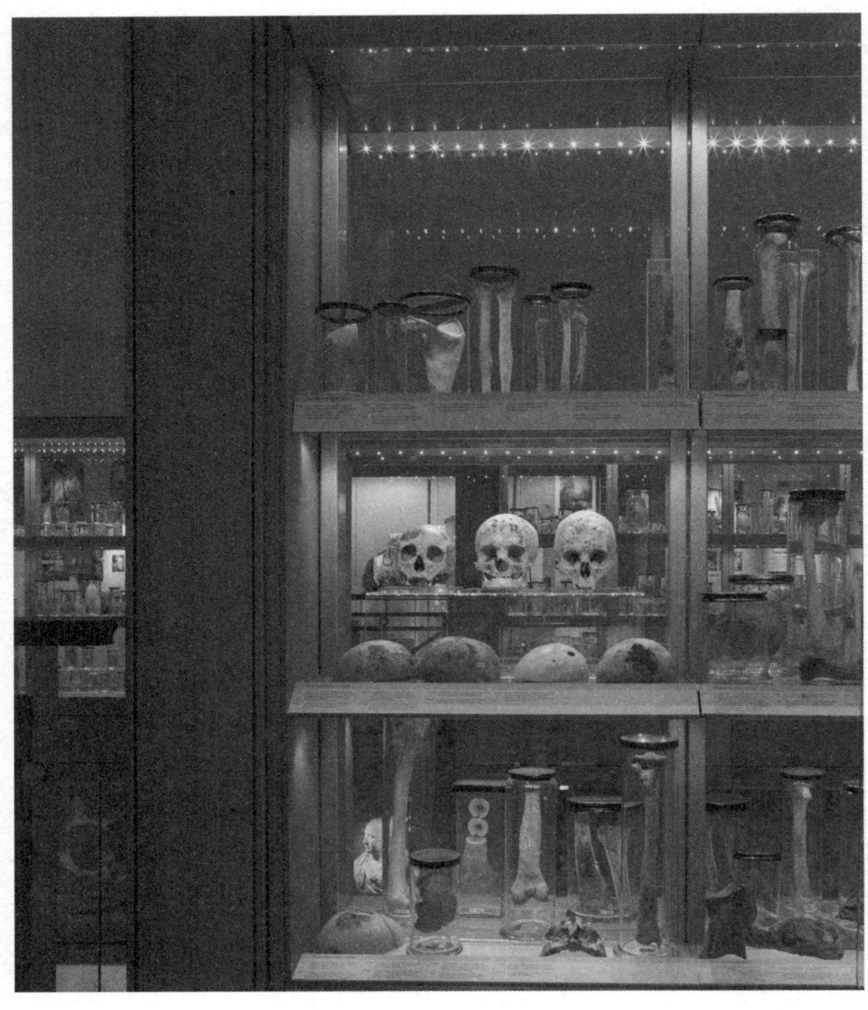

Osteological specimens from persons suffering from advanced syphilis at the Hunterian Museum, Royal College of Surgeons, London.

may be utterly indeterminate (a geological specimen, a souvenir, a ritual token?), but even something that clearly exhibits a defined purpose – a Viking sword, for example – stimulates diverse reflections, about a craftsman's skill, about actual fighting, about archaeological preservation and discovery, about what a European might make of the great reach and stereotypic violence of Viking history today. Material culture, in the museum setting, can be rich and suggestive but is also, paradoxically, positively unprescriptive: it stimulates and enables the imagination; it gives you a push into a space in which you can move and think.

Even an affecting exhibit visit that certainly is scripted, such as the confrontation with four thousand victims' shoes in the United States Holocaust Memorial Museum (drawn from the hundreds of thousands of pairs discovered when Auschwitz and other camps were liberated by Soviet soldiers in January 1945), is one that a visitor must come to terms with, in their own terms. One person may feel loss in relation to a close family history, meditating upon personal suffering and trauma that is understood to be uniquely Jewish; another may be prompted to reflect upon more recent instances of attempted genocide in Rwanda and elsewhere, and the larger evils of ethnic violence and racism. If memorial sites and collections represent a special case, most museums are not created to elicit reflection in such specific terms. Or, in any case, if directors or curators have an idea that their museum has a message – be it a narrative of national identity through art or of diminishing biodiversity – actual visitors are always likely to take away both less and more, to be idiosyncratic in their responses, to 'make their own mental collection'.

Observations of this kind – which substantiate and enlarge the senses in which museums afford 'spiritual uplift' – are framed largely in personal terms. It is the individual who may step away from day-to-day anxieties and be intrigued, delighted or absorbed, however briefly, by something wonderful, potent or just odd, in material form. Yet the museum may also be effective in a different way that is emphatically collective. This is evident, arrestingly so, if we leave aside grand metropolitan institutions and consider certain local museums, at the very opposite end of the spectrum, in their scale and resources. Annie Coombes has recently explored the projects of a number of grass-roots peace museums – amounting to a 'peace museum movement' – in Kenya, which gained momentum following the post-election violence of 2007–8, but which, in the case of the Lari Memorial Peace Museum, northwest of Nairobi, had been established some years earlier to address a deeper history – that of the anti-colonial Mau Mau insurgency.[41] In particular, Lari represented an effort to negotiate the legacy of one of the worst atrocities of the conflict, a notorious double massacre of March 1953, first perpetrated by Mau Mau adherents on those loyal to the British, and second, by way of revenge or reprisal, of those thought to be Mau Mau by the government and their supporters. Decades later, the community was said still to struggle with 'pain, suspicion, hatred and separation'.[42] The museum sought to address the 'unhealed wounds' and, subsequent to events of 2007–8, collaborated with a growing network of peace museums across Kenya to create a beaded peace tree that exemplified a commitment and capacity to live and work together. Coombes's analysis draws attention to the ways the Lari museum's modest collection of material culture – displayed in a fashion that may appear traditionally ethnographic – revitalized artefacts as a means of conflict resolution. Together with archival photos graphically representing the violent events of 1953, customary objects play one role that is familiar – that of affirming the value of local traditions – and another that is less so: the affinities of form and media across regions, in beadwork especially, reveal a shared cultural heritage, deeper than the separate ethnicities that were so fatally exaggerated during the post-election violence.

Coombes's argument – that the out-of-the-way case might point toward a radically different future for ethnographic collections in general – is suggestive. The Kenyan peace museums, as well as many similar small, volunteer-run institutions in other parts of Africa and

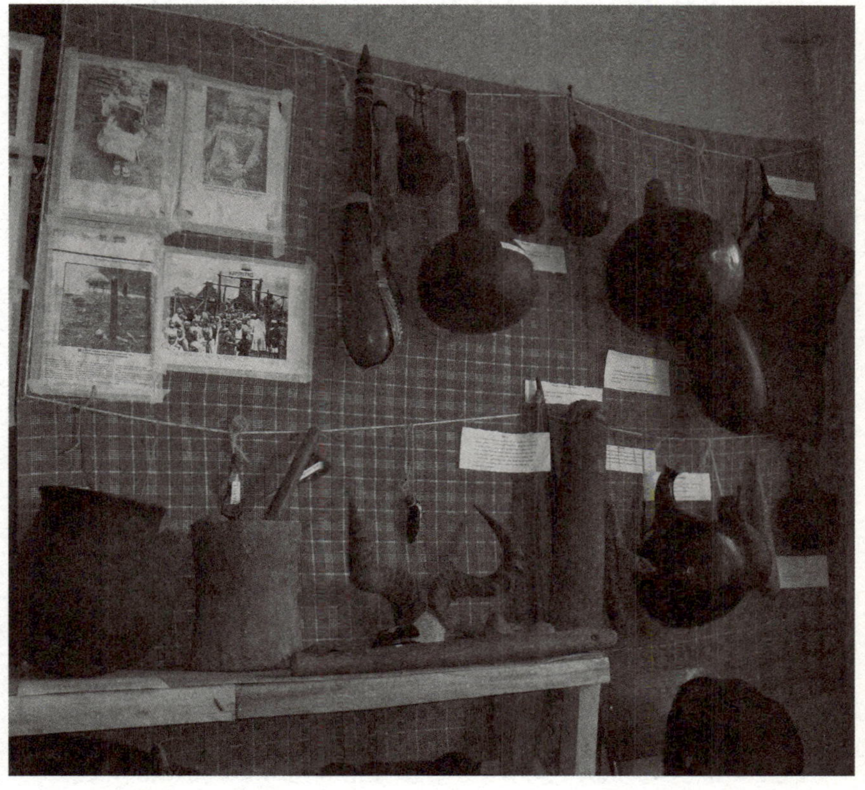

Exhibits at the Lari Memorial Peace Museum, Kimende, Kenya, 2009.

elsewhere, also raise a more fundamental set of questions. Why should a museum represent any kind of answer, any part of a solution, for those concerned with 'wounds and painful memories' of this sort? Why should a comparatively poor community make the effort to create an institution of this type that is supposedly the bearer of projects of imperial and cultural hegemony? What, in other words, is the museum good for, in this time and place?

If the answer has two parts, the first and less surprising is to do with the way museums usually validate what they contain and represent. They may (and often do) privilege art practices, a history of civilization, a story of a group or community, whether marginalized or not; they may present wonders of nature and science, or even celebrate a particular hobby or recreation. This is not and has not always been the case – during the imperial period indigenous weapons were sometimes displayed as proofs of the violent propensities of particular peoples. But in general collections are indirectly if not directly affirmative. A war museum is unlikely today to celebrate war, but instead suggests that it is important to understand and commemorate it.

The second part of the response is not at this level of content, of ideological or moral effect; it goes deeper and is a matter of sociality. What the museum is good for is its sustenance of civil society: it not only is part of the public sphere, but constitutes a space of participation in public life. Its visitors may be people of a place, citizens of a nation or members of a cosmopolitan community. They are drawn together by sharing an interest in encountering whatever the museum happens to contain, an interest in participating in that encounter. The space is one that they may visit for a particular event, and they may mingle or may choose to take things in more privately. In a small-scale, community institution such as the Lari Memorial Peace

Museum, visits will almost invariably involve interaction with others, discussion of some kind, directly related to the displays or not. But even in larger institutions, among tourists or school groups, a visitor is a co-visitor, implicitly acknowledging both the participation of others and their difference: they may come from somewhere else or have more or less profoundly different perspectives upon history, identity or faith.[43]

Bill Viola's *Tiny Deaths* (1993) is a triple video projection, over three of the four walls in a medium-sized, very dark room. For most of its duration the screens are themselves dark. They flicker, and shadowy figures are intermittently discernable; from time to time a person appears and disappears in a sudden flash of light. The audio is loud and consists of indistinct murmuring, as if from a number of different voices or sources. While the work may be captioned in conventional art-historical terms, as an evocation of the transience of existence, its arresting feature is rather the intensity of the experience of being present. The darkness and uncertainty, the suddenness of the figures' appearances and disappearances, may arouse fear, and certainly a degree of anxiety. Online comments prompted by the recent installation of this piece at Tate Modern suggest that viewers-cum-participants are rendered anxious by virtually invisible fellow visitors: you only momentarily sense how populated the space may be, who else is there; you may be unexpectedly close to others; awkwardly, you may bump into them. I take it that this awkward sense of others, of indistinct figures within the room, is not incidental, but important to the piece, and that the apprehensiveness is intended to be shared.

If the effect in the case of *Tiny Deaths* is distinctive to the darkness and the particular contemporary genre of the immersive large-scale, multiple-screen video, there is another sense in which it is

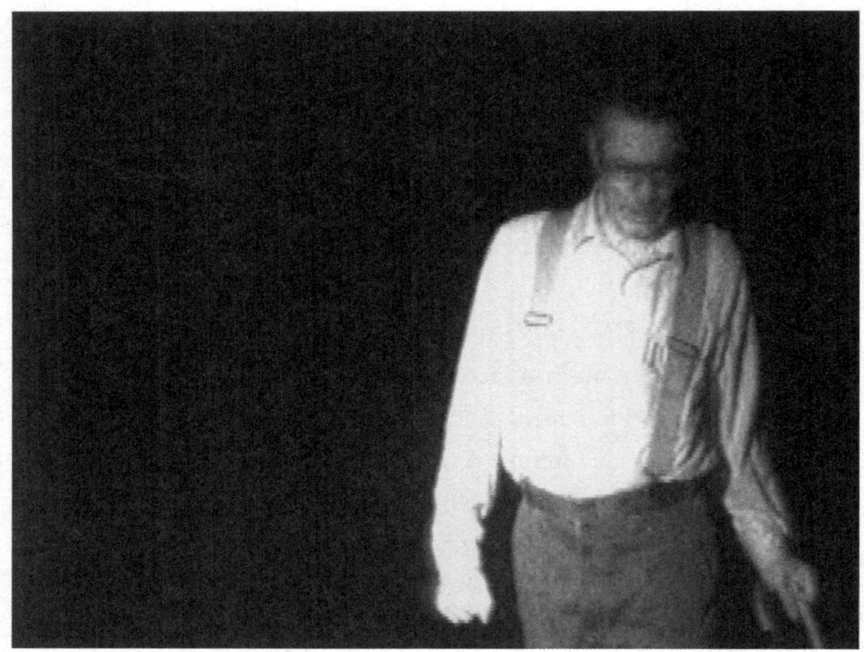

symptomatic of many types of works and exhibits. Most famously – a hallmark of Tate Modern's success – Olafur Eliasson's *The Weather Project* of 2003 fostered consciousness of and engagement with other visitors: people interacted. 'Countless documentary images of the work show spontaneous meetings, celebrations, people embracing or revelling in the artificial light, or lying on the floor to gaze at their own reflections in the ceiling, and even episodes of civil protest.'[44] Something similar has been true of other Turbine Hall installations, such as Rachel Whiteread's *EMBANKMENT* (2005), much enjoyed by children, among others. Through devices of scale and address, not only contemporary works but also other sorts of museum exhibits elicit shared awareness and a common responsiveness (not necessarily a common response) from disparate people.

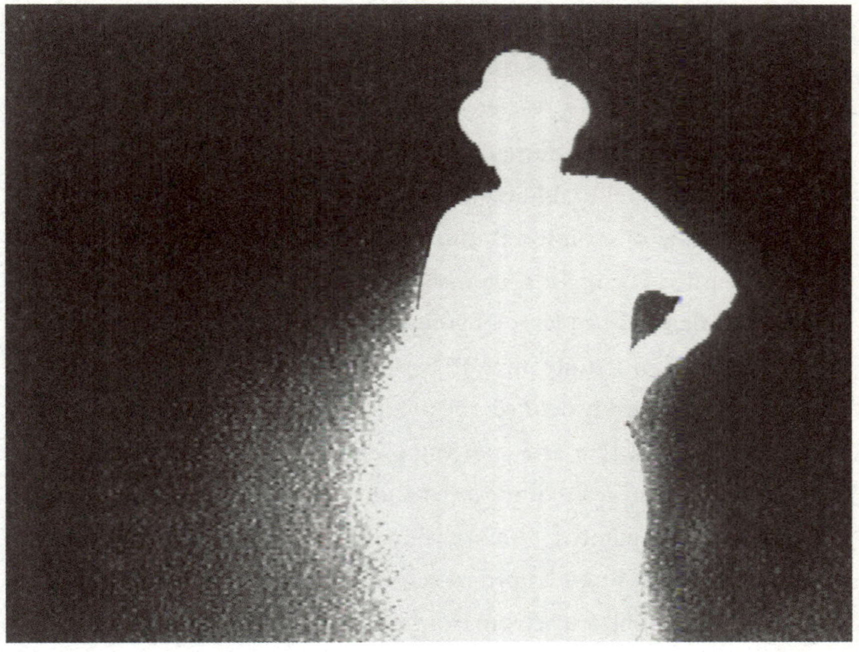

Still images from Bill Viola, *Tiny Deaths*, 1993, video, three projections, black-and-white and sound.

The kind of coming together that takes place before or among displays is not at all like the mixing of people in the bazaar or the shopping mall. The growth of museum retail and the commercialization of the museum experience have been much lamented, but entering an exhibition remains a fundamentally different experience to that of shopping. Shopping is the negotiation of personal needs or desires relative to the cash one can spend; some find it enjoyable but it is also risky – one may be duped by hard salesmanship, or by misleading packaging or apparent bargains; perhaps worse, one's reason may be momentarily eclipsed by desire. Whereas, even if you have paid to enter a gallery, your engagement with the works, the space, the stories, is just part of the unhurried walk that you undertake through however many rooms; it is not subject to a calculus of acquisition or affordability, or restrained by concern that one's careful management of one's purse may lapse.

Similarly, and again despite the supposed and often disparaged downgrading of exhibitions into entertainment, the gathering that a museum visit entails is likewise different to the coming together of an audience for a play, or a group of fans for a concert or a game. In the museum setting, interest, beyond the interest in entering the collection, is weakly defined; the predicate of attendance is precisely the opposite of that at a sporting event, at which you must be a supporter of one team or the other and appear dressed in colours, or with your face painted, to make your allegiance manifest. The point is not just that in an empirical sense, museum visitors are highly varied, embracing a spectrum from the retired connoisseur of medieval coins to the child eager to see the mummies. It is that *in principle* the museum accommodates and sustains a heterogeneity of interest; it *exists for* the heterogeneous bearers of those interests, who (despite all talk of museums and communities) are likely to be variously local residents, the inhabitants of a city, migrants, tourists and others. Their differences need not be negotiated or debated; their coming together is a matter of co-presence and mutual awareness, not one of solidarity or shared consciousness. Not reaching out, refraining from collective action, may make the museum appear a space of ineffectiveness, of conservatism – a disappointment. But this interpretation would overlook its particular character as a space that elicits and fosters empathy.

One looks because one is curious, because one wants to encounter something that is distant or distinctive. The simplest questions that we ask of objects – what is it? who made it? what was it for? – reflect an attempt to understand things, that is, to understand them on their own terms. As one makes that effort, implicitly acknowledging that those terms are not one's own, one reflects on distance itself. This is so, most obviously, of works and artefacts of a different, perhaps ancient, historical epoch, or from a remote and more or less unfamiliar cultural setting – and it is one of the paradoxes of artefactuality that one can get close, get a sense of the intimate thing, of something like a mummified baby crocodile from Egypt, remote in terms of its cultural and ritual inspiration as well as its time and place of origin. Yet distance may be equally manifest in a work of art by a person of one's generation, nationality and locality. Circumstances of biography or idiosyncrasy make us very different, yet responsive to difference. My imputation – of a visitor's interest and response – is admittedly speculative. And it is an ideal, like that nebulous notion of 'civil society' itself, conceived in conflicting terms since Aristotle first proposed, in a discussion foundational for pluralist political thought, that the distinctiveness of the state arose from it being made up of 'different kinds of men'.[45] The Platonic position, that civil society was a domain within which citizens might come together to discuss such matters as public virtue, can only, in our own time, invite the criticism articulated by Partha Chatterjee, that civil society is 'demographically limited', and that it has represented a realm of freedom for privileged classes and privileged populations.[46]

Yet the Kenyan groups, and others like them engaged in post-conflict reconstruction, have worked to create a space of sociality around artefacts and images arising from a particular history. Elsewhere, people may not have to negotiate such profound difficulties, but go to museums in part because they are 'the safest of places', as

Estelle Morris, formerly a senior member of Tony Blair's cabinet, put it in a policy paper.[47] The claim may be odd or off-key, for galleries are associated in most people's minds with a mix of education, aesthetic pleasure and entertainment, but it illuminates something both fundamental and elusive. There are times when expressions of solidarity and collective action are urgently necessary – the 'Je suis Charlie' demonstrations in the aftermath of the Paris attacks of January 2015 are a recent instance. But in a quotidian sense, as people get on with their lives, sociality, evoked by Richard Sennett, on the basis of the German social theorist Georg Simmel – implicit mutual acknowledgement and regard, the acceptability of difference, the response to the common humanity of those you don't know – is not just a characterization of good manners, but a precondition of an effectively functioning society.[48]

The point is not just that museums are the safest of places in which to take risks – to air, for example, intractable issues of identity, difference and faith – although it surely is true that they are: the same issue raised in a radio talk show and in an exhibit are far more likely to heighten temper in the first setting and elicit reflection, give pause for thought, in the second, because a verbal assertion and an artefact's mute oration are different in their nature and effect. Apparent exceptions – the few works of contemporary art that are deliberately blasphemous or otherwise offensive, that have occasionally been sufficiently controversial to prompt the cancellation or closure of exhibitions – actually underscore the sense in which people think of museums as places in which they should be stimulated and perhaps challenged, but not injured. What is at issue is not the content, or the actuality of the museum – which may occasionally or even often be overcrowded, irritating or frustrating – but what it promises. At the most banal level, the museum offers 'something interesting'. Underlying that, it holds out the promise of a place and space richly peopled by works and things, a realm in which you can pursue interest and discover interests you did not know you had, not alone, but in company – that is, in the company of strangers.

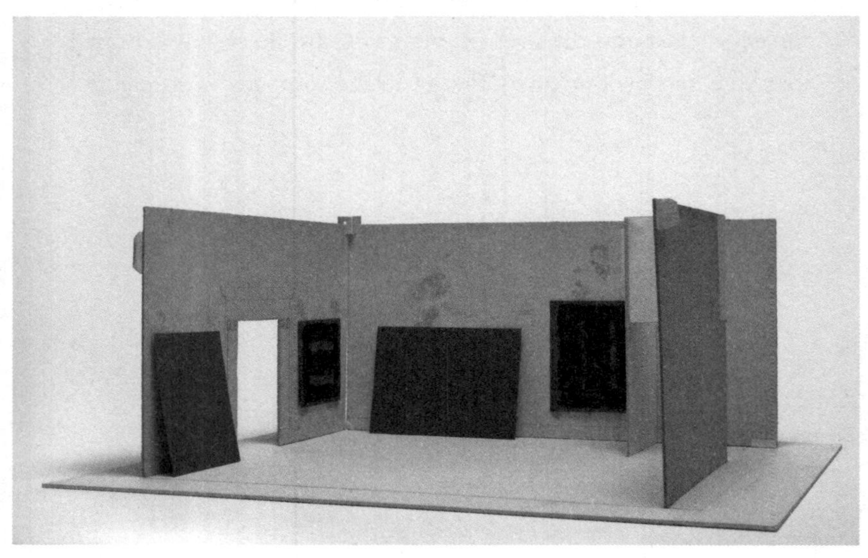

Mark Rothko, maquette for installation of Seagram murals at the Tate Gallery, London, 1970.

2

# THE MUSEUM AS METHOD

The debates about the politics of exhibitions and the negotiation of representation that have preoccupied commentators, curators and activists over the last thirty or so years have been of vital importance, but they have also passed over seemingly simple questions, such as, what do museums contain? What they contain – in most instances – are collections; what they exhibit are samples of those collections; what they do behind the scenes, out of public view, is called 'collections care'. Much of what is embraced by this term is practical and technical; it involves appropriate packing and pest control, for example. Yet, as with children or the elderly, 'care' has many dimensions: it involves a capacious, costly and contentious set of responsibilities. It may be clear that preserving an object in storage requires suitable racking, environmental monitoring and so on, but an artefact or specimen can't be said to be cared for if curators don't know they have it, if it can't be located or if it is otherwise miscatalogued. 'Care' is therefore, right from the start, a matter of knowledge and identification as well as an effort to manage physical risks. And if a collection is easier to care for if its value and significance are understood, that implies that research, interpretation, exhibition and access may all be important, alongside security and levels of light and humidity. In a world of uncertain funding, an effective curator has to be an ambassador for the collections in her or his care: unless people, from museum managers through visitors and school teachers to government ministers and other potential sponsors, are persuaded that these works or specimens are significant, indeed somehow revelatory, there can be no constituency of supporters whose positive interest will underpin the costs of looking after material, and indeed of the future acquisitions that keep a collection alive.

Day-to-day, curators and collections staff are often involved in managing loans for temporary and touring exhibitions. Most people who go to blockbusters or more modest temporary shows have no notion of the elaborate and protracted diplomacy that may be required to bring together the works displayed on the walls or in cases around them. These sorts of negotiations weigh up the significance and fragility of remarkable objects; they entail subtle and sometimes not so subtle forms of reciprocity; they may reflect wider diplomatic and political agendas, and sometimes involve large sums of money. In a more low-key fashion, curators adjust or refresh displays and spend time bringing pieces out from storage for study by researchers and community members, perhaps the descendants of the original creators, collectors or donors. These are not just occasions for dispassionate analysis or observation – they are often affecting encounters, especially but not exclusively when people have ancestral connections with the works or relics in question.

Collections are extended through new acquisitions; they may also be reduced, if material is 'de-accessioned' through transfer, sale, repatriation or whatever other form of disposal. Museums engage in fundraising, typically in order to buy more art, to conserve works they hold, to build or renovate facilities for collections care or display and to mount and market exhibitions. They offer public and educational programmes that may involve hands-on activities or tours of displays, or that take people behind the scenes. Collections are thus at the heart of more or less everything museums do, even if they are typically only very partially exhibited. The 'tip of the iceberg' is the obvious analogy, but it is, unhelpfully, an inorganic one. It may be more apt to contrast the look of a great forest from the edge with its vast and mysterious inner life. Those who don't know museums from within tend to suppose that a collections store is a sort of artefactual mausoleum, a dark space in which things languish unregarded, perhaps deservedly, it being assumed that they are second-rate relative to what is on display. In the past, it may well have been the case that reserve collections were left unexamined or unused for long periods. Very recently, the publicly accessible online catalogue has become considerably more common, comprehensive and easily navigable. This development has brought collections into view to an unprecedented extent, and also motivated and enabled more students, researchers and interested people to seek access to facilities such as print rooms and museum stores, which are becoming surprisingly busy, places of movement and animation.

At one time it was a protocol of museum security that the physical addresses of reserves were not published. A new model conceives them as collection study centres, open not only to professionals in the know, but to any member of the public who may make an appointment to see the actual objects of special interest to them. The trend to create 'visible storage' responds similarly to the challenge of conveying and opening up what is still largely an internal view – that of the collection as a realm of life and imagination.[1]

If a more versatile sense of what museums are depends on a deeper sense of what they contain, we need to move beyond an unhelpful trio of understandings, which I call a naturalism of heritage, a naturalism of the collection and a naturalism of the object. I have already mentioned, in the context of repatriation, the assumption that people (whoever, wherever) want their stuff back. Heritage is certainly a broad and elusive concept: according to a 1999 Charter on International Cultural Tourism,

> It encompasses landscapes, historic places, sites and built environments, as well as bio-diversity, collections, past and continuing cultural practices, knowledge and living experiences. It records and expresses the long processes of historic development, forming the essence of diverse national, regional, indigenous and local identities and is an integral part of modern life.[2]

Underlying wide-ranging definitions of such kinds are, however, assumptions that people have or should have an organic attachment to artefacts and practices associated with their ancestors or their nation, an attachment presumed to be important to their identity, that contributes to a sense of belonging. These notions amount to a naturalism of heritage. Of course, historic artefacts, as well as sites and intangible forms of heritage, may indeed be cherished by people in just these terms, but interests in the material culture of the past are often notably diverse and are as often marked by indifference or explicit rejection as by affirmation. Media commentators do not hesitate to assume that indigenous people are attached to the works of their ancestors but don't reflect on why, if that is the case, English people do not necessarily value the decorative arts or paintings made by their ancestors.

In many African nations, an aspiration to embrace and appropriate modernity is, and has long been, of profound importance, as is an (often linked) commitment to evangelical Christianity. Neither identification prompts people to go around talking about the importance to them of ancestral things; to the contrary, they may disavow such interest, associating it with backwardness and sin. In South Africa, traditional art and craft carries the double taint of Apartheid segregationism and tribalism, the latter anathema from the perspective of the ANC's ongoing nation-building effort. The picture on the ground is of course more complicated, but the short version is that money has been lavished on museums of struggle – sites of celebration, commemoration and conscience, of the kind cited earlier – while the ethnographic collections which might have been considered obvious expressions of the 'heritage' everybody is supposed to need and want appear, for the moment, to have little to offer collective imaginations and aspirations, and accordingly suffer a lack of both patrons and a public.[3]

The situation in parts of the Middle East is considerably more disturbing. Militants affiliated with the so-called Islamic State have funded their campaigns through the sale of looted antiquities – as early as June 2014 they were reported to have raised some U.S.$36 million in this manner – but have notoriously gone on to destroy works and edifices at enormously significant sites such as Nimrud and Palmyra.[4] The intention is evidently to repudiate, in the most categorical terms, the relevance of any modernist and universal language of heritage, at the same time as other freedoms and girls' right to education are similarly rejected. Like the Taliban's destruction of the Bamiyan Buddhas in 2001, these acts of iconoclasm were staged for a wider world and responded brutally to the international community's interest in the preservation of such monuments. If 'community' in that sense is too often an abstraction of diplomacy, there actually are many people in many countries who value such figures, edifices and remains, who sense a collective injury and loss, even with respect to sites they personally never visited and never anticipated visiting.

In the Pacific, while evangelical and millenarian faiths have many adherents, customary culture is commonly celebrated and showcased for tourists, but those Islanders who are keenly interested in the historic artefacts they may see in museums, in Suva, Nouméa, Auckland, Sydney or London, are not all affirmative for the same reasons. Someone may treasure a piece of barkcloth because it has particular associations with remembered people or a known place; a practitioner may be absorbed in the intricate examination of weaving or carving technique; a community leader may look to revive crafts to generate income, or consider that awareness of tradition will help keep young people out of trouble; a youth may seek a tattoo motif from an appropriately local source.[5]

If we need, therefore, to acknowledge the range, idiosyncrasy and sometimes absence of interest people have in 'their' heritage, even an antipathy to whatever it may be, we need conversely to recognize that people may be attached to artefacts that are not linked with their culture or nationality in this sense, but that may appeal by virtue of their strangeness, or their distant and even mysterious origins. The fundamental problem of the language of heritage is not that it somehow overrates the past – heritage patently is powerful – but the presumption that interest and value rest in a form of possession. This is not surprising, since heritage's history, and especially its legal safeguarding, are closely linked with the modern nation state. Nations and would-be nations, such as indigenous minorities, list, protect and limit the export of heritage. More generally, something matters to us because it is in a cultural or historical sense 'ours'. No doubt unintentionally, this is to presuppose, and even amounts to a charter for, a lack of curiosity – that we will not want to encounter what comes from elsewhere.

Turning from the claims made about collections to their make-up, the 'naturalism' that I signal is a numerical one; it is the presumption that a collection is a more or less vast set of objects – that is, of individual entities. In a sense, it is: an overwhelming number of specimens or artefacts may daunt the viewer of a crowded natural history, ethnography or decorative art display. If the mainstream art museum mostly presents work more sparsely, any larger fine-art institution displays considerably more than a visitor is likely to want to look at in the course of a single visit, and probably has a print room, with drawers upon drawers of etchings, aquatints, mezzotints, woodblocks, linocuts and screen prints. Some museums seem to contain not just too much stuff, but too many kinds of stuff – a sheer excess of categories and genres.

Yet hundreds of thousands or even millions of artefacts or specimens do not constitute 'the collection' any more than a physical territory of, say, 7.7 million square km or a population of, say, 22 million people constitutes a nation. A nation is a complex institutional and political entity – a form of governance – as well as an imagined and contested community – a narrative. Without pushing

*overleaf:* Mark Adams, *Downing Street, Cambridge. Museum of Archaeology and Anthropology. Bevan Store. Totokia style Fijian clubs, i-wau, collected by Baron Anatole von Hügel, Sir Arthur Gordon and others,* 2010, silver bromide prints.

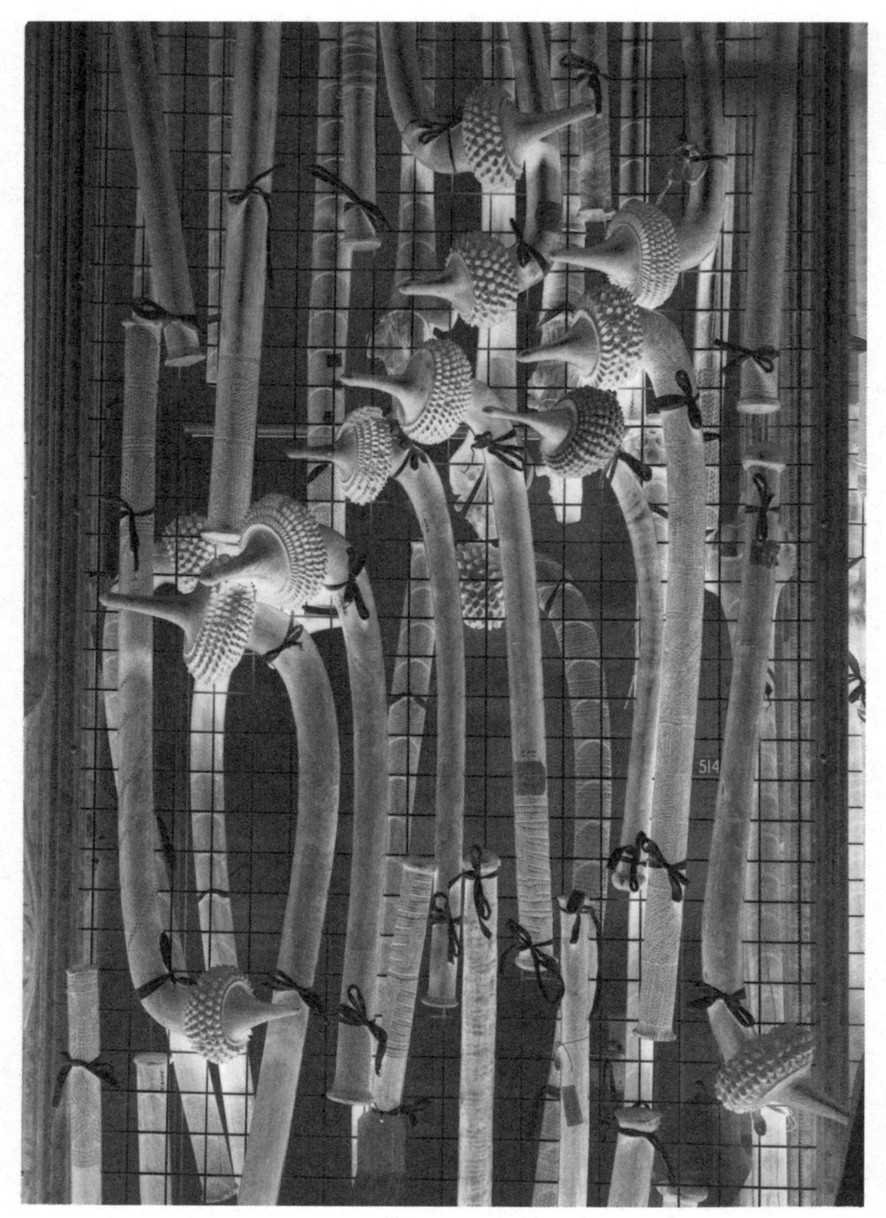
514

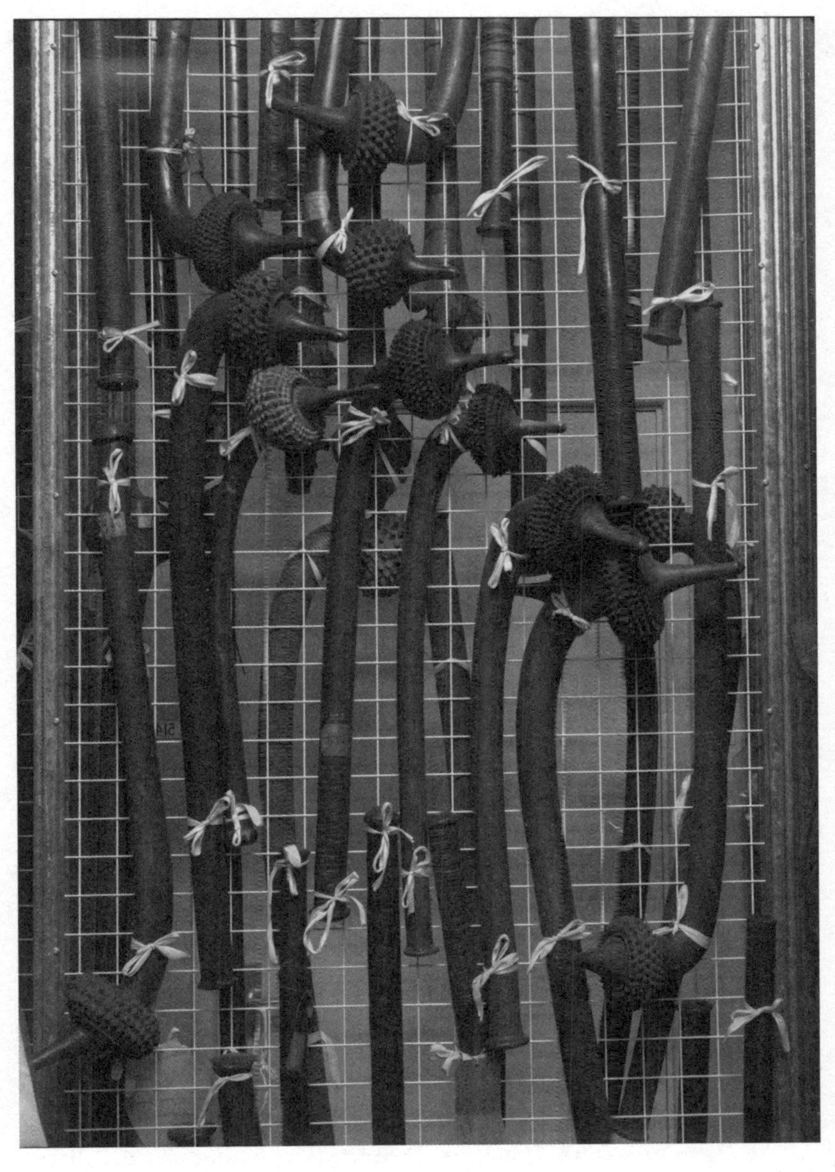

the analogy, a collection is likewise made up of complex associations, connections and representations.[6] A museum collection is rendered singular and unified through a kind of equivalent to national governance in an ideally coherent and complete cataloguing system, but also in an institution's constitution and administrative structure, which generally vests the responsibility to maintain, care for and display a collection – which may be owned legally by the nation, the public, a foundation or a university, rather than by the institution itself – in a board of trustees of some kind, which appoints a director and a staff of curators who actually do the work.

A collection, like a house or a person, thus has distinct legal and physical existences. The material and meaningful lives of houses, people and collections alike are less easily distinguished. And most museums do not hold 'a collection' as much as they do 'collections', in the plural, meaning that their total holdings are made up of bodies of material, reflecting the broadest categories of modern Western knowledge (natural history, technology), affinities of media, materials or genre (drawings, ceramics, coins and medals) and major periods and regions (medieval and modern; Asia and Africa). Yet museums' holdings, in these broad divisions, will in turn be made up of many specific collections, a collection of relics from Scott's Antarctic expeditions, a bequest of French Impressionist paintings and so on. Very often, what might be called a 'collection' – a group of works or specimens assembled at a particular time – has suffered division and distribution: the Benin Bronzes notoriously appropriated during the British punitive expedition of 1897 were auctioned to cover the costs of the mission and though there are major holdings in the British Museum and in the Ethnologisches Museum, Berlin, sub-collections deriving from this sale are now dispersed among dozens of institutions in Europe and elsewhere. Hence the 'collection' in one sense is both smaller and larger than the 'collection' in the other; it is at once a fraction of one museum's collection – something that occupies a specific and bounded space in a display case, gallery or set of storage drawers or racks in one museum – and a larger entity, which may populate many such spaces in different institutions (and private collections) in different parts of the world. An object diaspora is like a diaspora of people, distributed across a number of countries: we won't know for sure just how many individuals or artefacts from Samoa or Tanzania will be found in France, Germany or Canada. Their situations and experiences and relative marginality or privilege will vary a great deal; some may be 'lost' to censuses or catalogues unconcerned to identify origins or inaccurate in their mapping of them.

The core of this argument is that what we might call a positivist conception of the collection – an identity associated with its definite physical existence – will not take us far at all. Though collections are made up of works and things, and might therefore seem susceptible to precise enumeration and definition, in a deeper and truer sense they are also made up, like nations or communities, of relations. These relations in turn are of a number of kinds, some literal and amenable to straightforward description, others more at the level of conception or imagination, yet not necessarily less consequential for being so. Among the more literal, we can point to relations between objects that form distinct groups and series. A group of zoological specimens may all have been collected by one naturalist, a group of photographs by a connoisseur over a lifetime of acquisition. Four spears now in Cambridge were appropriated by Captain Cook and his companions from an Aboriginal camp not far from the water's edge, on the south shore of Botany Bay, within a short time of the navigator's first

Australian landing on 29 April 1770. Rothko's Seagram murals, some of which are now on permanent display at Tate Modern, were at first intended for display at an elite Manhattan restaurant. Such associations and sets appear simple enough, but may be doubly incomplete and overdetermined.

The journal of the naturalist Joseph Banks, who accompanied Cook, indicates that a much larger number of spears – some forty to fifty – were picked up, because some had earlier been thrown at the Europeans as they attempted to land and it was feared that their tips were poisoned. This was not so much collecting as disarmament. What happened to the rest is not known; some may have been destroyed, others might well have reached other museums, yet without documentation linking them to the *Endeavour*'s voyage. A drawing, made soon after the voyage by a draughtsman employed by Banks, is proof that representative examples were considered significant. It also helps establish that a shield in the British Museum was obtained on the same occasion; indeed it is clear from Banks's notes that it was picked up by one of the Aboriginal men who had thrown spears, to defend himself when the intruders opened fire – he dropped it as he withdrew. These quotidian things are related to each other and above all to the inauspicious inauguration of relationships between the British and indigenous Australians in a singularly specific sense: they were acquired not incidentally but as part of the practice of seeing off local resistance to the landing. The multi-pronged fish spear seems intimately apt to the shallow, sandy waters of Botany Bay, and just too ordinary an instrument of subsistence to bear the narrative of continental colonization with which we inevitably now associate it.[7]

Rothko's commission, on the other hand, was originally for a set of seven works, and he hired a studio space adapted to a scale specifically intended to simulate the proportions of the restaurant. The artist had, as is well known, misgivings about the appropriateness of the setting and withdrew from the arrangement, but went on to produce thirty more or less related paintings, nine of which he gifted to the Tate in a display he mocked up himself for a specific room in the Millbank gallery that is now Tate Britain.[8] The group now relocated to Tate Modern is precisely not 'the' set, from the perspective of the paintings' conception or genesis, but the works do manifest the revision of the project, its 'decommissioning', which Rothko admirers would interpret as its liberation from commercial constraint and debasement.

Artefacts, artworks and specimens not only bear relations with other objects and works, but with the forms of documentation that are as essential to a museum's existence as premises and spaces for display. Registration numbers may be impressed into seals, written onto the actual artefacts or the backs of paintings, or inscribed on labels that are stuck onto them or attached to them; objects may be stored within boxes or on racks that bear lists of the works within a particular container or on a particular support. It might be assumed that these identifying attachments are of no more interest than labels bearing prices in department stores, but they are often far stranger and can be unexpectedly revealing. The Ceres Borghese now on long-term loan from the Louvre to the Musée des civilisations de l'Europe et de la Méditerranée in Marseilles bears a red stamp in which M R indicates that it formed part of the *mobilier royal* – it was among the works 'restituted to', and around 1815 catalogued by order of, Louis XVIII following the Bourbon Restoration. Yet the sculpture (a portrait of Livia, wife of the emperor Augustus, which may not have been given the characteristics of Ceres, goddess of agriculture, until an eighteenth-century 'restoration') had actually been purchased by Napoleon from Prince Camillo Borghese (his brother-in-law) in 1807, and in due course the collection as a whole reverted to being that of the people and nation, not that of the king.[9] Labels and catalogues often preserve obsolete assertions of ownership and identification of this kind: they are replete with geographic and political anachronisms and mark orders and relations that existed at one time but do so no more.

Collections are supposed to be documented in accessions registers, which typically consist of a series of physical ledgers; many will have been accessed in the past through catalogue cards, which sometimes featured drawings of the pieces and in some cases multiple annotations by successive curators incorporating corrections, revisions or the opinions of visiting experts. An object file may also include conservators' reports and valuations prepared for insurance purposes. In general, museums do not insure their permanent collections, but works must be insured at the expense of the borrower when they travel to exhibitions elsewhere: museum pieces, defined by their permanent removal from circulation and the market, are nevertheless periodically assessed in market terms, though their valuations are usually confidential and do not normally form part of the catalogue record made available to the public, or to researchers. Documentation is thus layered – it has public and more restricted expressions.

Collections data of this kind, once all on paper and card, has generally now been transferred to electronic systems of various sorts, incidentally nearly always introducing at least a few 'misrelations' of mistranscription, partial transcription and the omission or duplication of records. Like collections themselves, which may be

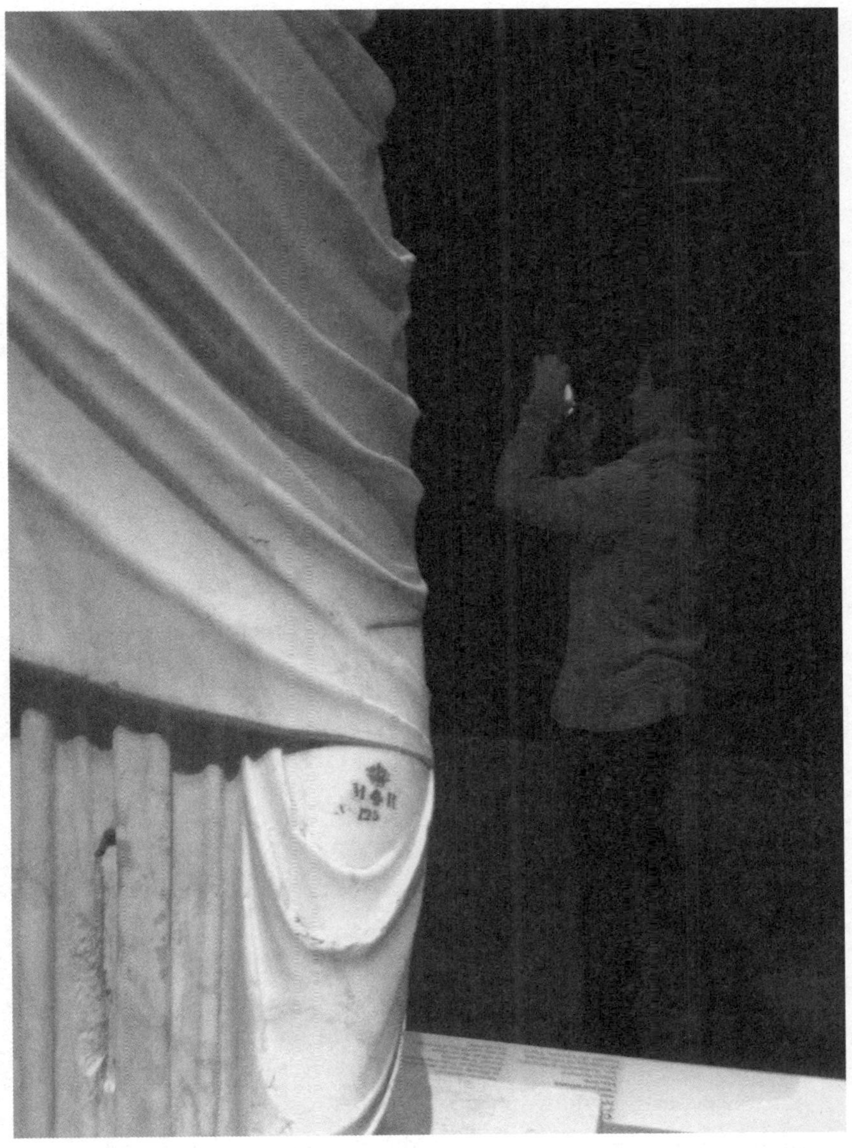

Detail of the *Portrait of Livia as Ceres*, Roman, *c.* AD 20, purchased 1807 from the Borghese collection, as exhibited at the Musée des civilisations de l'Europe et de la Méditerranée, Marseilles, with visitor and smartphone.

amalgamated through physical transfer, these databases are susceptible to inclusion in cross-institutional search platforms of various kinds. The data on old catalogue records, inherited by their modern online counterparts, may now be 'harvested' by other systems, such as the Reciprocal Research Network at the University of British Columbia, which assembles collection records associated with certain northwest-coast aboriginal groups, with the intention of making the digital collection accessible to those groups themselves as well as to other interested parties.[10]

The collections of, say, an art or natural history museum are often understood to include archives and photo archives as well as the works and specimens themselves. Documents and photos are thus related to each other and also to artworks, artefacts and specimens: letters may reveal the negotiation of an acquisition; photos may show a sculpture in the artist's studio, in an antecedent gallery or collection, or, for an ethnographic artefact in use prior to collection, even the moment and occasion of its acquisition. There is a wide range of such relations, ranging from those that may be formally captured within a modern museum's database of linked records, to relations of reference and context, like the association between the Parthenon marbles now in the British Museum and the travel narrative of Edward Daniel Clarke, who witnessed and lamented their detachment from the temple (but who had himself removed an important statue from the site of Eleusis against the wishes of locals who considered her presence auspicious, despite being Christians rather than adherents of some neoclassical polytheism).[11] Another such example is the association between a particular ornithological specimen and the biography of the naturalist pre-eminent in the public imagination, Charles Darwin.

Many of the relationships existing in and among museum collections could be described as latent or potential, like a relationship between myself and a cousin of whose existence and identity I am ignorant. Such a relationship, we could say, might as well not exist, but it does nevertheless: it retains the capacity to be discovered and activated, and many people's lives are marked at one time or another by encounters, often of an intensely interesting or affecting kind, with lost relatives or acquaintances of this sort. Similarly, curators or museum visitors may be unaware of both the relationships among artefacts and the relationships between them and people – the links may be latent in museum documentation or in sources that might be traced otherwise. Yet the connections can, through effort or accident, be discovered, altering the significance and interest of the object. In 2009, Liz Wetton, a long-term volunteer working through the egg collections of the Museum of Zoology in Cambridge, found one with Darwin's name written on it, which turned out to be the only egg extant from the *Beagle* voyage. It was collected in Uruguay, and belonged to the common tinamou bird; Darwin had cracked it by trying to get it into a box that was too small. Its rediscovery was much publicized and it has since been included in various exhibitions. Now, a specimen that on the face of it is unexceptional – despite uncannily having the appearance more of a bronze commemorative cast than the actual eggshell it is – gives visitors a sense of tangible connection with one of the legendary figures, and one of the legendary expeditions, in the history of science, as well as with the extraordinary naturalist's all too ordinary clumsiness.[12]

In this broader and certainly more nebulous sense, objects can be related to a host of people: those who originally created them or first used them; those creators' descendants; those who collected

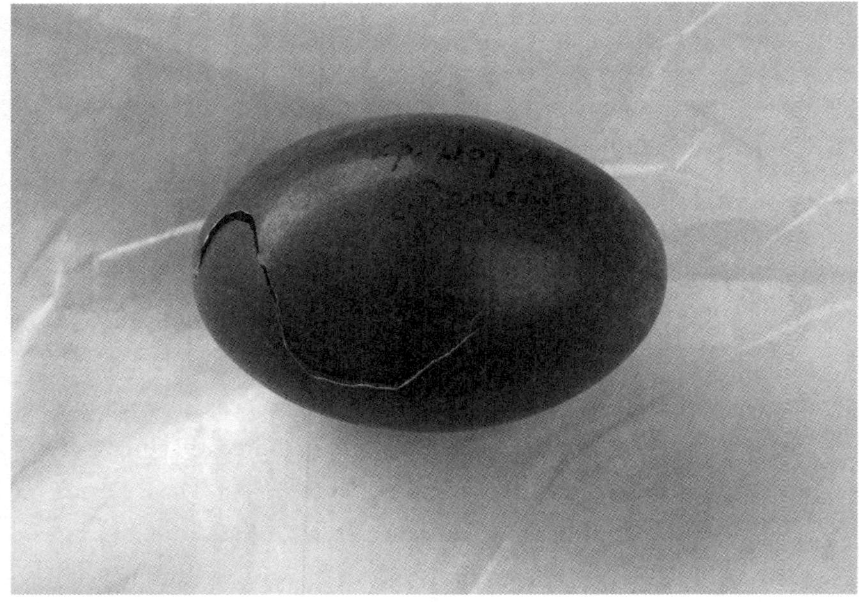

Tinamou egg, *c.* 1830. Found in Uruguay by Charles Darwin; Museum of Zoology, Cambridge.

them and their descendants; nationalists who consider that certain treasures may only legitimately be kept in their own country; the curators and scientists who work on the things; the artists who study and respond to the works of predecessors. It may seem improbable that relationships between relics of whatever sort and people long dead, or people who may never have seen or touched them, are real and consequential, but their management may be delicate and their mismanagement may bring about a crisis. In New Zealand, a bitter dispute in 2009 between the Auckland Museum and the children of Sir Edmund Hillary, who had bequeathed his manuscripts to the institution, was resolved only following the intervention of the country's prime minister; it loomed large among issues that brought the institution to breaking point and forced the director to resign the following year.[13]

These associations do not all take the form of straightforward attachment; even if we think of as strong a connection as that between maker and object, artist and work, there is abundant evidence that people regard their creations in various ways – sometimes they are ambivalent, sometimes they take the view that once a work is completed and out there, the rest is not their business. Such relationships are also culturally variable and may be shaped by precepts quite different to Western ideas of authorship and property. The reason that the extraordinary wooden sculptures from New Ireland known as malangan are found in such vast numbers in museum collections (there are thousands in Berlin alone) is that they were made for particular mortuary ceremonies. People were then done with them – they had no further value, they were left to rot in the forest or, from the colonial period onwards, were sold to travellers and collectors. In traditional terms, the relationships between artists or communities and carvings were finished, extinguished. If that was so, some people on or from New Ireland may now think about the question differently, and the nation of Papua New Guinea – of which New Ireland is a part – has the usual legal frameworks intended to prohibit or regulate the export of artefacts and antiquities.

If collections are made up of a bewildering variety of relations, what they speak of, most vitally, are human intentions. Consider J.M.W. Turner, at the age of 27 already wealthy, regarded as the outstanding British artist of his generation, and a Royal Academician. The artist opened Turner's Gallery, adjunct to his own city house, not far north of the department stores and fashion outlets that now line Oxford Street. Here he was able to order works as he wished, which he could not do in the crowded displays at the Royal Academy. He went on to refurbish the gallery, not as a showcase for new work, but as a museum displaying a representative range of his major paintings, and he formed the intention of presenting the collection to the nation. In order to constitute that bequest appropriately, he not only refrained from selling certain works but actually bought back others at auctions and otherwise.[14] While the collection's history following the artist's death in 1851 is complex, its transfer from the National Gallery to the Tate and the eventual inauguration in 1987 of the Clore Gallery – a wing of what is now Tate Britain – specifically to house the bequest, amounted not only to 'the most prominent national presentation of any one single artist' but also 'a huge step towards meeting Turner's own wishes'.[15] Collections are both the effects of, and evidence for, past intentions – in this case those of an artist with not only a vehement sense of his own place in British art history, but an interest in the nature and ambitions of national art institutions, such as the National Gallery, which had been founded in 1824 and opened its Trafalgar Square Galleries in 1838.

The Clore Gallery exemplifies a sense in which an individual's intentions may sometimes have remarkable impact over the long term: Rothko's gift, cited earlier, was partly inspired by his admiration for Turner and reflects similar interests in placing works considered outstanding and representative by the artists themselves in celebrated public settings. Yet the bequest could be seen as an exception that proves the rule: collections more typically result from layered and intersecting intentions. An ethnographer may seek ritual objects that people do not wish to surrender; the fieldworker may be given unsanctified copies instead, or things of different kinds, which people positively wish to barter. Of the things a field collector acquires,

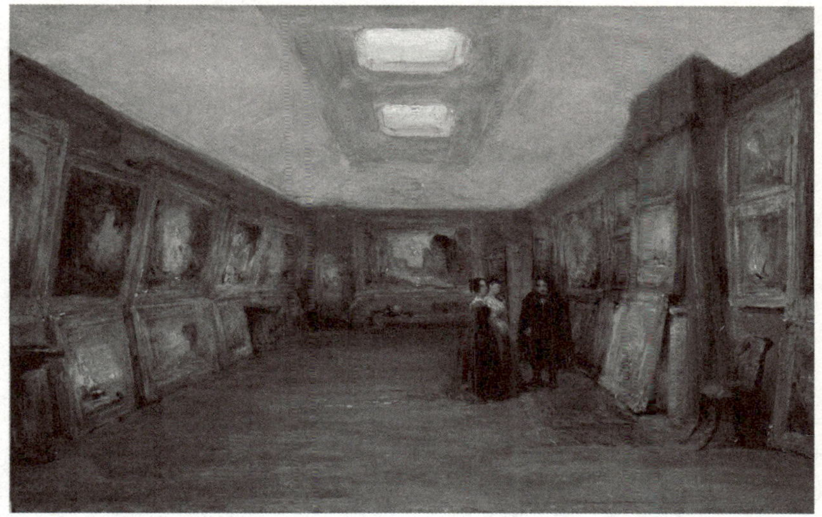

George Jones, *Interior of Turner's Gallery*, c. 1852, oil on panel, Ashmolean Museum, Oxford.

some may eventually reach a museum because a family or private collector did not want them, rather than because they were highly valued and thought appropriate to a public institution. And in fact, Turner's wishes are realized, to the extent that they have been, only because curators, museum leaders, fundraisers, architects and many others conceived and undertook a project that had its own rationale in the context of late twentieth-century art-museum development.

It is still commonly presumed in the media that ethnographic artefacts were mostly looted. While some objects, including famous ones such as the Benin Bronzes mentioned earlier, were indeed seized in the aftermath of violence, the bulk of what is in anthropological collections was obtained through purchase or exchange. Most field collectors were, like other travellers, comparatively vulnerable, reliant on host communities' help and hospitality; they did not have the capacity to steal artefacts, had they even wished to do so. Those who assume that collections were stolen would be surprised to discover quite how often locals were positively willing, not merely to sell things for prices that they considered reasonable, but to gift objects to collectors or museums, for various reasons, including an interest in seeing their tradition or their people represented in what they took to be a prestigious metropolitan setting.

Among the pieces from the Kingdom of Buganda (present-day Uganda) in the Museum of Archaeology and Anthropology (MAA) in Cambridge is a brass necklet worn by a royal bodyguard. Apolo Kagwa (1864–1927) was Katikiro or prime minister of the kingdom, and was regent for many years in place of the young heir. One of the Church Missionary Society's earliest converts, he was also a friend of the prominent missionary John Roscoe, whose book *The Baganda* (1911) is a classic early survey of customary life in the kingdom, though it owed a great deal to Kagwa's own extensive writings on history and folklore and drew on interviews with elders that the men conducted jointly. It was during a visit to England with his private secretary to attend the coronation of Edward VII in 1902 that Kagwa visited Roscoe in Cambridge and presented the necklet and sixteen other pieces to the museum, where they are now cared for alongside Roscoe's separate and more extensive donation, much of which he had probably received from or through Kagwa. When Kagwa assembled the group of pieces ahead of his trip to England, he was thinking diplomatically; he planned to leave the artefacts with appropriate recipients there, and perhaps had the museum in mind from the start.[16]

In November 1961, in the lead-up to Ugandan independence, Abu Mayanja, minister for education, wrote to Cambridge's vice

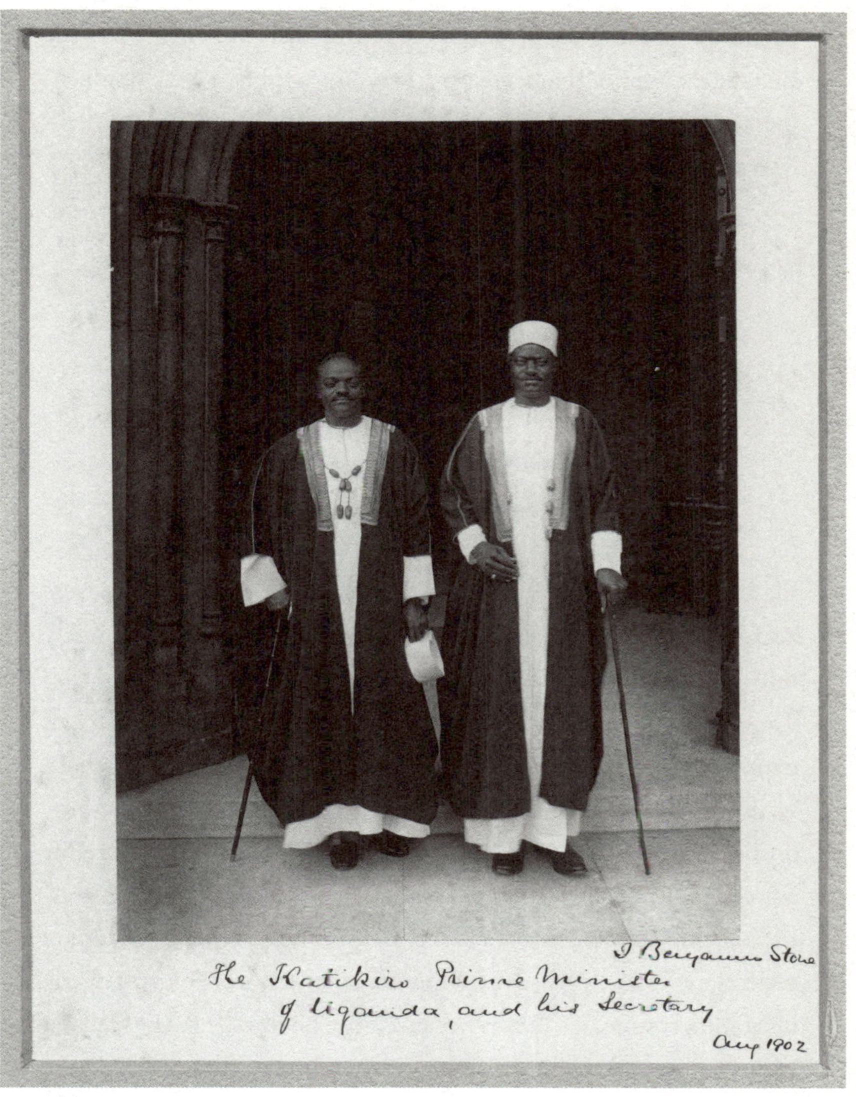


Sir Benjamin Stone, Apolo Kagwa, Katikiro of Uganda, and Ham Musaka [his secretary], August 1902, platinum print, National Portrait Gallery, London.

chancellor seeking the repatriation of the 'historic relics' from the Buganda kingdom that were held at MAA, singling out the regalia of the war god Kibuuka. A barrister and a Cambridge graduate himself, Mayanja expressed himself judiciously:

> We are not disputing the legal title of Cambridge to these relics although it is doubtful whether Sir Apolo had the right to give them away. On the contrary we are very grateful to the University for having preserved them. Our request is rather that [you] will consider sympathetically our great interest in these things especially now that Uganda is about to regain her Independence.

He also emphasized that the 'facilities' at the national museum were adequate and that the objects would not only be preserved safely but would remain accessible to 'scientific enquirers and others'.[17] The museum's committee, chaired at the time by Jack Goody, an eminent Africanist, were indeed sympathetic, 'so far as unique and sacred objects' were concerned. The 'general ethnological collection', on the other hand, was said to be 'of great value in Cambridge for educational purposes', and anyway, the committee believed, consisted mainly of objects already represented in the Ugandan national collection. In due course the Kibuuka relics went back to Kampala in Mayanja's suitcase. They have since been on display in the Uganda Museum, though Kibuuka followers have repeatedly called for the sacred objects to be handed over to them for cult purposes and in November 2007 a crowd stormed the institution, intending to seize the relics. Though they were prevented from doing so, the issue remains alive, and in part to forestall any renewed attempt, armed guards are routinely present at the museum's public entrance. Kagwa, Roscoe and Mayanja, like J.M.W. Turner, were all interested in placing objects in museums – institutions that had national or scientific status, or both. In 1961, there was a question, soon succeeded by consensus, that the appropriate museum for the relics, though not the collection as a whole, was in Kampala rather than Cambridge; the more enduring and bitter contention since has been about whether they should be in a museum at all, and the thwarted intentions of those cult followers now define the collection, as palpably as those of the Greek people and government do the Elgin marbles.

Just as a ring may be a materialization of a marriage vow, a collection is less a mass of individual things than a materialization of successive intentions. It represents a body of evidence rather like an archaeological deposit, a site-specific formation of things gathered and brought from elsewhere. The cultural theorist W.J.T. Mitchell influentially asked, 'What do pictures really want?' He sought to acknowledge and address the claims and demands that images all too often seem to make of us, to entertain what on the face of it might be considered a theoretical heresy – that paintings, photographs and other images may play active and forceful parts in our lives.[18] We might ask a comparable question: what do collections want?

Among the answers to this question is something like excavation, or even geomorphological investigation, that would draw out the collection's story of accumulation and loss. The archaeologist makes sense of a site by identifying its distinct and successive layers, and by demarcating areas of erosion or disturbance. These levels and features may reflect phases of human use and events such as immigration, evacuation or environmental change. Collections are likewise marked by phases of activity and dormancy. We typically imagine them steadily growing, but they may also have been subtracted from. In the late nineteenth and well into the twentieth centuries, so-called 'duplicates' in ethnography collections, such as clubs of ostensibly the same type, were extensively exchanged or sold. Art museums, especially in the United States, still de-accession and sell works that are considered of lesser importance, or perhaps those that have just become unfashionable, with startling regularity. Collections have also been shifted periodically across institutions and disciplines, and have been divided and freshly amalgamated. In Paris, the movement of material from the Musée de l'Homme to the Musée du quai Branly was a focus of heated debate, it being feared that an inclusive anthropology was to be displaced by a hierarchical and primitivist art history. But this was far from the first shift that some artefacts in the collections of the new institution had already undergone, or suffered. Some were previously in the Louvre, in a museum of colonial 'antiquities' or in the Musée de la Marine, as well as a variety of smaller institutions, each implying a distinct artistic, historical, ethnological or archaeological frame of reference. And the reconstitution of holdings and institutions continues apace; recently

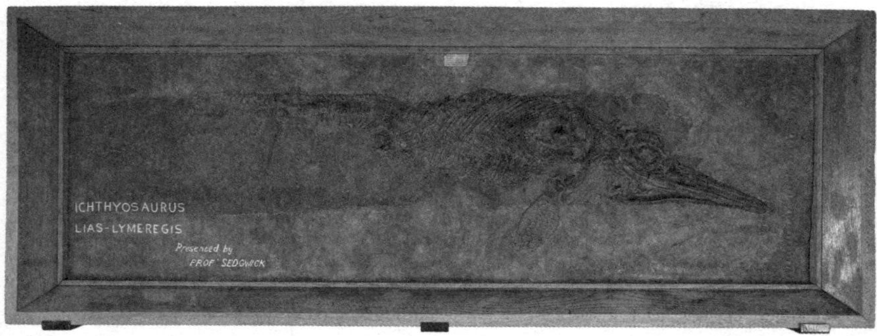


Ichthyosaur skeleton, collected in Lyme Regis by Mary Anning, early 19th century; Sedgwick Museum of Earth Sciences, Cambridge.

accomplished in Antwerp, Barcelona and Marseilles, it continues, as has been mentioned, in Berlin, where the Humboldt-Forum development is scheduled to open in 2019. Hence, if the collection may be compared to the nation, it is like the United Kingdom, South Sudan or even Donetsk – in other words it represents a totality of a temporary kind, the product of federation or division, and may prove susceptible, soon enough, either to further division or some fresh unification.

Which brings us to the naturalism of the collected artefact. Especially but not exclusively in ethnography collections, it is assumed that the objects in museums sample the stuff that people actually had and used, and that they were extracted from organic lives, from community use. Such artefacts were thus subjected to a process of 'decontextualization', a movement (we suppose) from significance and value within their original or natural context, to one of separation from context and life. While this rhetoric is associated particularly with things in world cultures collections, and with the assumption that artefacts were wrongfully appropriated, it has a wider range of expressions, for example in relation to the specimens that fill natural history museums. Whether we are thinking of birds, plants or fossils, what these are emphatically not are 'natural specimens'. To the contrary, they are artful creations. Among practitioners the word 'preparation' is used to refer to the rendering of residue in stone, a plant cutting or a dead creature in a suitably revelatory, visually dramatic or (in the case of taxidermy) paradoxically still but lifelike form. When I first encountered the dodo skeleton in Cambridge's University Museum of Zoology, I assumed that what I looked at was 'the' skeleton of a particular dodo, whereas it is in fact an assemblage, made from the bones of many individual birds that were gathered by islanders from the deep mud of the swamp known aptly as the Mare aux Songes in southeastern Mauritius.[19]

Many works in museums did indeed have 'contexts' in people's lives, and these include not only African or Oceanic works that were formerly caught up in the heat and dust of dance, but paintings that were once in churches or domestic settings. Yet just as other paintings and artworks were conceived for public institutions, a far greater proportion of the indigenous works in museums were made for collectors – and indeed specifically for museums – than is commonly understood. The great German museums *für Völkerkunde* that assembled their holdings in the closing decades of the nineteenth century and the period before the First World War, in part through undertaking large-scale, state-sponsored expeditions, are replete with model houses and canoes, made on commission for the ethnographers who took home many big things but could mostly not purchase or pack the full-scale originals. Such collections also include model human figures showing tattoos or appropriately scaled articles of dress. None of these were samples of things that their communities habitually made or used; they were novel creations, products of the cross-cultural encounter and of collecting itself, which looks less like a moment of appropriation and more like a space of redefinition and invention.

What I call the naturalism of the artefact also presumes that a thing's identity has something of the self-subsistence and fixity of the physical object, yet many museum objects are in important senses not just themselves – they are their citations. A citation may be a reference in a literal sense: a work or specimen may be published in a scholarly article or a catalogue, and some more obscure pieces may only be cited in that manner, or not at all. But others acquire lives

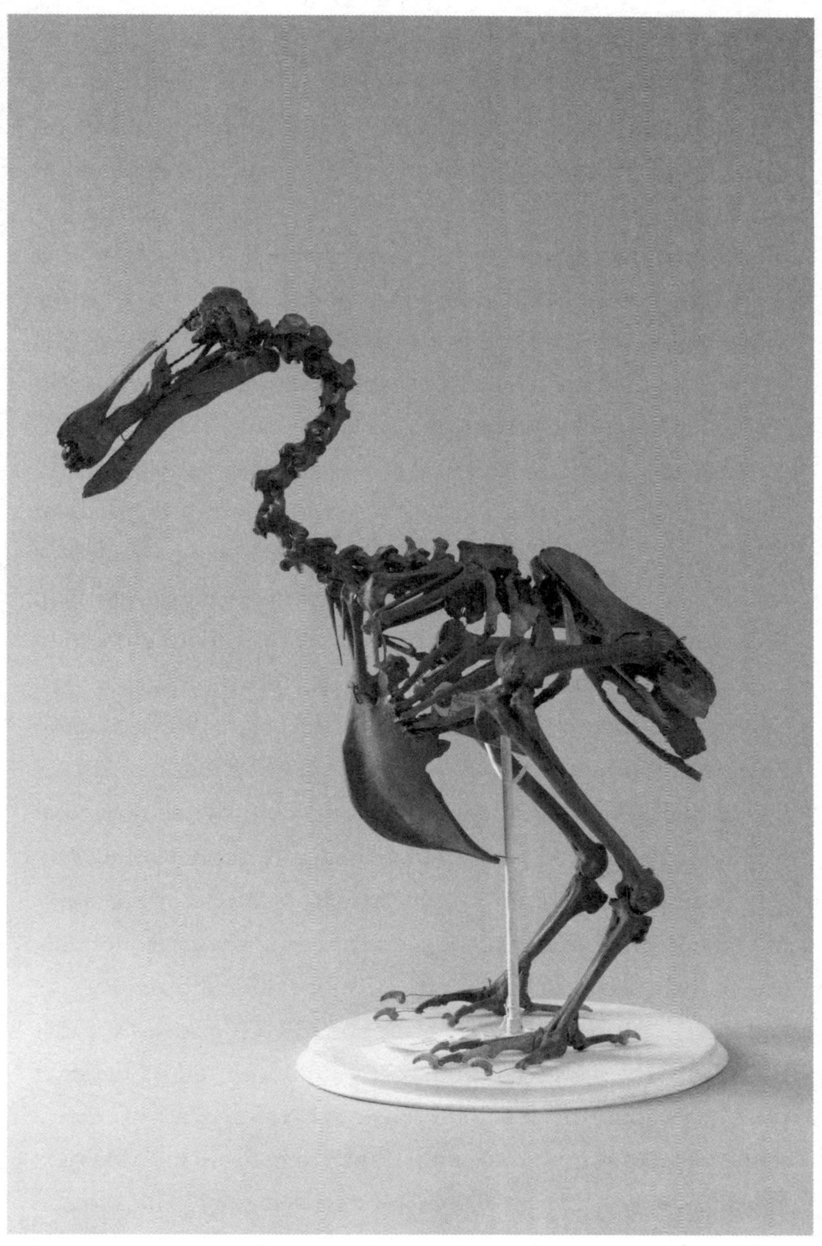

Dodo skeleton, composite. Bones found in Mauritius, *c.* 1870; Museum of Zoology, Cambridge.

through literary works or visual allusions. In Cambridge, a Roman-British Barnack stone coffin, excavated during the development of a new suburb, contained not only the skeleton of a woman but those of a shrew and a mouse; the woman's toes had apparently been gnawed by the latter. The coffin was displayed in the museum in the 1950s, and was evidently seen by Sylvia Plath, who was prompted to write 'All the Dead Dears', a powerful and fearful meditation on 'this antique museum-cased lady', 'no kin of mine, yet kin she is'.[20]

An Austral Islands sculpture of a god known as A'a, remarkable for the proliferation of smaller god images over the body of the figure, itself a hollow casket in phallic form that contained 24 smaller gods at the time it was surrendered to the missionary John Williams in 1822, is cited in a poem (by William Empson) and in innumerable texts on aesthetics in general and on Oceania in particular, and was also notably replicated. The first replica was cast in order to compensate the London Missionary Society (LMS) for the loss of the figure itself, which was among a number showcased as trophies at the LMS's Missionary Museum during the nineteenth century that by the end of the century were recognized as major works of Oceanic ritual art. Further casts were eventually made, not only for ethnographic museums but for artists including Roland Penrose and Picasso. Henry Moore, who had a bronze cast made, wrote that the sculpture was 'so powerful that it was difficult to find the right place in his house to put it'. One such cast has also been 'repatriated' to the island of Rurutu, where it is displayed in the island's Mairie.[21] Whereas the 'specimen' is in principle interchangeable with another, even the replicas of A'a are each seemingly unique.

A collection can be said to be made up not only of its internal relationships, but by the fame of individual pieces, which reaches many different milieux and is expressed in many diverse ways. Certain objects, such as the Rosetta Stone, possess the singular hyper-celebrity that we also associate with the *Mona Lisa*, the Rapa Nui statues and a few other works. Though the word 'iconic' is often used of such pieces, their distinctive characteristics are not those of icons. To the contrary, they seem constantly at risk of a total loss of sanctity or meaning, appearing as they do incessantly as tropes in

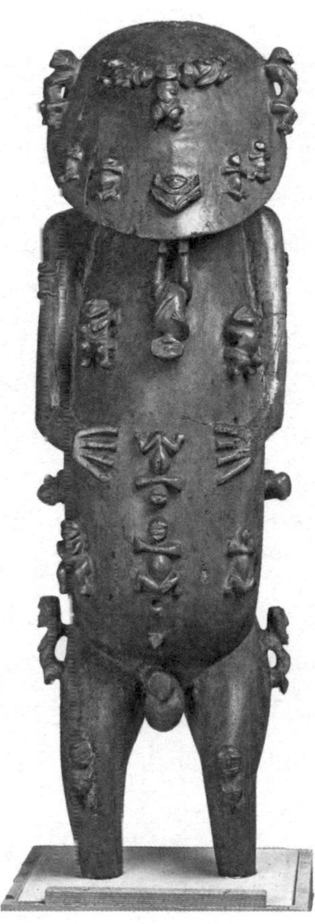

The god A'a, wooden sculpture, Rurutu, Austral Islands, Polynesia, made before 1821; British Museum, London.

newspaper cartoons, advertisements and allusions of every possible kind. If the proliferation of what might be called pseudo-citations, which are generally indifferent to any meaningful identity the work in question ever possessed, does not simply enhance the aura of the original in an extreme manner but converts its sighting into a tourist fetish, there remains a vestige of space in which the encounter with the actual piece may be surprising or revealing. Which is to say that a collection also exists in the before and after: of anticipated visits and expectations on the one hand, of souvenirs and recollections on the other.

If, to sum up, the 'three naturalisms' of heritage, the collection and the artefact are questioned, where are we left? First, we cannot presume *for whom* collections bear value and significance. Without diminishing the sense in which they are the creations of particular people, of a particular place and time, we would be wrong if we expected people of the place or culture, or their descendants – the 'source community' in museum jargon – to necessarily attach importance and value to historic things. Sometimes they do, yet there are many instances where they don't, or where they do so in qualified and very varied terms, reflecting issues of distance and dislocation from the past, as well as the present orientations of their practice, faith and politics. Conversely, communities and individuals adopt and appropriate things; they may sense connection with things, and value things, that are not part of 'their' heritage in a reified cultural, ethnic or national sense.

Second, a collection is considerably more, something other than, a smaller or larger group of individual objects. Its affinity with the archaeological site suggests an emergent quality: it is reshaped as we act on it; there is more to it than we thought and less than we may know in the future. Yet it may well be at risk, environmentally or politically: we hope, but can't be sure, that we will have the opportunity to revisit it. It – the collection – shifts shape as we approach it from different angles and activate it in its different aspects. Most vitally, it is *made up of relations* as much as it is of things, and those relations are themselves heterogeneous. Some are literal, such as a work or specimen's connection with a label; others, such as an association with an unknown creator or known former owner, may be nebulous yet potentially powerful. Relations may be hypothetical, latent or susceptible to activation: the relation is itself like an artefact such as a folded piece of fabric – for the time being unused, but with the potential of becoming a dress, a banner, a shroud.

The digital image, encountered online, is not meaningfully or effectively equivalent to any actual object. I am articulating something more than the preciousness of a connoisseur: the material thing, in its three-dimensionality, presence, scale, texture and tactility, is different in its nature and effect to any picture of it. Which isn't to deny that online images are nevertheless enormously useful. They not only enable ready reference for those already in the know, but democratize access for those who can't get to a particular museum for whatever reason, for school classes and many others (subject to levels of 'digital literacy', that is, the capability of making use of what the Internet has to offer). It is therefore understandable that cultural agencies are heavily committed to the expansion of museums' digital presences and offerings.

What it is important to add is that while the image inevitably fails to do justice to the individual object, digitization, in equal or greater measure, decisively enhances the collection. An online catalogue renders a mass of things visible and apprehendable to a greater extent than ever before. It has always been, quite simply, difficult to get a sense of what a mass of boxes or drawers contain; even of the range and extent of a collection of paintings mounted over many racks. Card indices and similar physical registers did not necessarily make the task a great deal easier, other than for the curators who worked with their catalogues, finding ways into them and in due course knowing them intimately. In contrast, where a museum's website permits a collections search, results in the form of a grid of 'thumbnails' reveal the number of relevant objects or specimens more or less immediately, as well as the relative preponderance of certain types and key attributes such as date or place of origin, depending on the database in question. If I have an interest in Gauguin's works on paper, I can establish the scope of the collections in New York, Paris and elsewhere within a quarter of an hour; I may also be struck that what are ostensibly impressions of the same print appear notably different.

It is vital to know that many such systems suffer quirks or glitches, and even the best seem capable of telling users that there are no records relating to objects that you know for sure are in the collection. But online databases have been genuinely transformative, and have empowered understandings that could in the past only be obtained on site, painstakingly and with the active support of curators and collections staff (who in the bad old days were sadly often obstructive). Hence, if collections have provided knowledge of some kind, for as long as they have been assembled and attended to, they have only now been revealed more broadly and become actually usable by the many rather than the few.

Finally, the question of a collection's 'representativeness' is highly uncertain. While the positivist collectors of the late nineteenth and twentieth centuries laboured to produce encyclopaedic assemblages, and while artefact collections were and still are understood as 'material cultures', presumed to typify or sample the stuff that a particular group of people made, had and used, their relationship with this 'actually used' material culture is evidently less direct, even oblique. Many travellers and fieldworkers were not really seeking to collect systematically and in any case obtained what they were given or what local people wanted to barter or were prepared to give up. Some collectors obtained artefacts mainly on commission – they were parties to the creation of new material cultures – while others concentrated on certain genres because they were fascinated by them, or they simply acquired things they personally liked, as did and do many art collectors.

Over the last twenty to thirty years, the history of collections has become the focus of a steadily growing literature.[22] Fascinating as the byways of object biographies and the tales of eccentric collectors may be, there is a risk that museum-based scholarship of this kind implies that institutional histories are somehow more significant than the bigger stories of culture and politics that motivated the creation of the artworks, artefacts and specimens that constitute collections. Yet archaeological method demands comprehension of a site's stratigraphy and chronology, not as an end in itself, but because without that understanding, the lens that the site (or collection) offers cannot be focused in a fashion that brings the wider world into view. Just as prehistory explores histories of migration, trade and environmental change on the basis of extant material evidence, the museum offers the oblique and partial but powerful perspective of the collection based upon similarly broad issues of human creativity, cultural diversity, politics and natural history. And – I turn to this theme in the next chapter – a collection is more than a historical resource; it is also something that we work with prospectively, a technology that enables the creation of new things.

Beyond the naturalisms of heritage, the collection and the artefact, the museum becomes visible not just as an edifice or institution, but as a method and a form of activity.[23] Curators typically identify themselves in disciplinary terms: they are art historians, archaeologists or entomologists. But in another sense their discipline is that of the curator. Insofar as their research is museum-based, it starts with objects, with material culture in the distinctively assembled form of the collection, and the way the curator finds inspiration, insight or knowledge is in some sense through the collection. Their enquiries aim to document collections or interpret and contextualize specific works; their artistic or scientific experiments treat the collection as a kind of 'big data', mapping variety, testing possibilities and somehow activating the mass of objects in relation to a set of issues or aims. If the world of research embraces a bewildering range of methods, there is nevertheless something peculiar (I mean both distinctive *and* odd) about that of the museum, which begins less with discourse or theory, with a problem inherited or framed, than simply with stuff – with works, artefacts or specimens of whatever kind.

There are, of course, museum methods in a literal and technical sense, which could be reviewed here. While conservation is probably still associated in most people's minds with preventative or remedial work on fragile things – with restoration – it has come to embrace a wide range of analytical techniques that now enable pigments and residues to be precisely identified, which use imaging techniques such as CAT scans that we associate above all with medicine to see the insides of complex assemblages, microphotography to reveal how things were made, isotope analysis to work out where wood was from and so on. These techniques may be revelatory, and in some cases enable us to 'know', for the first time, or far more deeply, artefacts that have been in collections for decades. But I am interested here in the 'museum as method' in a more general and figurative sense. The method – that is, the activity of knowing in a museum setting – has, I suggest, its moments, and those we might reflect on are the moments of discovery, captioning and juxtaposition.

The canonical curatorial act is that of selection: a work is chosen to form part of a display. It is picked out of a mass of potential others, removed from the collection as a whole and placed within another series or set that will be arranged in exhibition form. This act represents a basic element of curatorial practice, not because selecting works or pieces for exhibition is necessarily something curators do every day, or the most vital thing that they do. It would not matter if the selection being made was of works that might be reproduced on postcards or some other sort of museum merchandise, or of pieces relevant to the interests of a particular group of visitors. In a primary sense, things are selected as foci of our attention, irrespective of whether we subsequently go on to choose to include them in a display or among the highlights discussed in an audio guide, or for whatever other further use. But 'selection' and 'choice' imply an activity that is conducted rationally, in an uncomplicated manner. That might occasionally be apt, if for example one was seeking the earliest work by a certain artist in a particular collection, or the impression of an eighteenth-century aquatint most free of foxing or discoloration. Yet curatorial activity is not, in general, directed by specific or measurable criteria in this manner. Its principle is that it is driven by curiosity, which is to say that it is open to the unexpected, to whatever one may encounter.

What we do in collections is 'discover' things: we uncover and reveal them. Discovery often involves finding things that were not lost, identifying things already known to others, being disappointed by the piece you thought you were seeking but intrigued by something that happens to be on the same shelf or in the same box. The encounter with arrays of objects should unsettle one's models and expectations. For example, a search for a 'good' or 'representative' example may put at risk an idea of a genre. One may be distracted by a piece that is neither 'good' nor typical but interestingly odd or that has an intriguing story attached to it. This is in one sense utterly unremarkable, it is the contingency of dealing with things, but in another sense it represents a method, powerful because it engages with works and things that may be not simply surprising, but that might have appeared beside the point, inconsequential, embarrassing or irrelevant. That therefore raise challenges, at least momentarily, to one's sense of the point – of what was consequential, appropriate, relevant.

I'm asserting that there might be value in looking for, at, or into things, in a manner only weakly guided by theory, or literally misguided, in the sense that direction given by theory is abandoned as things are encountered along the way. This admittedly sounds like the affirmation of an antiquarian curiosity, an indiscriminate and eclectic approach to knowing, and one surely long superseded by rigorous disciplines and critical theories. But there are two reasons why 'happening upon' things might have methodological potency. The first is that a preparedness to encounter things and consider them amounts to a responsiveness to forms of material evidence beneath or at odds with conceptions of artistic value, canonical ethnographies, national histories, reifications of local heritage and even the narratives of 'subalterns' – that is, the oppressed. In other words, all kinds of received wisdom and expectations may be complicated or disturbed by this 'happening upon' artefacts that manifest visions, situations, stories, intentions and identifications that may not have been previously recognized or acknowledged. 'Happening upon' brings the question of 'what else is there?' to the fore. That question has confronted, and should continue to confront, claims about great art, cultural traditions, historical progress and celebrated acts of resistance.

Second, the antiquarianism that this discovery licenses is not that of Casaubon (in George Eliot's *Middlemarch*), but that of W. G. Sebald; not the self-aggrandizing accumulation of ancient citations or specimens, towards some ideally comprehensive and authoritative treatise, chart or catalogue, but a meditation on, and enquiry into, larger histories of culture, empire, commerce and military enterprise. In *The Rings of Saturn*, Sebald undertakes a walk around the Suffolk coast, past neglected seaside resorts, obscure stately homes and out of the way small towns. He reads, he notices things, he takes photographs, he drops off in front of television documentaries. These sites, relics, documents and images provoke personal reflections and historical enquiries – enquiries that engage esoteric detail in a manner that might be considered extravagant, were Sebald's style not notably austere, restrained and mostly matter-of-fact. His method, unambiguously, is that of curiosity: he goes out to look for things, he comes across them, he pauses before them, he writes about them.[24]

If no one else has 'written up' an itinerary, at once a walk and an unsystematic investigation, in quite this remarkable way, and if the method is a model for a walk around a museum or a foray into a collection, the disposition that unifies Sebald's writing is not one that I would particularly advocate. Sebald is, above all, disturbed by loss and by the limitless chronicles of natural and human destruction; he is the numbed but articulate narrator of the grotesque and miserable toll of warfare upon various human populations at varied times in the past. The rings of Saturn are the frozen fragments of past worlds; the sites encountered around the Suffolk coast are the detritus of past absurdities and atrocities, marked by madness and violence, as well as more obscure personal projects, humanitarian missions and idiosyncratic enquiries. The characters Sebald celebrates are mostly those who renounce the world, who commit themselves to some harmless pursuit or to an arcane scholarly project that they alone value. His disenchantment, indeed his horror, is understandable in light of the twentieth-century European history unavoidably present for his generation. But – from the perspective of society rather than that of the individual artist – the museum must today be other than this and more than this. If different kinds of collections and different spaces within them – different temporary exhibitions – each have their own narratives and orientations, the museum in general must be a space of wonder and hope, humour and creativity, as well as the pain and shock that Holocaust displays and others dedicated to historic violence prompt, or the jaundiced meditation on inequality, exploitation and vanity that one can imagine Sebald taking away from almost any display dedicated to an ancient or more recent civilization.

If the moment of discovery gives us a good deal to think about, that thinking must be deliberately and carefully depleted in the act of captioning. By captioning, I mean not only the literal composition of a line of text that might accompany an image or object, but the seemingly simple matter of describing any museum piece. That description might be the answer to a question that in turn is deceptively simple: 'What is it?' Even to begin to respond, by identifying a work as a painting by or a painting of somebody or something, advocates a particular form of engagement with the object, in one case encouraging a viewer to understand it as an expression of an artist's creativity (conventionally citing its association with that artist's other work, its position in a chronological series of stylistic shifts or experiments), in the other presuming an interest primarily in the subject, in Elizabeth I, or the landscape or city depicted.

There are actual captions and there are captions implied by context and setting. In an art museum, the assumption is made that a painting of a naval battle is on display because it is by Turner, and the viewers' interest is in what the particular work reveals of the painter's handling of marine subjects, explosive light and so on. Yet a few years ago the huge work on show in the Nelson Gallery at the National Maritime Museum was presented entirely differently, less as an ambitious, experimental painting by an artist very prominent at the time, than as a visual representation of Trafalgar, of the famous naval engagement in which the hero of the display meets his end – to the extent that an audio narrative was synchronized with spot lighting that drew attention to details across the surface of the painting, depicting particular moments of the action as it unfolded.

Hence captions are implied and reinforced simply by institutional setting. There has been too much circular discussion about ethnography versus art, as though these were the only, or mutually exclusive, frames for non-Western artefacts. If by now it is clear that there are many contexts for objects and that their adequate cultural contextualization need not be represented at the expense of their presence and effect (their aesthetic impact), it was certainly once the case that there was a clear divide, indeed an antagonism, between the approaches of art and natural history museums. If this overused and battered institutional and hierarchical baggage is being discarded only piece by piece, it makes it all the more important that curators now caption deliberately. The words we use matter. Is a figurative representation of a man or woman a 'sculpture' when it is made by a European, but only a 'carving' when it is made by an African or a Pacific Islander? Are Polynesian barkcloths decorated fabrics or paintings? Is a shield a weapon? What is a dance club? Is a walking stick an orator's staff or a souvenir? Is a certain carving a spirit figure or a copy of a spirit figure commissioned by an ethnologist? The question is asked not only to seek the 'right' answer for the particular piece. The method is the use of the object in the exploration of what these categories and distinctions might mean, where they come from, where they mislead and where they remain useful or unavoidable.

The moment of juxtaposition arises because objects are seldom exhibited on their own. Whatever 'it' may be, one has to ask what it goes with, what it may be placed in a series with or what it may be opposed to. Again, it goes without saying that a chronological ordering of works by a single artist, a group representing a particular place or period or a set of specimens representing the fauna of a region, each respectively ask objects to speak to familiar conventions. But museum scenography does more than this – it develops arguments not through sequences of linguistic propositions, but through the arrangement of things. These arguments are not linear because the spaces employed are not usually linear; even in a corridor gallery or a rectangular room, which is occupied by what might be considered the simplest of display formats – a series of two-dimensional works around the walls – those who enter may focus first on left or right, and respond to lines of sight, rather than simply examining each work in whatever order may have been intended.

The analysis that the museum offers is thus generated through associations, through the staging of similarity, difference, progression, disruption, equivalence, hierarchy, singularity and accumulation, among other relations between works, artefacts and exhibits. Among the oldest geological displays which are in some sense intact are the cabinets of the antiquarian and naturalist John Woodward (1665 or 1668–1728), part-bequeathed / part-sold to the University of Cambridge, the founding elements of what was at first the Woodwardian Museum, now the Sedgwick Museum of Earth Sciences. Woodward was a follower of Agostina Scilla (1629–1700), who argued vigorously that fossils were the remains of once-living organisms rather than stones that mystically or fortuitously resembled them. Woodward made extensive collections that he grouped in his drawers, in part to illuminate this thesis. In particular he juxtaposed very ancient fossils, such as those of shark teeth, with examples procured from recently deceased sharks: his display thus constituted a scientific instrument, a revelation of the affinity between things.[25]

Franz Boas was the greatest anthropologist of the discipline's formative period of professionalization, over the late nineteenth and early twentieth centuries. His commitment was to challenging racial theory, social evolutionary thought and similarly hierarchical conceptions of human variety, advocating in their place a cultural relativism that had many antecedents in German philosophy. This was at the time far from widely accepted, yet went on – not least through the influential popularization of Boas's followers, Ruth

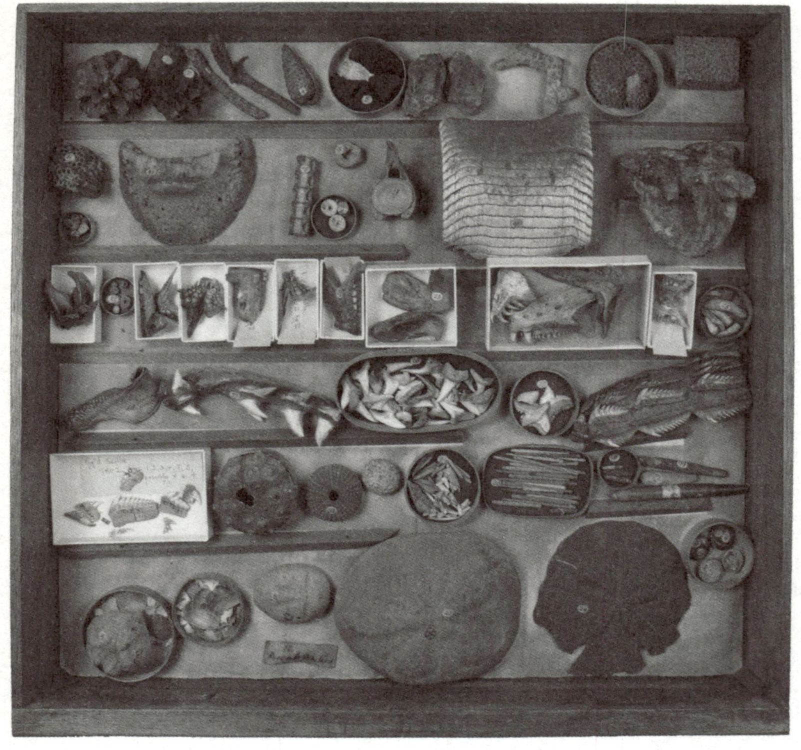

Woodward cabinet drawers: Cabinet E, Drawer 27: 'Bones, teeth etc of fishes'; Cabinet B, Drawer 17: 'The extraneous Fossils, Shells, and the rest, compared with those produced at this Day'; Sedgwick Museum of Earth Sciences, Cambridge.

Benedict and Margaret Mead – to underpin the late twentieth- and twenty-first-century political discourses of multiculturalism. Boas's own field investigations were focused on the American northwest coast, and his achievement during his tenure as a curator at the American Museum of Natural History was the creation of a hall dedicated to the cultures of the region. This gallery, which is extant in a modified form, is distinguished by a comparatively simple yet profoundly

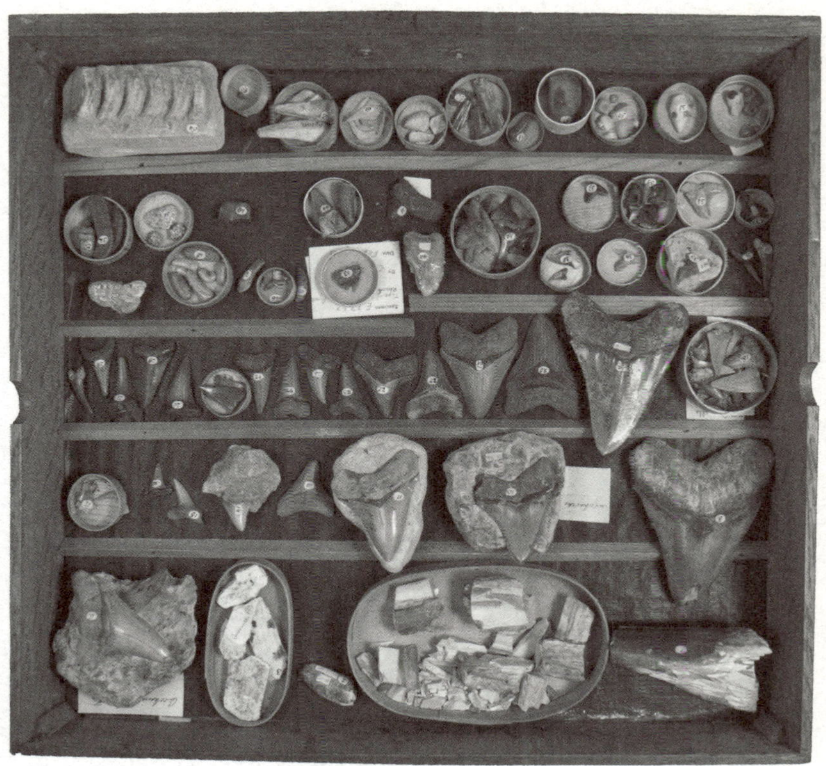

important organizational principle: each of ten generous bays off the central axis is dedicated to a single major cultural group.[26] In his interventions in a famous debate of the period, Boas had earlier written,

> the main object of ethnological collections should be the dissemination of the fact that civilization is not something absolute, but that it is relative, and that our ideas and conceptions are true only so far as our civilization goes . . . this object can be accomplished only by the tribal arrangement of collections.[27]

This was as opposed, Boas meant, to typological or psychological arrangements that implied developmental series or grouped artefacts by function, fragmenting the representation of any particular cultural group. His fullest articulation of the argument was the hall itself, which remains what Lévi-Strauss famously called it, 'a magic place', one that would strike visitors today as more progressive and remarkable had its propositions not gone on to form part of a broad (if chronically qualified and conflicted) public understanding of cultural diversity and cultural value.[28]

The term 'juxtaposition' may be inappropriate if it implies a dramatic placement of exhibits that in some sense sets one against another, and is hardly apt, for example, for a gathering of similar things, such as Chinese ceramics or Egyptian shabti – a gathering typical of many museums. But I prefer 'juxtaposition' to an anodyne word such as 'ordering' or 'grouping' precisely because it implies a placing-side-by-side that may be argumentative, that may entail ambiguity or tension, that may take a risk. Perhaps the most controversial of all major late twentieth-century exhibitions was '"Primitivism" in Twentieth-century Art', curated by William Rubin for the Museum of Modern Art in New York over 1984–5. Immediately hailed as 'an immensely important show', it was subsequently interrogated by such eminent figures in cultural theory, art history and anthropology as James Clifford, Hal Foster, Thomas McEvilley and Sally Price.[29] A false universalism, a hierarchic relation of heroic Western artists and anonymous tribal ones, an understanding of modernism as something unconnected with empire and ethnographic collecting and a contrast between the supposedly direct or unchecked creativity of 'primitive' art and the deliberate refinement of traditional Western art were among the aspects and implications of the project that attracted censure. Those of us who have cited or taught the debates (which continue to be reviewed in art-history classrooms, thirty years later) now mostly know the exhibition through Rubin's catalogue, which placed modern and tribal works side by side on the covers of each of the two volumes.[30] In a sense, the debate was about nothing more or less than the point of this juxtaposition, or what it inadvertently implied. Were the works commensurable, or did their pairing underscore their difference? Was one of interest only, or primarily, because it had interested the creator of the other? Why, and for what gain, or at what cost, were they placed together?

Much more could be said about the particular questions that the term chosen by Rubin – 'affinity' – raised. What is more generally suggestive is that juxtaposition tends to be at once argumentative and unclear, powerful and ambiguous, nothing if not open to question.

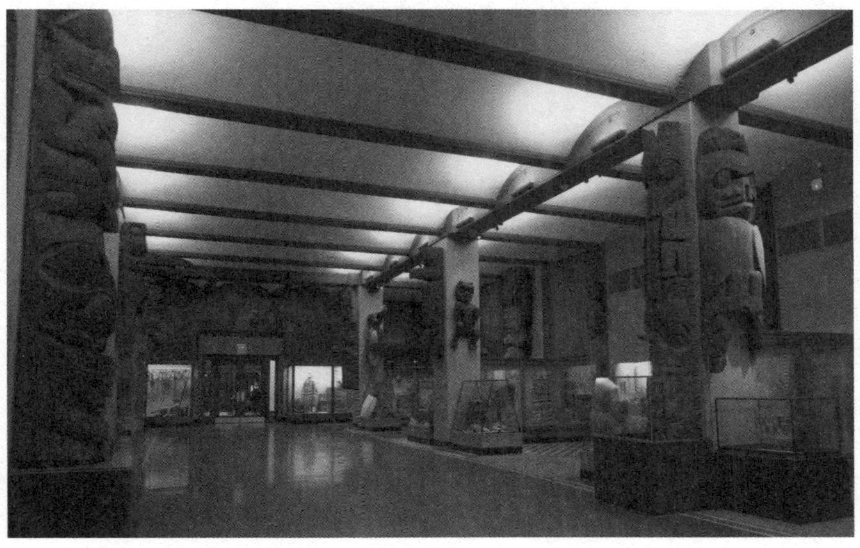

Hall of the Northwest Coast Indians, American Museum of Natural History, New York, April 2015.

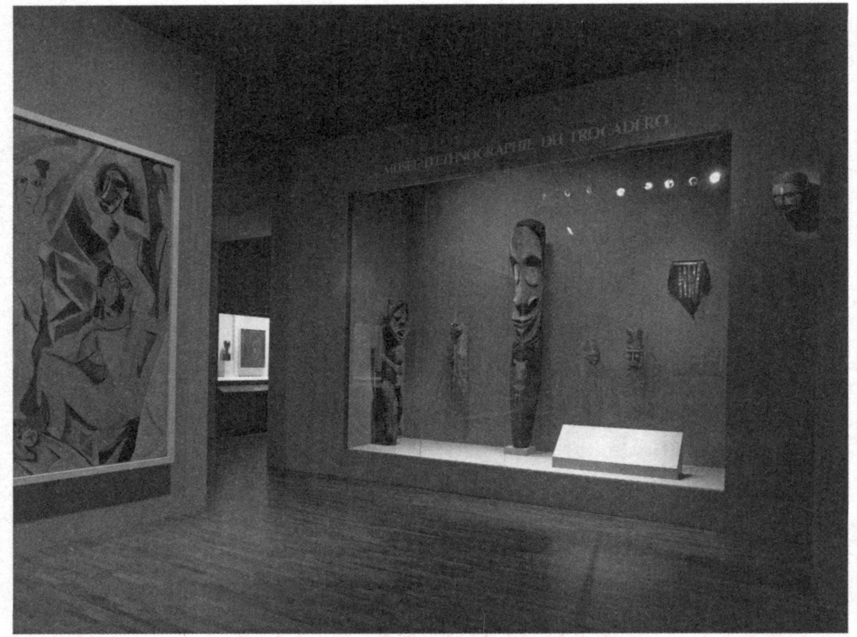

Installation view, '"Primitivism" in Twentieth-century Art', Museum of Modern Art, New York, 1984–5.

Even if one sides with the critics (at best the show was marred by ethnocentrism), the 'Primitivism' exhibition succeeded like no other in inflaming an enduring debate. The fact that both Woodward's drawers and Boas's hall were at one time provocative but now appear unremarkable indicates that juxtaposition's effects are mutable. What was stimulating at one moment may become less so; it may become embarrassingly dated, just uncontentious or even unintelligible. If museums feature too many galleries that are, for better or worse, no longer of their moment, the museum 'as method' is restless; it seeks to renew displays, not necessarily through the full-scale refurbishments that take place too infrequently, cost too much and are too long in planning and development. By introducing works and objects from one collection into another, thus cross-cutting the usual distinctions of genre and discipline, and by inviting and staging artists' responses, among other strategies that are now well established, the museum 'as method' reactivates permanent exhibitions that time may have been unkind to. In whatever form, via whatever technique or practice, the activation of the collection is the museum's beating heart.

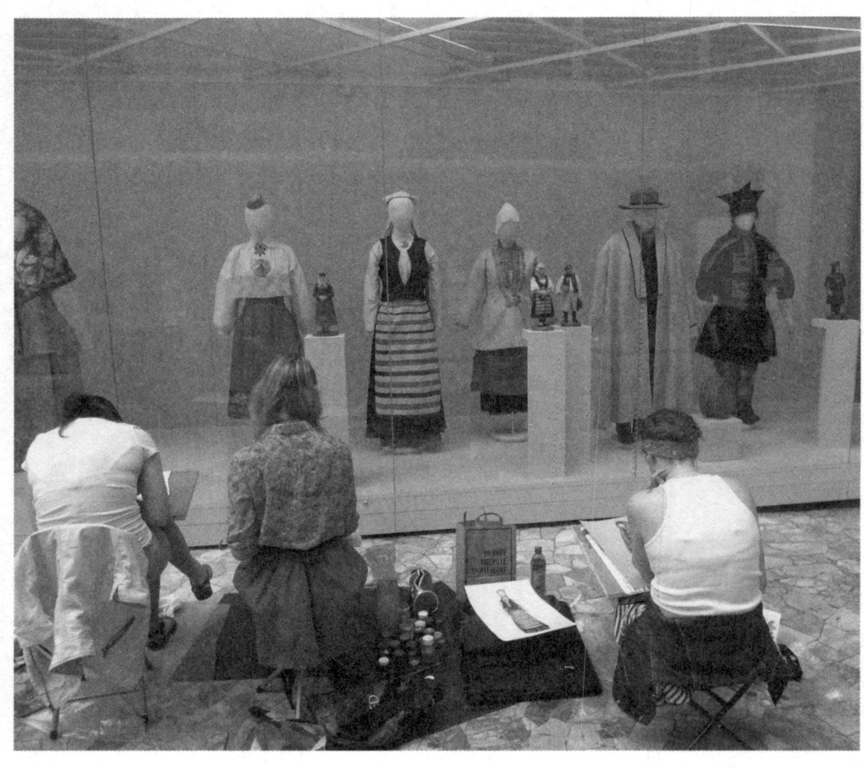

In the gallery featuring costumes of the Russian nationalities, Museum of Ethnography, St Petersburg, July 2013.

# 3

# THE COLLECTION AS CREATIVE TECHNOLOGY

In the autumn of 2011, the Turner Prize-winning British artist Grayson Perry (potter, transvestite, commentator on contemporary society, TV personality and so on) filled one of the British Museum's temporary exhibition galleries with his 'Tomb of the Unknown Craftsman', an exuberantly varied personal selection from across the institution's collections, interspersed with his own works and stories. Conceived by the artist as an inversion of a well-established model – that of the contemporary artist's 'intervention' in, or response to, the museum – Perry saw himself selecting things that conversely seemed to respond to his own works, that resonated with his narratives of emotional life, pilgrimage and imaginary religion. The pieces he found were mainly small things: pilgrims' tokens, figures of deities, grave goods, portable shrines and cross-cultural representations, such as Chinese and Haida sculptures depicting Europeans. Among many enthusiastic commentators, one noted that the historic works acquired 'new freedom and force' precisely because they were taken 'out of context', out of the periods, regions and cultures through which curators would, more usually, have presented them. Artefacts became more surprising and revealing:

> Is this onyx cameo that looks so like the artist really Roman or did Perry carve it himself? . . . This incidental guessing game goes to the heart of the show – Perry is collapsing time through art. For what is really out of date here? Not the shrines, coins, reliquaries, embroideries, pilgrim badges and maps that reach backwards and forwards through the millenniums.[1]

The 'museum as method' renders the collection a realm of discovery. 'Method' implies systematic scholarly activity, and I intend it to. If museums have too often been potential rather than actual research resources, because they have been difficult to enter and navigate, it is now the case that online catalogues are genuinely usable and informative, and curators more inclined to open doors than they once were. Other developments such as enhanced imaging and analytical techniques have enlarged the scope for collections-based investigations that make use of museum collections and pieces as diverse as Egyptian mummies, European paintings and Devonian fish. A recent project in palaeontology found a decisively significant 415-million-year-old specimen from Siberia in a geological collection in Tallinn. Newly revealed through CT scanning, *Janusiscus* enables fresh consideration of the evolutionary relationships between bony fish and cartilaginous species like sharks: a common ancestor, it suggests that sharks are specialized species rather than (as is commonly presumed) more 'primitive' types. Other current studies are using collections from the Natural History Museum and Manchester Museum to model the macroevolution of birds, and to experiment with automated identification of butterfly species to explore biodiversity and climate change.[2]

Yet entering collections, finding things, connecting and juxtaposing them is emphatically not a set of activities that specialists of whichever kind monopolize. The 'museum as method' is a business that ordinary visitors and others interested in collections can make their own, motivated by very diverse interests and to very varied effect. Artists' uses of museums are of special interest here because they bring into view, particularly powerfully, the sense in which a collection can be a creative technology. In certain respects, this is obvious. Curators in art museums choose works from their collections and others available to them, and create exhibitions out of those selections. Projects such as Grayson Perry's reveal the potentiality of the collection in a richer and less familiar register. The perforce vast, uneven mass of stuff that constitutes the collection, the arcane relations that connect things, some obscure, some celebrated, amounts to an apparatus, itself a strange hybrid of the all-too physical and the virtual, the archaic and the advanced; a nearly unintelligible amalgam of a Heath Robinson contraption and the smartest of devices, its search results somehow always offering both more and less than you asked for. Artworks and collections do not just inspire, as museum advocates routinely, if rightly, claim; the collection is more particularly a technology that, quite simply, enables people to *make new things.*

While 'The Tomb of the Unknown Craftsman' evoked a pilgrimage or cult that was at once highly personal and deliberately transhistorical, collections are also vital instruments of historical reimagining. All museums are history museums, whether they are ostensibly museums of science, art or anthropology. They bear traces of all kinds of, and are often highly expressive of, their formation, not always in ways (in the case of older institutions) that their present curators are comfortable with. If, in some cases, new buildings or comprehensive renovations have rendered a former organization invisible, sweeping away dated or unfashionable orderings, it is considerably more common – given the long timescale over which museum 'improvements' tend to evolve, and the unhappy propensity for promised funds to be scaled back or withdrawn altogether – for institutions to exhibit, at any one time, approaches to design, display and interpretation reflecting different periods and the perhaps starkly different preoccupations of museum managers and curators over time. The Pitt Rivers Museum in Oxford is the most celebrated 'museum of a museum', though the general understanding that its Victorian displays are unchanged is inaccurate.[3] Many of its cases have in fact been recurated at various times, largely but not entirely adhering to the famous typological paradigm. In any event, the Pitt Rivers is often cited as though it is a unique 'period piece', whereas many museums, in less obvious ways, actually reflect successive phases of establishment, enlargement, neglect and perhaps subsequent renewal; they also manifest changing conceptual frames, the biographies of people and objects and the microhistories of particular collections. More broadly, architecture, signage, gallery names, plaques and portraits, which are not strictly elements of the exhibitions as such, may express the entangled histories of art, travel, science and civic culture that prompted town councillors, university grandees, philanthropists and others to join forces and create or enlarge the suitably impressive buildings that housed collections, that drew visitors and that entered people's experiences and memories.

Pierre Nora suggests, in one of the introductory texts to *Les Lieux de mémoire*, his magisterial project of collaborative historical rethinking, that history meant something very different to the French after the 1960s than it had before. Previously, history had been an 'intellectual operation that eliminated the distance between us and the past'; in other words it established a sense of genesis, of identity through continuity, of what has since been referred to as national narrative. But decolonization and economic growth produced a radical reorientation. The rationality of the West was, Nora claimed, destabilized by the confrontation with other cultures and mentalities, while the rapidity of change 'made the past totally foreign', establishing the need for a history 'that dealt with the sense of loss . . . and of permanent separation'. The work of history, indeed the project of *Les Lieux de mémoire*, became 'the operation that put that distance [between past and present] into relief'.[4] This statement could imply the sort of understanding of self that history traditionally offered, on the basis of difference rather than identity.[5] But the wording is more suggestive and implies interest, not so much in *what* has become distant, but in distance itself, in the fact and nature of a relationship with a past no longer readily assimilable to the state of things today.

Perhaps because they were so long considered dull and dusty, or even as dead places, museums have engaged ambivalently with memory. Yet they are, in many cases, *lieux de mémoire par excellence*, and in a richer and less predictable sense than many of the national monuments and similar sites that may be more commonly considered bearers of a collective past. As realms of memory, they can be seen from the perspective suggested by Nora: the histories they manifest are notable for their unfamiliarity. But they may be unfamiliar in a fashion itself less familiar than Nora's. History of the 'school curriculum' kind addresses national genesis, defining events and great transitions: kings and battles, revolutions, the emergence of parliaments, decolonization and national independence. The *Lieux de*

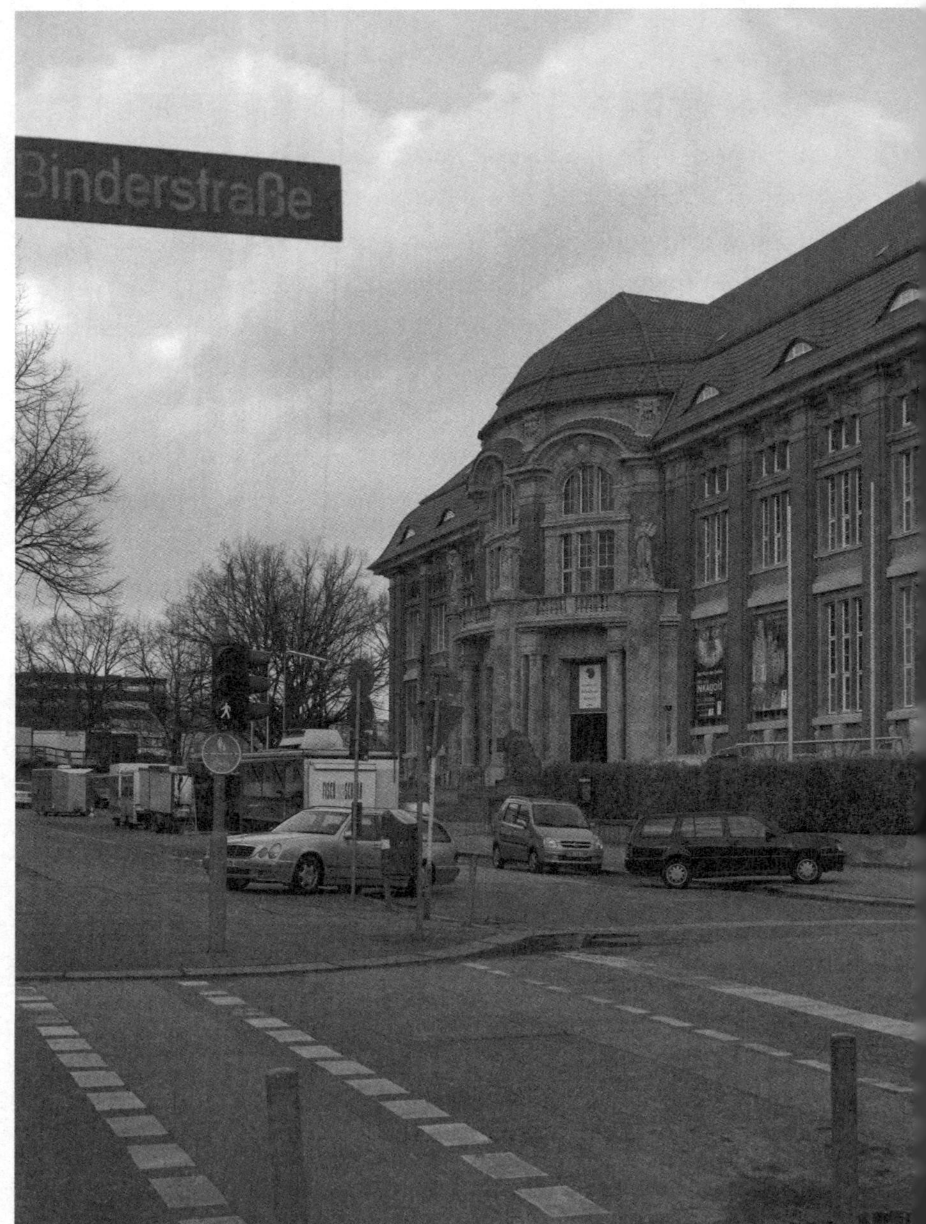
Binderstraße

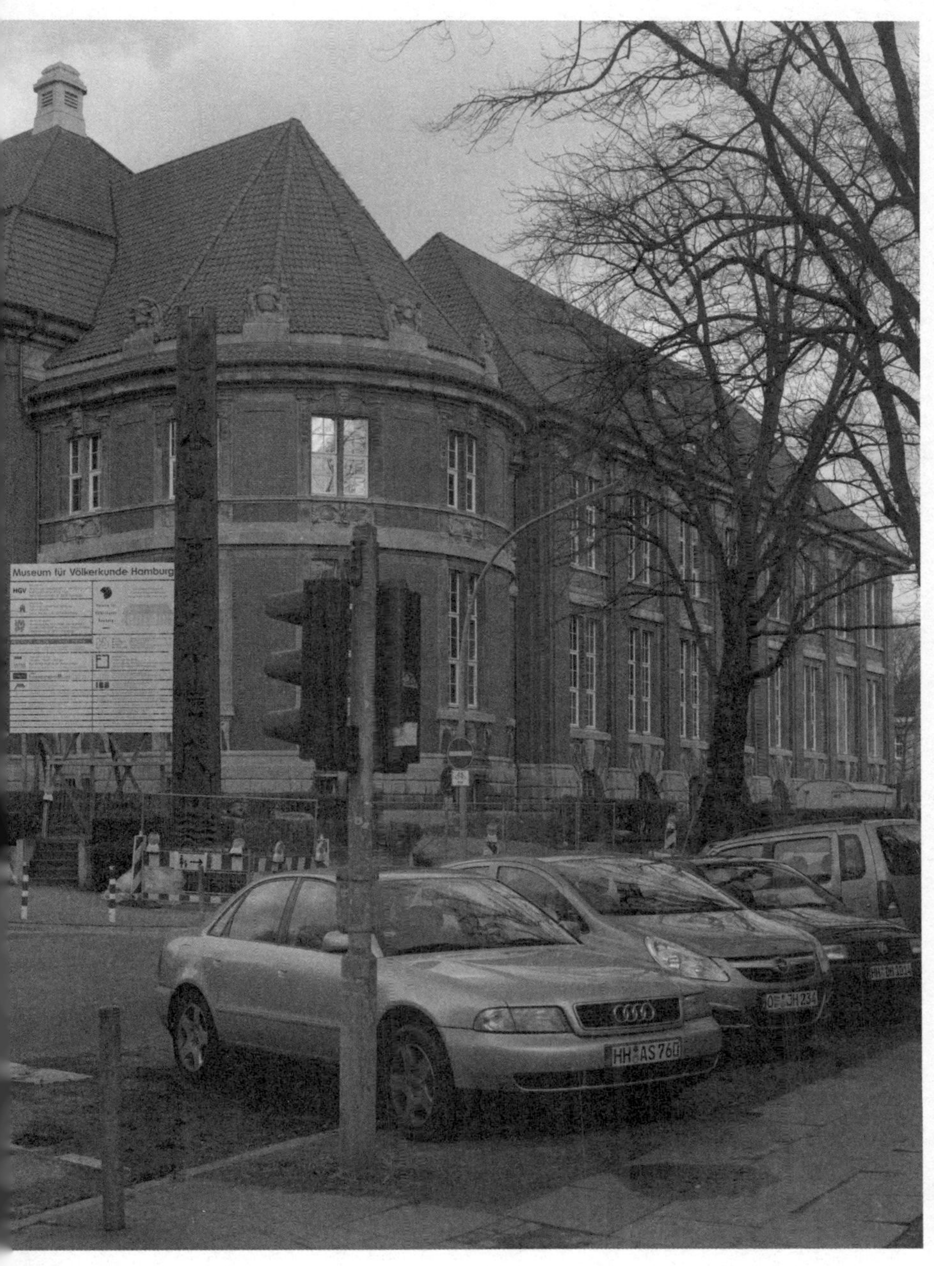


Mark Adams, *12.1.07 Museum für Völkerkunde, Hamburg,* black-and-white print.

*mémoire* project started from the sense of a sheer disconnect between the present and past that rendered even comparatively recent history nearly incomprehensible. Art and science museums are not overtly historical, but their artefacts and collections speak of histories of culture, travel, science and civic imagining that are not, or not only, separated from our time by rupture. Material artefacts, for the most part, do not directly represent the events and developments foregrounded in conventional historical narrative, but often have oblique and incidental relationships to them; they bring particular and curious aspects of past life into view.

While the discipline of history is often concerned to render the public life of the past alive, for readers or the viewers of television documentaries today, collections often reveal dimensions of former experience that were not common or public knowledge in their period. We can never know a time in the full sense that those who were then alive did, but we can paradoxically know things about it that they didn't, not for the obvious reason that we have the perspective of hindsight, but because museum collections contingently preserve many things that may have been private, unimportant or otherwise off the record, relative to what may have been publically visible. It is true that archives of all kinds are replete with information that was initially personal or confidential, in a sense part of social life at a particular time yet not known to society, but artefact and art collections are of another order; they evidence material and embodied aspects of existence seldom registered in documents of any kind.

At times the 'unrepresentative' nature of both art and anthropology collections has been lamented, for different reasons. Over the mid-twentieth century, ethnologists distanced themselves from the museum as an institution and repository of knowledge, in part because artefact collections were considered too tangential or partial as expressions of social practice. They also observed that some societies made much of material culture – representing clan identities or statuses through architecture or images, for instance – while others did not, perhaps articulating such relationships through dance, oratory or body art. Hence artefact collections in themselves were of little use in informing cultural comparisons. More recently, the constitution of art collections, their hierarchies and their multiple exclusions, have been extensively criticized, though acquisition policies have only incrementally been extended in order to redress elitist and canonical orientations. There are two implications: the first is that the 'failure' of ethnographic and folk-art collections to be more genuinely representative reflects the unrealistic nature of positivistic expectations, rather than a poverty on the part of the collections themselves. In hindsight, it was naive ever to expect that an assembly of objects could be any sort of objective, comprehensive or encyclopaedic expression of a historic period or a way of life, any more than a set of costumes and stage props could represent a play or an opera. Collections do, however, represent the histories of their own formation and the wider histories of art, science and travel that stimulated that formation; they are powerful, if awkward, instruments for the interpretation of those wider histories as well as of conditions and processes of other kinds. Second, cross-disciplinary enquiry, meaning in this context cross-generic and cross-museum, can give them fresh and different significance, working beyond the paradigms and agendas that framed them in the first place. Objects and collections speak past lives and encounters in the heterogeneous and unpredictable fashion of Sebald's images and observations.

In Cambridge, there are three Maori carvings collected by Baron Carl von Hügel, which are not simply specimens of Maori art or culture but bearers of intersecting biographies and histories. Von Hügel was an Austrian soldier and diplomat renowned for his botany and gardening. In the late 1820s, he was engaged to a Hungarian princess, said to be one of the great beauties of the age, who then became the third wife of the great Austrian statesman Prince Metternich, a family friend of von Hügel's. He dealt with his apparently acute distress by embarking upon an extended voyage through Kashmir, Ceylon and eventually Australia and the Philippines, which included a short but rich visit in March 1834 to the Bay of Islands in northern New Zealand. There, von Hügel spent a good deal of time in the company of William Yate of the Church Missionary Society, a gifted linguist, an enthusiastic student of Maori culture and author of some of the earliest insightful commentaries upon Maori tiki – objects of personal adornment that he recognized were powerful memorializations of deceased kin. Yate, who soon afterwards was disgraced by the exposure of his sexuality, proudly entertained the aristocratic traveller and presented him with pieces from his own collection, which mostly later reached the state museum in Vienna. A few were retained in the family; sixty years later, von Hügel's son, Anatole von Hügel, had undertaken his own long voyage to the Pacific, in part a project of piety, had made his own great collections and been appointed the founding curator of the Museum of Archaeology and Ethnology (later Anthropology) in Cambridge, to which he donated the three pieces his father had obtained.[6]

The largest was a tekoteko, an apical carving from the facade of a house, in the style not of the Bay of Islands, where it had been collected, but of the Te Arawa tribe of the central North Island. The work, moreover, has naturalistic fingers and hands, an innovation of the period. It was probably newly carved at the time of von Hügel's visit, and may have been the work of a man he called 'the lame tattooist', whom von Hügel met, exchanged gifts with and even asked to inflict a small sample tattoo on his arm. The work's Te Arawa style reflects the decades of turbulence prior to this particular encounter. Traders had been visiting the region since the 1790s; local competition and conflict had intensified and, most crucially, the warrior chief Hongi Hika had visited England and Australia and imported firearms on an unprecedented scale. The musket wars of the 1820s were marked by sustained invasions of Te Arawa territory, and so-called slaves were taken in considerable numbers and resettled among the tribes of the north. Those captives included a good many carvers, perhaps including the 'lame tattooist', and by 1830 the art tradition particular to the north had been all but abandoned; the work of carving in the region was given to these subordinate, assimilated Te Arawa instead. The sculpture's authorship and acquisition history cannot be absolutely specified – it may or may not have been this man's work, it may have been given to von Hügel directly, it may have been acquired first by Yate – but we do know for sure that it is a product of these meetings, this milieu, and that its unfinished state reflects the first of its recontextualizations; the work's Maori maker took the view that what he had started, an incarnation of an ancestor intended to speak tribal authority from an elevated architectural setting, might rather be gifted, traded, sent to Europe.

In 2005–6, an exhibition was developed at Cambridge's Museum of Archaeology and Anthropology entitled 'Pasifika Styles'; it brought a number of New Zealand artists to the museum and enabled them to respond both to specific works and to the institutional context. Lisa Reihana was among the group and she created work related to Hongi Hika's visit to Cambridge – he had helped the linguist Samuel Lee prepare an early form of Maori grammar – but also an installation that incorporated the tekoteko. Her project – *He Tautoko* – bore a symmetrical relationship to an act of repatriation. She undertook extensive filming and gathered a variety of audio materials – 'the Manukau Institute of Technology Maori choir, and the "tap-tapping" sounds as Maori artist Lyonel Grant carves the pattern found on the mouth of the *tekoteko* onto another work'. As she wrote,

> The *tekoteko* is erected inside a vitrine, contextualized by sounds and images of home. Footage of blue skies signifies that he was once seen on top of a meeting house, silhouetted by New Zealand skies. On the *tekoteko* are 1960s headphones, and when the viewer listens to the Nokia phones [that is, to handsets attached to the display], the combination of the two, visually and conceptually, evokes conversing with this ancestor.[7]

While the artist will say light-heartedly that she has a thing about the clunky design of 1960s and '70s technology, the inclusion of handsets with coiled leads that telephones, before the cordless kind, always had, also recalls, for her, her grandmother's work in the local telephone exchange. The work stages a deliberate disconnect; had the project been simply to enliven the figure in the present, the artist could have introduced the ubiquitous earphones we associate with iPods or other new headphones. Often, we relate to artworks by associating them in some way with our lives or interests: Christianity or

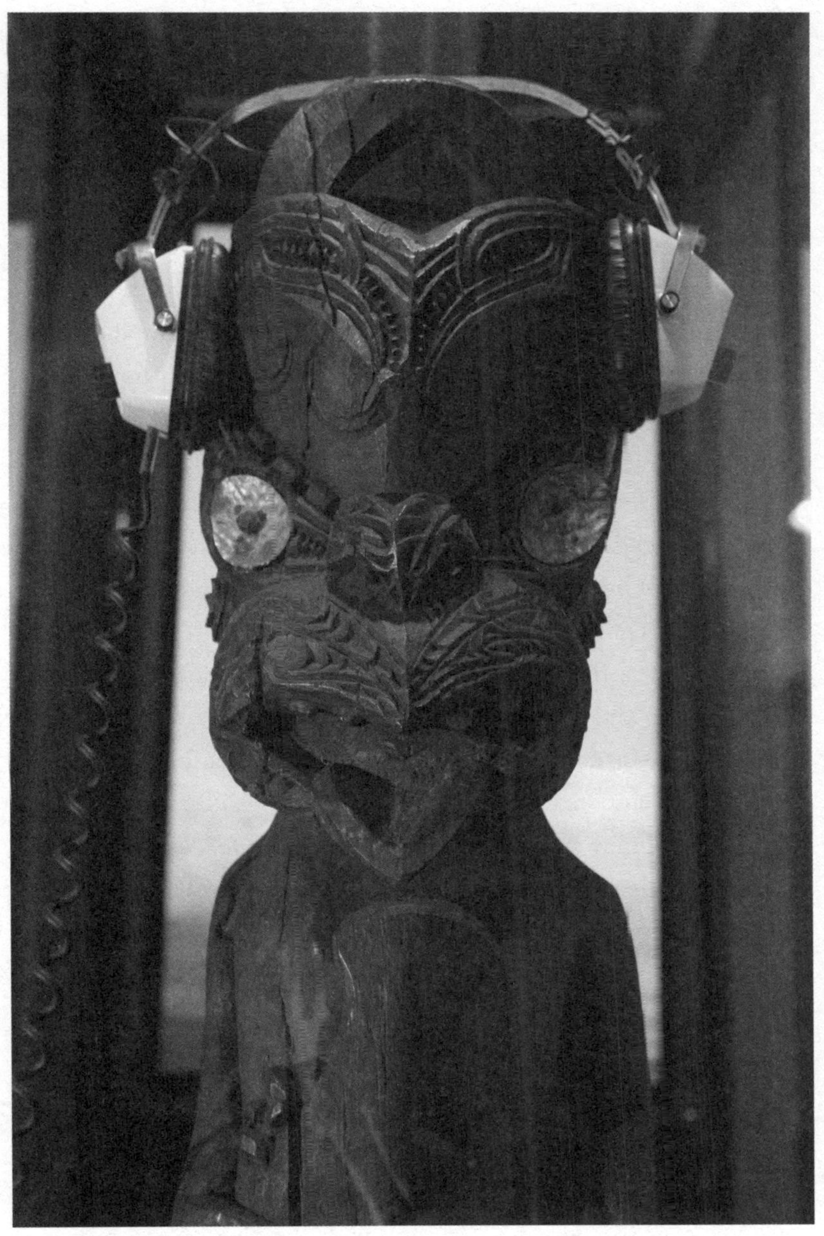

Lisa Reihana, *He Tautoko*, mixed-media installation with historic tekoteko (gable sculpture), as exhibited in 'Pasifika Styles', Museum of Archaeology and Anthropology, Cambridge, 2006–8.

Islam may connect us with works of religious art, land- or cityscapes may represent places we inhabit or have visited, and there are many other personal, biographic and idiosyncratic kinds of associations that make images and artefacts present to us, that bring them home to us. If *He Tautoko* is evidently concerned with bringing home the tekoteko, and bringing this work from the past to life now, the artist would seem to have him inhabit not our own time, just now, but a time both within the span of our own lives and contemporaneous with her childhood in the 1960s and '70s. Which is to say that ancestral art forms may indeed be things that we can make our own, but we 'have' them, as we 'have' our own lives, which are made up of earlier and more recent passages, the former prone to recede and become less familiar to us.

Since 1995, the indigenous Australian artist Brook Andrew has been visiting and studying anthropological collections in Australia, the United Kingdom and elsewhere. His interest has been in bringing old and obscure images of indigenous people 'into the light'; an early prizewinning work rendered one man *Sexy and Dangerous* (1996); more recently the mood of these works has typically been more elusive and enigmatic. Andrew has responded to collections associated with William Blandowski, a natural historian in the tradition of Alexander von Humboldt, who arrived in Australia in 1849 and began to make a name for himself in scientific circles, and over 1856–7 led an expedition to the confluence of the Murray and Darling rivers, a region then little known to white settlers. He gathered a massive collection of new natural specimens on the basis, he was happy to acknowledge, of close collaboration with the Nyeri Nyeri people, whose activities and ceremonies were studied and depicted by the expedition artist, Gerard Krefft.[8]

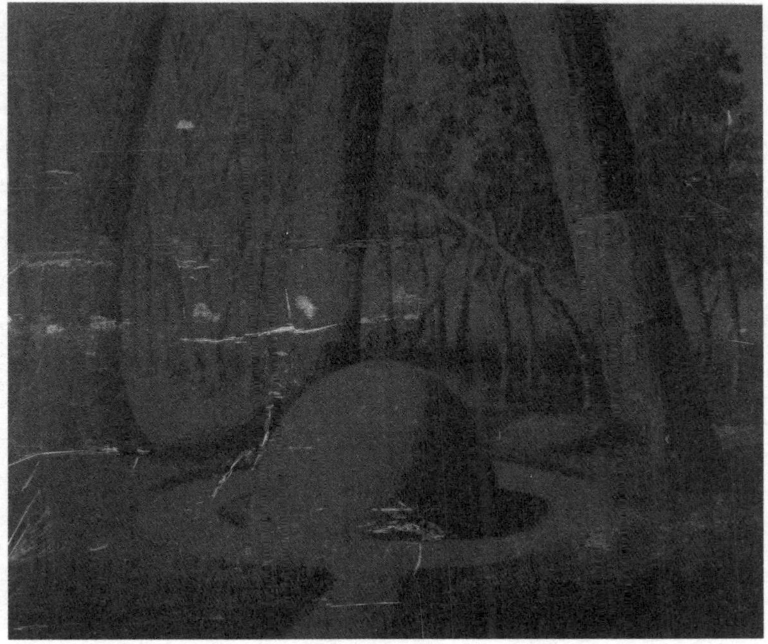

Brook Andrew, *The Island I*, 2008, mixed media on Belgian linen, Museum of Archaeology and Anthropology, Cambridge.

On his return to Melbourne, Blandowski was initially feted, but was swiftly caught up in controversy and compelled to return to Europe. Over 1860–61 he employed a draughtsman to rework Krefft's drawings, together with illustrations from other sources, and planned an ambitious visual encyclopedia. But he failed to gain financial backing and only two copies of the album, *Australien in 142 Photographischen*, are today known to exist, one in the Staatsbibliothek, Berlin, and the other in Cambridge. In addition, some three hundred faded and flimsy copy prints are in MAA's photographic archive, and it was these that Brook Andrew came across and was immediately excited by when he first visited the Museum in June 2007. Only a couple of weeks later, back in Australia, he wrote to me requesting high-resolution scans that he could manipulate and develop, and within six months he had begun producing a series of works on a spectacular scale, 3 m wide and 2.5 m high.

Blandowski's title was misleading. No doubt he hoped to capitalize on photography's status at the time, as an advanced technology with a unique capacity to represent nature. But the album was made up of photographs of drawings, derived from a variety of sources, including illustrations in earlier exploratory works: the representation of the burial mound was adapted from the frontispiece of Charles Sturt's *Two Expeditions into the Interior of Southern Australia* (1833). The image was thus at some remove from field sketches that might themselves have been imaginative or inaccurate. Yet, in however distorted a fashion, the colonial imagery acknowledged an indigenous Australian landscape architecture, an aesthetic also represented in the carved trees surrounding what was essentially a mortuary monument. Hence the obscure print stands as an affirmation of customary culture, which Andrew's work literally magnifies, to billboard scale, making commensurate claims upon the attention of the public. In Australia, these works aroused great interest, were critically discussed in arts journals, acquired by several of the major state art galleries, exhibited and toured.[9]

I cite Reihana's and Andrew's work here not because I am seeking to add to a now twenty-year-old discussion regarding contemporary artists' interventions in museums: the staging of residencies and the exhibition of their outcomes is now not innovative, but business as usual. It no longer makes sense to argue about whether such projects are authentically disruptive or co-opted: some, as Hal Foster indeed acknowledged in an influential critique at an early stage of this debate, are genuinely provocative, others less so; there is no efficacy or complicity inherent in the genre.[10] The projects, like Grayson Perry's, that have been most successful have not just been strong works of art that could have appeared anywhere; they have been works, collections and installations genuinely responsive to the museums that hosted them, and they have emerged from dialogue with institutions' identities, with the places and nations in which they are situated. Hence there is more to this sort of artist's project than the appropriation of an *objet trouvé* or any routine artistic stimulus. Artists respond to institutions, sometimes institutions' hidden histories, but also and especially to collections; they engage gatherings of artefacts, draw things from them and caption and juxtapose them provocatively. Reihana and Andrew, among others who have produced powerful work in the museum setting, draw attention to the sense in which the collection is not only a relational assembly in manifold senses, but a creative technology, something that can be used to make new things, such as works of contemporary art that can be internationally circulated, shown, critically reviewed and sold.

Fertile as these works are, I am interested here less in their distinctiveness than in their affinity with the uses visitors of all kinds make of museums. It is now notable that people constantly make visual notes with their smartphones, which they may simply keep for themselves or post and share online, captioned by any sort of observation: a comment on the composition of a thing, a political remark, a postcard-like 'wish you were here'. This is another dimension of museum life that has changed dramatically and recently: only a few years ago, many institutions prohibited taking pictures. If photography is still often disallowed in temporary exhibitions (usually because of the restrictions imposed by lending institutions), in general the practice is now more or less enthusiastically encouraged. Museums are keen to be 'liked', in the sense of cited, voted for or positively reviewed, via whichever social-media platform. These online expressions are motivating new strategies in museum marketing and public engagement, but could also be seen to be making visible ways of using collections that have long been significant. Visitors of all kinds have always entered exhibits, made connections between things, formed impressions and understood their own interests and preferences better through having encountered collections and visited or revisited objects significant to them. At one time these uses and responses had lives in notebooks, in conversations, even just in private thoughts. The 'museum as method', to reiterate, amounts to a powerful and distinctive kind of research that curators and others with access to, and interest in, material culture and collections can engage in. But it is also an activity of discovery and reflection in which anyone, not necessarily just those who are scholars or specialists, can participate, even if their access is limited only to what is on display, and not to the richer but less readily intelligible and less ordered realm of stored collections. We all have the capacity to move around museums, make discoveries, caption things and put them into series or juxtapose them with other works, exhibits or images, in whatever terms happen to be salient to us.

It is important to add that this argument is not a voluntarist one that implies that ideologies have no impact on us, that they do not constrain our ways of seeing in many crude but also more subtle ways. It is rather an affirmation that wherever people start from, whatever habitus shapes their values, attitudes and interests, or blinkers their perceptions of the foreign, cross-cultural or unfamiliar, they nevertheless possess a certain ability, a considerable ability, to make a museum their own. They may refuse to make it – as can a genuinely uninterested child who wants only to be outside – but for the most part they find ways of making, out of their engagement with a collection, a sense that is somehow enjoyable, rewarding or productive; which is to say that they have made connections between their own prior concerns and whatever they may have encountered.

There is a practice associated with museums that is not new but very old, and it exemplifies the sense in which the collection is a creative technology: it is that of object drawing. For as long as they have existed, museums have been visited by professional and amateur artists who sketch artefacts and specimens; the activity is as alive as it ever has been, and there are few institutions that do not regularly host classes or in which individual artists are not to be found, sometimes in negotiation with gallery attendants ('wet' media are mostly discouraged), making marks, producing studies of objects and occasionally of other visitors and gallery environments. Drawing is at once intimately attentive to material culture and empowered by the museum setting, yet indifferent to curatorial ordering and interpretation. This, again, underscores the weakly scripted quality of the exhibition, and especially of the usually wide-ranging permanent exhibition, as opposed to the (supposedly, ideally) more focused temporary show. If a temporary project may quite appropriately be concerned to present a thesis or theme, there is a wider sense in which the museum, the collection, the work or artefact count as things out of which other things can be made. The sense in which the museum is *for* illustrators and artists, among other visitors, reflects the sense in which it admits a heterogeneity of interest. Irrespective of the unrealistic expectations of some curators or museum-makers, who anticipate the public grasping particular narratives of art history, national history or environmental change, the museum is (either deliberately or inadvertently) responsive to society's make-up, its constitution out of 'different kinds' of people, who perforce bring different perspectives (maybe even particular wounds or grievances) to its collections. All 'make something of it', as the idiom has it, meaning that they form an impression. This may go without saying; my argument is the converse – that the museum and more specifically the collection is something out of which things can be made. Some of us are content to leave with ideas and impressions, others wish to create and circulate sets of photos, intended to be shared online and bear commentary, or put together arguments in our minds, celebrating particular artists, regarding a so-called civilization, in favour of repatriation, against globalization, or whatever. And others of us intend to draw on paper, or work towards more ambitious works of art that make claims on the attention of an international art public, like those of Reihana and Andrew.

The gatherings of people we refer to as museum visitors are heterogeneous in distinct senses. *In principle*, I have suggested, the museum visitor's particular interest is open and unspecified, because the museum is an institution of civil society and it exists for that heterogeneous community, which is divided not only by class, race and gender differences but by age and generation and by far more particular aspects of biography and personal interest. *In practice*, the capacity of particular museums to appeal to and attract varied populations, among them people alienated or effectively excluded by discrimination and inequality, is another matter. But if art institutions were long censured for their elitism, most publicly funded museums now vigorously seek a wider range of visitors, especially from minority ethnic and lower-income groups. In a time of growing domestic as well as international tourism, their core middle-class audience is no longer drawn mainly from one city, region or nation, but from many. A museum that any proportion of its varied visitors will enjoy or value (that is, in other words, one that is more or less successful) *may* be 'of difference' (if it represents diverse natural phenomena, cultures or arts of various kinds) but *must* also be 'for difference'. That is, it ideally offers something to everybody who might visit, and in fact probably does so, by accident if not by design. Even if curatorial agendas and captions fall short in rendering what is displayed salient to the full range of those who enter, the artefacts exhibited may nevertheless speak to them; material culture being constituted mutably, the collection is a versatile technology. We – whoever we may be – can treat the museum as an apparatus that helps us 'collect our thoughts'. We select the few things out of the many we encounter, we may be guided by curators' captions, we may revise, resist or disregard them, we may take away something incommunicable, a memory of a childhood moment of wonder before a spectacular work, or a clearly articulated political view. One may, for example, walk away from a pottery dish entranced by its simple form, or one may frame a sense of outrage that a display of late nineteenth-century masks from the Congo includes no mention of rubber, Leopold or empire.

All that said, there is a deeper level at which museums of the kind that range over cultures and histories do bear values. They affirm the significance of what they exhibit, and where they exhibit works from diverse regions, works that are in some sense impressive, they almost inevitably do something of the work that Franz Boas advocated in 1887, affirming, as he put it, 'that civilization is not something absolute'. They point to common humanity and to the universality of human creativity. Irrespective of whether a particular museum offers its visitors an explicit narrative of cultural diversity, globalization or even the contribution of immigration to the nation in which it is situated, and regardless of whether any such narrative is persuasive, historically diverse collections manifest human movement and interaction – what's involved in the formation of culture and society over time. In a world marked by reactive cycles of violence, the acts of states provoking those of terrorist militias and vice versa, as well as by attendant forms of religious extremism and anti-immigrant nativism, the museum thus has vital potential to inform alternative, affirmative understandings of difference. It does not just point to difference or diversity in principle, but at best offers a textured, materialized sense of culture, of (for example) place, seasonality, social relationships, belief, craft, aesthetics. The aspiration to do this kind of thing is one few curators or museum-makers would disavow. How effectively museums actually foster respect for difference and cross-cultural understanding, diminish the political legitimacy of anti-immigrant rhetoric or otherwise challenge racism, is another matter. No doubt many people would like to know, but this efficacy isn't easy to assess, and shouldn't be. The influence that museums may have upon broader understandings of such issues is unlike the effect of a marketing or party-political campaign; it can't be tested through a poll to gauge brand recognition or the popularity of a message or a leader.

There are instances of major exhibitions making a difference to the politics of race and ethnicity. There is no doubt, for example, that the celebrated 'Te Maori' show of the 1980s, which was acclaimed in the United States and then toured all the main city museums in New Zealand on its return home, captivated its domestic public, dramatically enhanced the status of Maori art and culture and helped build respect and support for Maori interests and claims. One can imagine exhibitions dedicated to the formation of culture and society in Syria and neighbouring countries fostering more compassionate responses to refugees. But in general the efficacy that museums have is slow and diffuse. They may inform understandings of conflict and crisis, but what they also do implicitly and less immediately, yet perhaps more consequentially, is offer an encounter with material culture, with works of art, artefacts and specimens, and with telling assemblages and institutions themselves. That encounter enables and nurtures curiosity, particularly a curiosity beyond the space and society one happens to inhabit. Ideally, they inspire an interest in going the distance to consider difference that is more potent than any particular moral or message that a curator or museum-maker may have articulated. What, in other words, collections say to us is less important than the difference they make to who we are.

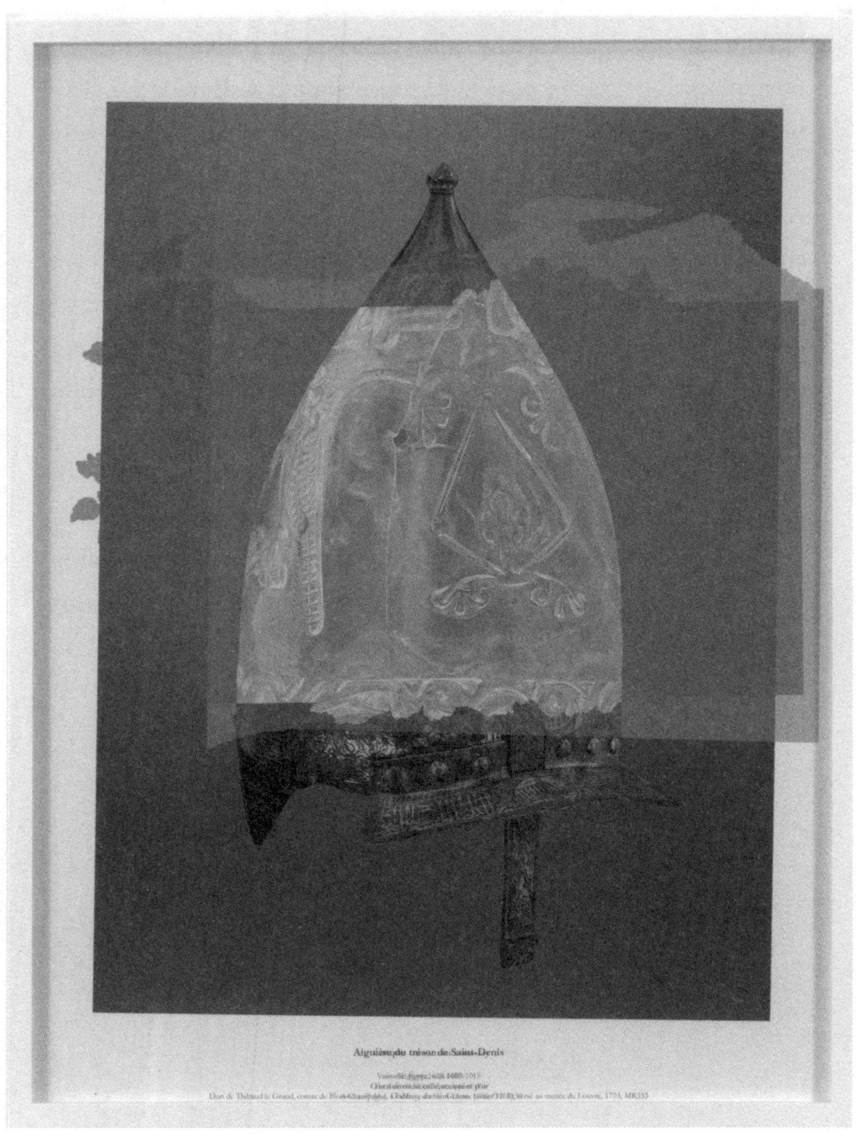


Walid Raad, *Preface to the Third Edition (Édition française), Plate* I, 2012, archival colour inkjet print.

# CONCLUSION

*And how far is it from the point where we find ourselves today back to the late eighteenth century, when the hope that mankind could improve and learn was inscribed in handsomely formed letters in our philosophical firmament?*

W. G. Sebald, *Campo Santo*

The ambition of museum development in the Middle East is impressive but also disconcerting. The rush to establish institutions on a scale that emerged over centuries in Europe stimulated the works by Walid Raad referred to earlier in this book. In his prints, installations and performances, the identities of the cultural treasures that museums are supposed to care for, exhibit and interpret are confused and rendered unintelligible.[1] The great precincts and museums in the making may be simply expressions of a will to power, of Ozymandian hubris – or they may manifest more sincere concerns to promote culture. For Raad, it is impossible, for now anyway, to adjudicate between these contradictory interpretations. This book is guardedly optimistic about the shape-shifting world of culture and its institutions; importantly, this world includes many modest and volunteer-run collections, as well as these implausibly grand projects. If the initiatives in the Emirates demand some scepticism (will the migrant workers who built them be welcome alongside other visitors?), my general sense is that there is more to be gained than lost from the momentum that museum development now possesses. Irrespective of what exactly motivates the enlargement and redisplay of old museums or the foundation of new ones, the creation of more spaces in which people can encounter and engage with significant art, history and science collections can be no bad thing.

Yet encounter and engagement can only be of value if the identities of things are not suppressed, lost or rendered meaningless. This is not to imply that any particular style of captioning is necessary or correct. It has been made abundantly clear that artefacts, artworks, assemblages and specimens have mutable identities that can be revealed and activated in a variety of ways. But it does raise the question of how museum- and exhibition-making projects need to be constituted if their potential and fertility is to be realized. This book is not a policy paper and it would not be in keeping with its style to conclude with recommendations, but there are broad principles that emerge from the issues and cases I have considered.

The first is that museums should foreground the object – the artefact, the artwork, the historical document, the scientific instrument, the natural specimen – in a manner that enables viewers, visitors and audiences to engage with its physicality and materiality, its particular identity and history. What is special about museums is that they gather together things that are remarkable, singular or telling in whatever way; people should be able to get close to those things and make what they are inclined to of them. There is nothing wrong with science centres in which interactive exhibits of various sorts proliferate, and such devices can render a whole range of processes and principles visible, entertaining and spectacular. But these techniques exemplify a distinct exhibitionary mode that is not museological in the strict sense. Material culture offers what John Berger (writing on photography) called 'another way of telling', and museums are the places in which it is given the opportunity to speak, and in which we are most susceptible to its surprises and its eloquence.[2]

Second, museums should reveal the complexity of collections – that is, of the masses of material from which particular exhibits are drawn. People should have the opportunity to encounter not only artworks, presented as singular things, but the histories of acquisition and exchange that have drawn them together, ostensibly systematized them, perhaps subsequently fragmented and redistributed them. This is so, not because everyone needs a lesson in the history of collections, but because the strange gathering of related stuff that constitutes the collection has a certain magic; it amounts to a realm of exploration that people ought to have the opportunity to enter and enjoy as well as understand.

These general points have an organizational correlate. As institutions, museums should be structured in a way that sustains curatorial expertise at their heart. Unfortunately, this is often no longer the case, most obviously because of funding constraints but also because of misguided strategies. In many medium-scale city and town museums, the technical care of material may be in the hands of a collections manager and its public presentation dealt with by designers, education or outreach staff, in institutions with no curators at all. On the other hand, in some national museums curators are researchers who work in a manner close to those of university-based colleagues, but do not work on collections or contribute to public programmes. The museum is only a method, the collection only genuinely a creative technology, if it is sustained and enlivened by enquiry, by exploration of its history and by experimentation with its possibilities in the present. Research, exhibition and public engagement ought to be in dialogue but they cannot be if curators are no longer researchers, or if research curators are disconnected from collections, displays, events and educational programmes. This is also why new acquisitions are still important. Those aware that collections are already too vast to be exhibited other than highly selectively might consider it absurd that they continue to be enlarged. But new works such as contemporary African textiles, for example, have things to tell us about their precursors, about historic fabrics in collections, and may help audiences consider larger issues, such as the continuing heterogeneity and vitality of world culture despite globalization. And in any case, digital access and the new turn toward creating study centres opens up collections as totalities, promising to bridge the divide between displays and what is in stores or reserves. Access is absolutely essential to the effectiveness and value of the museum, and so too is activation, but activation takes many forms, including those that are implicit and subtle.

The fourth principle is that museums should 'be themselves', in the sense that new architecture and new displays should not efface their particular stories and identities. Museums are interesting not only because they hold exceptional things, but because they are expressions of local interests, of the intentions and preoccupations of individual travellers, collectors and scholars. More collectively, they reflect projects of patronage, passages of city history, commercial and imperial connections, interests in civic 'improvement' and moments of academic ambition that may be at some remove from us now. Their setting, accommodation, presentation and architectural inflection, the range and peculiarities of their collections, are lenses that look upon the human interests and interactions that brought them into being over the longer term, that offer us more nuanced recognition of places we inhabit or visit, places that we thought we knew. The city collections that typically range over various orders and disciplines – of art, natural history and ethnography, among others – speak of biographies, travels and global engagements beyond the 'community' that supposedly gave rise to the collection. The more attentive it is to its particular story, the more revelatory and deterritorializing a cultural formation the museum may be.

Museums thus have the capacity to tell stories of lives and communities that are interconnected over space and time, at odds with the nationalist narratives that are periodically reasserted, and that appear to become more compelling, in times marked by insecurity and uncertainty. But it has been a theme of this book that museums are more than the stories they tell – they are also places to be. They are places that implicitly foster and sustain civil society, and that prompt us to be curious. Curiosity and sociality are not conventionally linked, but my tentative suggestion is that the one prepares us for the other; that an interest in what is novel, singular or different is conducive to empathy, to a readiness to encounter and acknowledge difference. Conversely, the encounter with difference that defines experience in any heterogeneous society can, but does not necessarily, prompt curiosity, or prompt us to travel imaginatively if not literally. Retreat is, to be sure, always an option.

More than any other recent social or economic study, Thomas Piketty's *Capital in the Twenty-first Century* has highlighted the question of inequality in the present. Irrespective of whether Piketty's much-debated analysis is robust from the perspective of economic science, the implications of the current level of inequality and the claim that it is again increasing are far-reaching.[3] Without needlessly claiming cause and effect, the trends that Piketty refers to heighten other dangers. It is no more than common sense that, insofar as a substantial proportion of any nation's population is actually, or perceives itself to be, left behind, the national and international order risks an exacerbation of poverty, social exclusion, crime, extremism, racism, failures of governance, environmental damage and sundry other threats to the well-being of the world's citizens and the sustainability of our societies.

Notwithstanding his emphasis on the role of inherited capital, Piketty accepts that skills are vital to income inequality and its amelioration, and that 'the best way to increase wages and reduce wage inequalities in the long run is to invest in education and skills.'[4] When economists debate these issues, they focus on specific technical expertise: the textbook instance is that of the engineer, able to obtain a price for his or less commonly her labour, ideally commensurate with the scarcity of his or her skills. Yet if we step back from the specific frame of the labour market, it is evident that skills of all kinds, from basic literacy and numeracy to the capacity to cooperate, negotiate and calculate political risk are, by definition, vital to occupations that we call skilled, that bring people better wages and, they hope and believe, better lives.

It is emphatically not the argument of this book that museums have the capacity to solve the world's problems. But alongside, and indeed as part of, the investment in 'education and skill' that Piketty calls for, they already do something, and can do more, to make the world a better place. More or less frequently, in schools as well as in higher education, the drive to focus investment in STEM subjects – science, technology, engineering and mathematics – and the reduction of support for the arts and social sciences are debated and lamented. Too often, advocates of the humanities are content to argue, with more or less elaboration, that the arts are good because they are good. There is another kind of argument, which takes the battle onto our opponents' terrain.[5] It is that the real world of our social and economic lives demands much sensitivity to culture and difference, in both the multicultural milieux the vast majority of people now locally inhabit, and in the regional, national and international relationships we need to initiate and sustain whatever kind of work we may be engaged in. In this context society needs not only technological innovation, scientific expertise and powerful calculation, but interpretive and analytical acuity. A British education secretary once dismissed medieval history, as a subject that might be sustained to ornament the offerings of one or two universities; Barack Obama similarly expressed doubts regarding art history's usefulness.[6] But these are precisely the kinds of disciplines that enable people to go the distance conceptually, to consider the consequences of acting or failing to act, to acknowledge alternate visions of rights, value and efficacy.

Advocates of museums have long argued that the institutions address societal needs, in terms that may be broadly apt but that are often excessively instrumental. If such capacity as museums may have to foster cosmopolitan citizenship is of enormous value, their deeper effectivity may arise not from their particular disciplinary orientation or content, but from the very fact that we cannot predict or prescribe what visitors make of them. Whether young or old, people enter collections and ask apparently obvious questions of objects, such as, 'What is it?', 'What is it for?', 'Why is it here?', 'Should it be here?' and so on. This curiosity, this questioning, *is* a skill. We might consider the ability to respond to difference a survival skill in the connected but heterogeneous, dangerous but fragile, world we inhabit. Many institutions, sites and experiences help people acquire skills of various kinds, but the museum promises something distinctive, as a place of encounter in which our sense of the possibility, the hazards and the necessity of encounter can grow. That is what, for all their faults, museums are good for in the twenty-first century.

# REFERENCES

## INTRODUCTION

1 I cannot provide anything approaching a fair overview of this literature here, but it may be helpful to point to a few key or representative texts. Among reviews of current trends, Fiammetta Rocco's 'Temples of Delight', a special report on 'Museums' published in *The Economist* (21 December 2013), is both valuable for its overview of data and issues, and symptomatic of the level of interest among that influential magazine's readership. Several substantial anthologies have brought together key critiques of museums from the 1980s on, together with more recent essays; see Peter Vergo, ed., *The New Museology* (London, 1989); Donald Preziosi and Claire Farago, eds, *Grasping the World: The Idea of the Museum* (Aldershot, 2003); Bettina Messias Carbonell, ed., *Museum Studies: An Anthology of Contexts* (Malden, MA, 2004); and Sharon Macdonald, ed., *A Companion to Museum Studies* (Malden, MA, 2010). The most current perspectives (and the burgeoning quality of the literature) are well represented in a four-volume set of *The International Handbooks of Museum Studies* under the general editorship of Sharon Macdonald and Helen Rees Leahy (New York, 2015), made up of Andrea Witcomb and Kylie Message, eds, *Museum Theory*; Conal McCarthy, ed., *Museum Practice*; Michelle Henning, ed., *Museum Media*; and Annie E. Coombes and Ruth B. Phillips, eds, *Museum Transformations*. Victoria Newhouse, *Towards a New Museum* (New York, 1998) is written from the perspective of architectural history. Other books that have been important to me, from various angles, have included: James Clifford, *The Predicament of Culture* (Cambridge,

MA, 1988); Annie E. Coombes, *Reinventing Africa: Museums, Material Culture and Popular Imagination in Late Victorian and Edwardian England* (New Haven, CT, 1994); Mary Bouquet, *Museums: A Visual Anthropology* (London, 2012) and Ruth Phillips, *Museum Pieces: Toward the Indigenization of Canadian Museums* (Montreal, 2011).

2 The idea that the museum is or should be a forum rather than a collection or temple has become commonplace, and was aired first at least 45 years ago (see Duncan F. Cameron, 'The Museum, a Temple or the Forum', *Curator*, XIV (1971), pp. 11–24). If the idea of the forum has been rendered banal, including as it does any sort of discussion space, the claim becomes more arresting, at least for Europeans, if its historical significance is recalled: within the classical political society, the forum was *the* place in which matters of consequence were discussed. Berlin's major city-centre museum development, the Humboldt-Forum (see p. 25 below) lays claim to this foundational concept twice, first in its title and second in the creation of an Agora which occupies the central precincts on the building's ground floor. The Greek equivalent, moreover, evokes democratic origins, commensurate in political theory with the Humboldt brothers' scientific and ethical pluralism, which in turn complicates the more straightforwardly negative evaluation of the age of empire that brought the forum's ethnographic and Asian collections to Europe.

3 Among important volumes in these areas are, respectively: Carol Duncan, *Civilizing Rituals: Inside Public Art Museums* (London, 1995); Reesa Greenberg, Bruce W. Ferguson and Sandy Nairne, eds, *Thinking about Exhibitions* (London, 1996); Christopher Hitchens, *The Parthenon Marbles: The Case for Reunification* (London, 2008); and Michael M. Ames, *Cannibal Tours and Glass Boxes: The Anthropology of Museums* (Vancouver, 1992).

4 For broader argument around these themes, see Ian Leslie, *Curious: The Desire to Know and Why Your Future Depends on It* (London, 2014) and the catalogue of a stimulating exhibition, *Curiosity: Art and the Pleasures of Knowing*, exh. cat., Hayward Touring (London, 2013).

5 Edmund Burke, *A Philosophical Enquiry into the Origin of Our Ideas of the Sublime and Beautiful*, ed. J. T. Boulton (Oxford, 1958), p. 31.

6 Stuart Hall, 'Introduction: Who Needs Identity?', in *Questions of Cultural Identity*, ed. Stuart Hall and Paul du Gay (London, 1996), and reprinted in, for example, *Identity: A Reader*, ed. Paul du Gay, Jessica Evans and Peter Redman (London, 2000).

7 Burke, *A Philosophical Enquiry*, p. 31.

## I
## THE ASCENDANCY OF THE MUSEUM

1 Allan Kaprow, 'Death in the Museum', *Arts*, XLI (February 1967), pp. 40–41.

2 Theodor W. Adorno, 'Valéry Proust Museum' [1967], in *Prisms* (Cambridge, MA, 1981), p. 175. Commissioned by the seminal journal of the culture of decolonization, *Présence Africaine*, in 1950, Chris Marker and Alain Resnais' remarkable film – the first of Marker's 'film essays' – was awarded the Prix Jean Vigo in 1954 but was then subject to censorship and not publically shown again in its original version until the late 1960s. Intriguingly and strangely, the film appears to have been completely overlooked by the critique of primitivism that was so conspicuous in art theory, cultural studies and postcolonial debate in the late 1980s and subsequently.

3 At the opening of the Design Museum, Margaret Thatcher upheld its character as a 'living exhibition' relative to the usual museum – 'something that is really rather dead' (speech given on 5 July 1989, available at www.margaretthatcher.org, accessed 7 June 2015).

4 Douglas Crimp, *On the Museum's Ruins* (Cambridge, MA, 1993). The title essay, published in *October*, XIII (1980), pp. 41–57, was concerned with what the author took to be the disruptive effects of photography with respect to the knowledge-claims of the museum.

5 Gyan Prakash, 'Museum Matters' [1996], in *Museum Studies: An Anthology of Contexts*, ed. Bettina Messias Carbonell (Malden, MA, 2004), p. 208.

6 When Rogers received the Pritzker Architecture Prize in 2007, the Pompidou came first in the list of his defining achievements. According

to the jury's citation, 'The Centre Georges Pompidou in Paris (1971–1977), designed in partnership with Renzo Piano, revolutionized museums, transforming what had once been elite monuments into popular places of social and cultural exchange, woven into the heart of the city.' See www.pritzkerprize.com, accessed 7 June 2015.

7 There are now commonly said to be 55,000 museums worldwide, relative to about 23,000 twenty years ago. For these broad statistics, see Fiammetta Rocco, 'Temples of Delight', *The Economist* (21 December 2013).

8 For a sampling of local, often niche-interest or otherwise idiosyncratic museums, see Christine Redington, *A Guide to the Small Museums of Britain* (London, 2002); the vitality of some among these institutions was reflected in the Narberth Museum (Pembrokeshire, Wales), resurrected in 2003 by local volunteers following earlier closure, being shortlisted for the (UK) Museum of the Year Prize in 2013. There are listings and online networks available for similar 'small museums' in the United States, among other countries.

9 Darryl McIntyre and Kirsten Wehner, eds, *National Museums: Negotiating Histories* (Canberra, 2001) exemplified debate at the time, and particularly conversations across Australia, Canada, South Africa and New Zealand.

10 Among affirmative responses, see Simon Schama, 'The Rijksmuseum Reopens', *Financial Times* (29 March 2013).

11 For a programmatic discussion, see T. Flierl and H. Parzinger, eds, *Humboldt-Forum Berlin: Das Projekt* (Berlin, 2009). The concept and work in progress are showcased at the Humboldt Box, an interim presentation, and via www.humboldt-box.com, accessed 7 June 2015. Commentaries include Friedrich von Bose, 'The Making of Berlin's Humboldt-Forum: Negotiating History and the Cultural Politics of Place', *Darkmatter*, XVIII (November 2013), www.darkmatter101.org, accessed 7 June 2015.

12 The architectural concept appears on relevant pages of the Ateliers Jean Nouvel site (www.jeannouvel.com, accessed 7 June 2015). Laurence des Cars et al., *Louvre Abu Dhabi: Birth of a Museum* (Paris, 2013), initially

unveiled the collection. Among dozens of news reports, see Alan Riding, 'The Louvre's Art: Priceless. The Louvre's Name: Expensive', *New York Times* (7 March 2007); Jonathan Jones, 'Why the Louvre Abu Dhabi is Worth Celebrating, Despite Its Dark Side', *The Guardian* (9 March 2015). In Jones's opinion, the creation of 'a new global museum in the Arab world with an Arab perspective is a revolutionary subversion of the old European imperialism of knowledge'.

13 Shown at the Carré d'Art, Nîmes, May–September 2014. See also Eva Respini, *Walid Raad*, exh. cat., Museum of Modern Art, New York (2015).

14 Rocco, 'Temples of Delight', pp. 8–9.

15 Daniel Libeskind et al., *Daniel Libeskind: The Space of Encounter* (London, 2001), provides an overview of projects up to the date of publication. See also Annie E. Coombes, *History after Apartheid: Visual Culture and Public Memory in a Democratic South Africa* (Durham, NC, 2003), and Paul Williams, *Memorial Museums: The Global Rush to Commemorate Atrocities* (Oxford, 2007). See also the web pages of the International Coalition of Sites of Conscience, www.sitesofconscience.org, accessed 1 February 2016.

16 These figures are derived from annual reports, government statistical publications and other sources. In the UK, visits to the institutions directly supported by the Department of Culture, Media and Sport are published on a monthly basis (see www.gov.uk/government/statistical-data-sets/museums-and-galleries-monthly-visits); in France the Ministère de la Culture et de la Communication publishes an annual report, 'statistiques de la culture', which breaks visits down by institution, and so on.

17 Douglas Crimp, 'On the Museum's Ruins', *October*, XIII (1980), p. 45. In 'The Exhibitionary Complex', Tony Bennett made this passage a departure point for an entirely different Foucauldian analysis, and one deservedly influential, of museums' part in the business of governance. See Bennett, 'The Exhibitionary Complex', *New Formations*, IV (1988), pp. 73–102, and Chapter Two in Bennett, *The Birth of the Museum: History, Theory, Politics* (London, 1995).

18 Pierre Bourdieu and Alan Darbel, *L'Amour de l'art: les musées et leur public* (Paris, 1966) and *The Love of Art* (Cambridge, 1990), trans. Caroline Beattie and Nick Merriman. The specific study informed Bourdieu's major subsequent treatise, *La Distinction: Critique sociale du jugement* (Paris, 1979).

19 'Half UK's Adults Have Been to a Museum or Gallery in Past Year', *The Guardian* (26 September 2013); 'Taking Part 2013/14', statistical release, Department of Culture, Media and Sport (September 2013).

20 This position was advocated among and by indigenous Kanak leaders in the lead-up to the opening of the Centre Culturel Tjibaou outside Noumea in 1998; interview with Emmanuel Kasarherou, *Mwà Véé*, special edition (October 2000). Marie-Claude Tjibaou, widow of the independence leader Jean-Marie Tjibaou, also presented this affirmative view of dispersed heritage in addresses at and around the opening of the Musée du quai Branly in Paris in 2006. Similar arguments have been made by Maori in various contexts. Lyonel Grant has described the meeting house named Rauru, in the Museum für Völkerkunde in Hamburg since the early twentieth century, as 'the very, very best ambassador we could ever have' in Germany and Europe, in Nicholas Thomas, Mark Adams, James Schuster and Lyonel Grant, eds, *Rauru: Tene Waitere, Maori Carving, Colonial History* (Dunedin, 2009), p. 53. Similarly, Paul Nchoji Nkwi, a senior academic from Cameroon, stated with respect to works of African art in European and American museums, 'Let them stay where they are, for the time being' (Cambridge-Africa collaborative programme conference on 'Art and Museums in Africa', University of Ghana, September 2013). The qualification is significant: it's not necessarily permanently right for these works to remain in Western institutions, but it is acceptable that they do so for now.

21 Hugh Eakin, 'What Went Wrong at the Getty', *New York Review of Books* (23 June 2011); 'NGA Removes Dancing Shiva from Display', *Canberra Times* (26 March 2014). A number of projects and websites research and publicize developments in this area, for example traffickingculture.org, lootingmatters.blogspot.com and

chasingaphrodite.com. James Cuno, in *Who Owns Antiquity? Museums and the Battle over Our Ancient Heritage* (Princeton, NJ, 2010), and in other works, has sought to make a global case for the moral precedence of encyclopedic museums over what are seen as the claims of currently nationalist regimes. Contests over heritage, of course, also relate to more recent indigenous artefacts and works seized during the Nazi period; hence there are several intersecting debates, not just one. I would question the effort to establish general precepts since all cases are different; as I have noted, not all potential claimants seek the repatriation of any or all expatriate objects, while in other cases they do on varied grounds, and there are contexts where museums have more to gain than to lose by returning works where the case is considered valid. It would be a mistake to imagine that such debates will ever be definitively resolved, and in fact they should not be: museum visitors may wish to, and should be enabled to, reflect on how collections crossed the world to reach institutions and what may be gained or lost as a result.

22 Stephen D. Lavine and Ivan Karp, 'Introduction: Museums and Multiculturalism', in *Museums and Communities: The Poetics and Politics of Museum Display*, ed. Lavine and Karp (Washington, DC, 1991), p. 1.

23 Laura Peers and Alison K. Brown, eds, *Museums and Source Communities: A Routledge Reader* (London, 2003).

24 James Clifford, 'Museums as Contact Zones', in *Routes: Travel and Translation in the Late Twentieth Century* (Cambridge, MA, 1997).

25 'Salmond Plots First Move in Scottish Battle to Win Back Lewis Chessmen', *The Scotsman* (22 December 2007). On the broader field see Jeanette Greenfield, *The Return of Cultural Treasures*, 3rd edn (Cambridge, 2013).

26 Peers and Brown, *Museums and Source Communities*; Lissant Bolton et al., *Melanesia: Art and Encounter* (London, 2013).

27 'A Lasting Difference for Heritage and People: Strategic Framework, 2013–2018', www.hlf.org.uk, accessed 8 June 2015.

28 'The Rise of the Global Middle Class', BBC News, www.bbc.co.uk/news, accessed 8 June 2015.

29 See the data pages of the UN's World Tourism Organisation, www2.unwto.org/facts/en/vision, and those of the World Bank, data.worldbank.org, accessed 8 June 2015. The figures referred to count 'arrivals'.

30 Beatriz Plaza, 'Evaluating the Influence of a Large Cultural Artifact in the Attraction of Tourism: The Guggenheim Museum Bilbao case', *Urban Affairs Review*, XXXVI (2000), pp. 264–74; David L. Prytherch and Laura Huntoon, 'Entrepreneurial Regionalist Planning in a Rescaled Spain: The Cases of Bilbao and València', *GeoJournal*, LXI (1/2) (2005), pp. 41–50. There is, needless to say, a critical take, which sees initiatives of this kind as expressions of cultural globalization and/or the cultural imperialism of the United States that are said to offer local art no space. See Joseba Zulaika, *Crónica de una seducción: El Museo Guggenheim Bilbao* (Madrid, 1997). Opposition along such lines has been more vigorous and sustained with respect to a current development in Finland; see 'Helsinki v Guggenheim: The Backlash against the Global Megabrand Is On', *The Guardian* (11 September 2014); 'Can the Guggenheim Charm Finland?', *New Yorker* (12 May 2015). One website (www.guggenheimhki.fi, accessed 8 June 2015), careful to declare that it is not an official Guggenheim site, but one maintained by a Finnish communications consultancy on behalf of the foundation, offers 'a basis for public debate about the terms and conditions on which a Guggenheim museum could be established in Helsinki and how that museum could benefit Helsinki and Finland.'

31 Within the arts and heritage sector in the UK, reference is commonly made to the role of institutions of this kind in 'place making', contributing to strong communities and perceptions of local identity. According to the sector group the Museums Association, museums 'make a place worth living in and worth visiting', in *Museums Change Lives: The MA's Vision of the Impact of Museums* (London, 2013), p. 8.

32 Julian Stallabrass, *High Art Lite: British Art in the 1990s* (London, 1999), was a refreshing diatribe, part of a wider, considered reaction against New Labour and the political, economic and cultural trends of the 1990s, but it did not explore the extent to which the British case

exemplified the double phenomenon of the international popularization of contemporary art and the ongoing art-market boom.

33 C. P. Snow, *The Two Cultures* (Cambridge, 1959); the Wellcome Trust continues to support art projects that specifically engage the biomedical sciences – see www.wellcome.ac.uk, accessed 24 June 2015.

34 Joanna Bowring, *Chronology of Temporary Exhibitions at the British Museum,* British Museum Occasional Paper 189 (London, 2012).

35 'Art History and the "Blockbuster" Exhibition' (editorial), *Art Bulletin,* LXVIII (1986), pp. 358–9; Giles Waterfield, 'Blockbusters: Too Big to Fail?', *Art Newspaper,* 224 (May 2011).

36 Chris Smith (Lord Smith of Finsbury), keynote address at 'Invaluable? The Value of Museums in a World of Prices', Art Fund Museums Summit, National Gallery, London, 9 July 2014. For details of this event, see *Invaluable? The Value of Museums in a World of Prices: A Summary of the Art Fund Prize for Museum of the Year 2014 Museums Summit,* www.artfund.org, accessed 24 June 2015.

37 Carol Duncan and Alan Wallach, 'The Universal Survey Museum', *Art History,* III (1980), pp. 447–69; Carol Duncan, 'From the Princely Gallery to the Public Art Museum: The Louvre Museum and the National Gallery, London', in *Grasping the World,* ed. Donald Preziosi and Claire Farrago (Aldershot, 2003), pp. 250–78.

38 This is a minor but nevertheless notable strand in visitors' comments on the British Museum posted on the travel agency and tourist forum TripAdvisor, www.tripadvisor.co.uk, ranging from the overtly censorious to the more neutral ('It's appalling that the British Museum won't give back stolen artefacts'; 'It was a little odd wondering whether some of the exhibits should have stayed in their country of origin but I enjoyed the museum nonetheless').

39 Jonathan Bate, *Shakespeare: Staging the World* (London, 2012); Neil MacGregor, *Shakespeare's Restless World: An Unexpected History in Twenty Objects* (London, 2012). The latter was the book version of a BBC radio series, reproducing the model of the *History of the World in 100 Objects,* probably the single most successful museum project of the twenty-first century thus far.

40 Arjun Appadurai, ed., *The Social Life of Things: Commodities in Cultural Perspective* (Cambridge, 1986); see also Nicholas Thomas, *Entangled Objects: Exchange, Material Culture and Colonialism in the Pacific* (Cambridge, MA, 1991) and Janet Hoskins, *Biographical Objects: How Things Tell the Stories of People's Lives* (New York, 1998).

41 Annie E. Coombes, 'Making a Difference: Ethnographic Interventions from the Post Colony', plenary lecture, 'The Future of Ethnographic Museums' conference, Oxford, July 2013; Annie E. Coombes, Lotte Hughes and Karega-Munene, *Managing Heritage, Making Peace: History, Identity and Memory in Contemporary Kenya* (London, 2013).

42 See the Memorial Peace Museum's site, www.amanikenya.com, accessed 26 June 2015.

43 This section of the discussion, and this book as a whole, are indebted to Richard Sennett, *Together: The Rituals, Pleasures and Politics of Cooperation* (London, 2012).

44 Marcella Beccaria, *Olafur Eliasson* (London, 2013), p. 71. The theme of the museum and sociality was enlarged on in Eliasson's own text, 'Museums Are Radical', published in the catalogue of the project – Susan May, *Olafur Eliasson: The Weather Project* (London, 2003).

45 Aristotle, *Politics*, book II, chap. 2.

46 Partha Chatterjee, *The Politics of the Governed: Reflections on Popular Politics in Most of the World* (New York, 2004).

47 Baroness Morris, *Review of the Arts Council's Strategic Framework*, July 2011 (undertaken at the time the Council assumed new responsibilities for museums), www.artscouncil.org.uk, accessed 26 June 2015.

48 Sennett, *Together*, pp. 37–8.

## 2

## THE MUSEUM AS METHOD

1 Visible storage was an initiative in particular of Michael Ames and the Museum of Anthropology at the University of British Columbia. See Michael M. Ames, 'Visible Storage and Public Documentation', *Curator*, XX (1977), pp. 65–80. There has recently been increasing interest

not only in making reserve collections accessible through some form of walk-in or walk-around storage, but in architectural features that dramatize the mass of material, such as the glass tower containing the library of George III in the British Library, and the similar cylinder of musical instruments in the Musée du quai Branly in Paris.

2 *Significance*, adopted by the International Council on Monuments and Sites at the 12th General Assembly in Mexico, October 1999.

3 Thanks to Annie Coombes for discussion of this point, and Nessa Leibhammer, 'Traditional Southern African Art at the Johannesburg Art Gallery', seminar presentation, Centre for African Studies, Cambridge, October 2012.

4 'The Terrifying Rise of ISIS', *The Guardian* (16 June 2014).

5 Varied interests of this kind, in relation to historic painted barkcloths in particular, are discussed in John Pule and Nicholas Thomas, *Hiapo: Past and Present in Niuean Barkcloth* (Dunedin, 2005).

6 On this front, two recent books are useful: Chris Gosden and Frances Larson, *Knowing Things: Exploring the Collections at the Pitt Rivers Museum, 1884–1945* (Oxford, 2007) and *Reassembling the Collection: Ethnographic Museums and Indigenous Agency*, ed. Rodney Harrison, Sarah Byrne and Anne Clarke (Santa Fe, NM, 2013).

7 J. C. Beaglehole, ed., *The Endeavour Journal of Sir Joseph Banks* (Sydney, 1962), vol. II, p. 55. For the context, see also Nicholas Thomas, *Discoveries: The Voyages of Captain Cook* (London, 2003), and Maria Nugent, *Captain Cook Was Here* (Cambridge, 2009).

8 See 'Room 1: The Seagram Murals between New York and London', www.tate.org.uk, accessed 30 June 2015.

9 Cécile Giroire and Daniel Roger, *Roman Art from the Louvre* (New York, 2007), p. 70.

10 See www.rrncommunity.org, accessed 1 February 2016.

11 Edward Daniel Clarke, *Travels in Various Countries of Europe, Asia and Africa* (London, 1818), vol. VI, p. 223.

12 Nicholas Thomas et al., *Discoveries: Art, Science and Exploration from the University of Cambridge Museums*, exh. cat., Two Temple Place (London, 2014), p. 38.

13 'Controversial Museum Chief Quits', *New Zealand Herald* (16 March 2010).

14 David Blayney Brown, 'Joseph Mallord William Turner, 1775–1851', artist biography, December 2012, in *J.M.W. Turner: Sketchbooks, Drawings and Watercolours*, ed. David Blayney Brown (December 2012), www.tate.org.uk, accessed 30 June 2015.

15 Sandy Nairne, *Art Theft and the Case of the Stolen Turners* (London, 2011), p. 28.

16 Mark Elliott and Nicholas Thomas, eds, *Gifts and Discoveries: The Museum of Archaeology and Anthropology, Cambridge* (London, 2011), pp. 24–5.

17 Abu Mayanja, AA 4/5/15, archives, Museum of Archaeology and Anthropology, Cambridge. I am grateful to Derek Peterson for drawing my attention to this repatriation, which is the subject of his own fuller research.

18 W.J.T. Mitchell, *What Do Pictures Want? The Lives and Loves of Images* (Chicago, IL, 2005).

19 Thomas et al., *Discoveries: Art, Science and Exploration*, p. 6.

20 Sylvia Plath, 'All the Dead Dears', in Plath, *Collected Poems* (London, 1981); Elliott and Thomas, *Gifts and Discoveries*, pp. 90–91.

21 Steven Hooper, 'Embodying Divinity: The Lives of A'a', *Journal of the Polynesian Society*, CXVI/2 (2007), pp. 131–80.

22 Represented in the *Journal of the History of Collections* (1989–).

23 This discussion draws on Nicholas Thomas, 'The Museum as Method', *Museum Anthropology*, XXXIII (2010), pp. 6–10.

24 W. G. Sebald, *The Rings of Saturn*, trans. Anthea Bell (London, 1995). Sebald has also referred to a gift from the artist Jan Peter Tripp of an engraving 'showing the mentally-ill senatorial president Daniel Paul Schreber . . . and much of what I have written later derives from this engraving, even in my method of procedure: in adhering to an exact historical perspective, in patiently engraving and linking together apparently disparate things in the manner of a still life' – see 'An Attempt at Restitution', in W. G. Sebald, *Campo Santo*, trans. Anthea Bell (London, 2005), p. 210.

25 David Price, 'John Woodward and a Surviving British Geological Collection from the Early Eighteenth Century', *Journal of the History of Collections*, I (1989), pp. 79–95; Kenneth J. McNamara, *The Star-crossed Stone: The Secret Life, Myths and History of a Fascinating Fossil* (Chicago, IL, 2010); Thomas et al., *Discoveries: Art, Science and Exploration*, pp. 40–41, 52–5.

26 Ira Jacknis, 'Franz Boas and Exhibits: On the Limitations of the Museum Method in Anthropology', in *Objects and Others: Essays on Museums and Material Culture*, ed. George W. Stocking Jr (Madison, WI, 1985); Ira Jacknis, 'The Ethnographic Object and the Object of Ethnography in the Early Career of Franz Boas', in *Volksgeist as Method and Ethic: Essays on Boasian Ethnography and the German Anthropological Tradition*, ed. George W. Stocking Jr (Madison, WI, 1996). I am grateful to Aaron Glass for advice on this front.

27 Franz Boas, 'Museums of Ethnology and their Classification', *Science*, IX/229 (17 June 1887), p. 589.

28 'There is in New York a magic place where all the dreams of childhood hold a rendezvous' – Claude Lévi-Strauss, in 'The Art of the Northwest Coast at the American Museum of Natural History', *Gazette des Beaux-Arts*, VI (1943), p. 24.

29 'Discovering the Heart of Modernism', *New York Times* (28 October 1984); James Clifford, 'Histories of the Tribal and the Modern', in *The Predicament of Culture*, James Clifford (Cambridge, MA, 1988); Hal Foster, 'The "Primitive" Unconscious of Modern Art', *October*, XXXIV (1985), pp. 45–70; Sally Price, *Primitive Art in Civilized Places* (Chicago, IL, 1989).

30 William Rubin, ed., *'Primitivism' and 20th Century Art: Affinity of the Tribal and the Modern*, exh. cat., Museum of Modern Art (New York, 1984).

## 3
## THE COLLECTION AS CREATIVE TECHNOLOGY

1 Grayson Perry, *The Tomb of the Unknown Craftsman*, exh. cat., British Museum (London, 2011); Laura Cumming, 'Grayson Perry: The Tomb

of the Unknown Craftsman – review', *The Observer* (9 October 2011). The exhibition was shown from October 2011 to February 2012.

2 Viviane Callier, 'Ancient Fossil May Rewrite Fish Family Tree', sciencemag.org (12 January 2015); for the birds study, see macroevolution.group.shef.ac.uk, accessed 14 September 2015; the National Science Collections Alliance is a U.S.-based association supportive of natural science collections and institutions, and research generated by them (nscalliance.org, accessed 14 September 2015). I am grateful to Paul Brakefield (Cambridge), Paul Smith (Oxford) and Henry McGhie (Manchester) for information concerning these projects and resources.

3 Michael O'Hanlon, *The Pitt Rivers Museum: A World Within* (London, 2014).

4 Pierre Nora, *Rethinking France: Les Lieux de mémoire*, vol. I: *The State*, trans. David P. Jordan et al. (Chicago, IL, 2001), pp. xvii–xviii. There is no exact equivalent to this passage in the French edition, Nora, *Les Lieux de mémoire*, vol. I (Paris, 1984).

5 See also Marc Augé's discussion in *Non-lieux: Introduction à une anthropologie de la surmodernité* (Paris, 1992), p. 37.

6 This draws on a longer account, Nicholas Thomas, Julie Adams, Billie Lythberg, Maia Nuku and Amiria Salmond, eds, *Artefacts of Encounter: Cook's Voyages, Colonial Collecting and Museum Histories* (Dunedin, 2016). See also Baron Charles (Carl) von Hügel, *New Holland Journal: November 1833–October 1834*, trans. and ed. Dymphna Clark (Melbourne, 1994).

7 Rosanna Raymond and Amiria Salmond, eds, *Pasifika Styles: Artists Inside the Museum* (Dunedin, 2008).

8 Harry Allen, ed., *Australia: William Blandowski's Illustrated Encyclopaedia of Aboriginal Australia* (Canberra, 2010).

9 'Brook Andrew: The Island', exh. cat., Museum of Archaeology and Anthropology (Cambridge, 2008).

10 Hal Foster, 'The Artist as Ethnographer?', in *The Traffic in Culture: Refiguring Art and Anthropology*, ed. George E. Marcus and Fred R. Myers (Berkeley, CA, 1995). See also James Putnam, *Art and Artifact:*

*The Museum as Medium* (London, 2009), and Jennifer Barrett and Jacqueline Miller, *Australian Artists in the Contemporary Museum* (Farnham, Surrey, 2014).

## CONCLUSION

1 Walid Raad, 'Walkthrough' performance accompanying the exhibition 'Walid Raad', Museum of Modern Art, New York, various dates, October–December 2015.

2 John Berger and Jean Mohr, *Another Way of Telling* (London, 1982).

3 Thomas Piketty, *Capital in the Twenty-first Century*, trans. Arthur Goldhammer (Cambridge, MA, 2014). For related arguments, see Joseph Stiglitz, *The Price of Inequality* (New York, 2012).

4 Piketty, *Capital*, p. 313.

5 It will be apparent that my argument complements but is different from that of the STEAM campaign, which advocates 'placing Art and Design at the center of STEM'. See stemtosteam.org, accessed 6 September 2015.

6 The distinction between the two cases is that Charles Clarke's observations were considered, and trenchantly in favour of state support only for subjects of 'clear usefulness', whereas Obama made an off-the-cuff comment in the context of affirming the importance of technical training, for which he subsequently apologized. See 'Clarke Dismisses Medieval Historians', *The Guardian* (9 May 2003), and 'President Obama Writes Apology to Art Historian', *New York Times* (18 February 2014).

# ACKNOWLEDGEMENTS

This book has been written in the context of a collaborative, comparative project, 'Pacific Presences: Oceanic Art and European Museums', in part concerned with the making of world cultures museums and what they offer to European publics today. The project has received funding from the European Research Council under the European Union's Seventh Framework Programme (FP7/2007–2013) / ERC grant agreement n° 324146. Work towards the book has also been supported by a Cambridge Humanities Research Grant; I am very grateful to both the ERC and the University for these awards.

I thank Remke van der Velden, who undertook bibliographical and data searches, and the 'Pacific Presences' team at the Museum of Archaeology and Anthropology for sharing museum visits and conversations: Julie Adams, Alison Clark, Lucie Carreau, Alana Jelinek and Maia Nuku. I owe a great deal to colleagues at MAA and in the University of Cambridge Museums partnership, especially Paul Brakefield, Wendy Brown, Kate Carreno, Mark Elliott, Sarah-Jane Harknett, Anita Herle, Liz Hide, Tim Knox, Jody Joy, Heather Lane, Ken McNamara, Andrew Nairne, Robin Osborne, Liba Taub and Chris Wingfield. My sense of the curatorial imagination owes much to work on recent and continuing projects with Martin Caiger-Smith, Peter Brunt and Adrian Locke.

By way of disclosure I should acknowledge links with institutions discussed here, as a member of the conseil d'orientation scientifique of the Musée du quai Branly and of the International Advisory Board of the Humboldt-Forum, but mention these groups mainly to thank Stéphan Martin and Yves Le Fur, and Hermann Parzinger and Viola

König respectively, for their invitations to participate in really stimulating exchanges. I have learned a great deal over many years through conversation with, and the work of, Lissant Bolton, Jim Clifford, Sean Mallon, Michael O'Hanlon and Ruth Phillips, and more recently from colleagues in European museum networks, including Wiebke Ahrndt, Laura van Broekhoven, Inés de Castro, Yuri Chistov, Steven Engelsman, Guido Gryseels, Emmanuel Kasarherou, Wayne Modest and Boris Wastiau. I have been lucky to undertake much of my research in dialogue with art practice, and it's been a particular pleasure to work with Mark Adams, some of whose images are included here. Special thanks also to Walid Raad and to Anthony Allen and Laura Hunt of the Paula Cooper Gallery, New York, for their generosity and help with images.

Over almost twenty years, Annie Coombes and I have visited museums of all kinds. I have benefitted enormously from our conversations and from her insights and advice, and owe her more than I can say, for the shared journey and her love and support. Our son, Nicky Coombes-Thomas, wouldn't have chosen to visit so many museums, but his responses have also been thought-provoking; without him, the journey would not have been as surprising and wonderful as it has been.

# PHOTO ACKNOWLEDGEMENTS

The author and publishers wish to thank those listed below for illustrative material and/or permission to reproduce it. Some locations of artworks are also given below, in the interests of brevity.

Courtesy Mark Adams: pp. 6, 72, 73, 120–21; Ashmolean Museum, Oxford: p. 85; courtesy Ateliers Jean Nouvel: p. 27; photos author: pp. 79, 111, 114; The British Museum, London (Oc,LMS.19): p. 95; photo courtesy Annie Coombes: p. 55; © Hunterian Museum of the Royal College of Surgeons: p. 52; Museum of Archaeology and Anthropology, Cambridge: pp. 127 (photo courtesy Kerry Brown), 129 (courtesy Brook Andrew); © 2015 The Museum of Modern Art, New York/Scala, Florence: p. 112; Museum of Zoology, Cambridge: pp. 82 (photo Paul Tucker), 93; National Portrait Gallery, London (x125433): p. 87; images Kira Perov, courtesy Bill Viola Studio: pp. 58, 59; © Walid Raad, courtesy Paula Cooper Gallery, New York, photo Steven Probert: pp. 2, 138; Sedgwick Museum of Earth Sciences, Cambridge: pp. 90 (CAMSM J.35187 – photo Mark Box), 108 (photo Eva-Louise Fowler), 109 (photo Eva-Louise Fowler); photo Pete Souza/White House: p. 20; and Tate Archive Collection © Kate Rothko Prizel and Christopher Rothko/DACS 1998, photo J. Fernandes, Tate Photography: p. 64.

# INDEX

Page numbers in *italics* indicate illustrations

# The Infinite

# Books by the Author

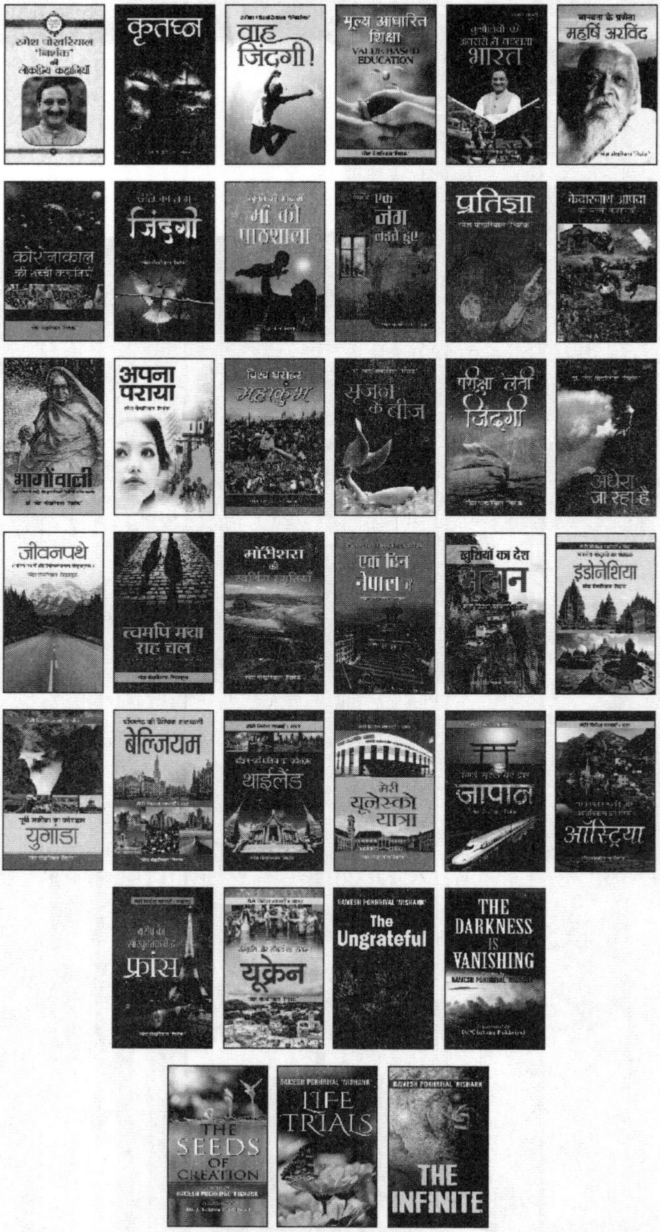

रमेश पोखरियाल 'निशंक' की लोकप्रिय कहानियाँ
कृतघ्न
वाह जिंदगी!
मूल्य आधारित शिक्षा VALUE BASED EDUCATION
भारत
मानवता के प्रणेता महर्षि अरविंद

कोरोनाकाल की सच्ची कहानियाँ
जिंदगी
माँ की पाठशाला
एक जंग लड़ते हुए
प्रतिज्ञा
केदारनाथ आपदा

भागोंवाली
अपना पराया
विश्व धरोहर महाकुंभ
सृजन के बीज
परीक्षा लेती जिंदगी
अँधेरा जा रहा है

जीवनपथे
त्वमपि मया सह चल
मॉरीशस की
एक दिन नेपाल में
खुशियों का देश भूटान
इंडोनेशिया

युगांडा
बेल्जियम
थाईलैंड
मेरी यूनेस्को यात्रा
जापान
ऑस्ट्रिया

फ्रांस
यूक्रेन
RAMESH POKHRIYAL 'NISHANK' The Ungrateful
THE DARKNESS IS VANISHING

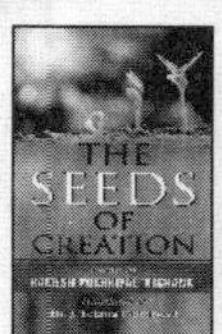


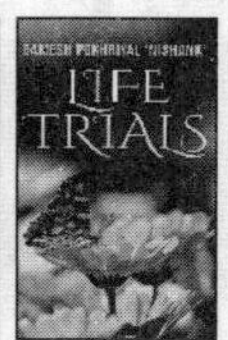


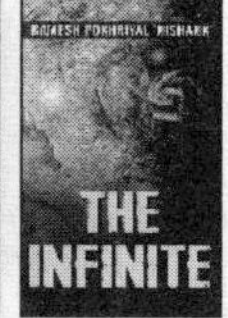

# The Infinite

Ramesh Pokhriyal 'Nishank'

Translated by
**Dr. Chetana Pokhriyal**

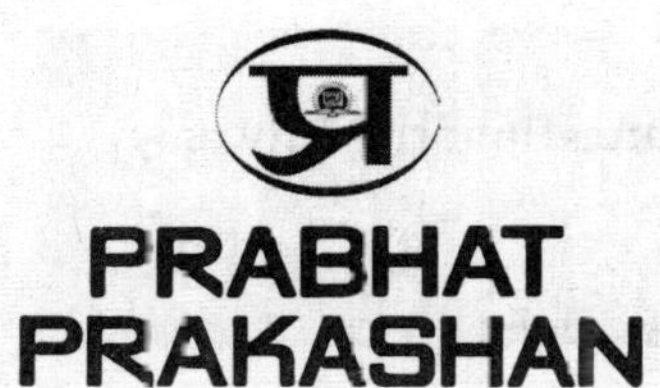

*Published by*
**PRABHAT PRAKASHAN PVT. LTD.**
4/19 Asaf Ali Road,
New Delhi-110 002 (INDIA)
e-mail: prabhatbooks@gmail.com

ISBN 978-93-90923-78-6
**THE INFINITE**
*novel* by Shri Ramesh Pokhriyal 'Nishank'



*Edition*
2025

*Price*
₹ 350.00 (Rupees Three Hundred Fifty only)

*Printed at*
R-Tech Offset Printers, Delhi

# Contents

# 1

# The Shadows of the Past

It was an icy-cold winter night. Regardless of the cold-shuddering winters, Bhagirathi was comfortably snugged in deep slumber, in the balmy warmth of hot burning coals and dung cakes in the fireplace. At that moment, the somnolent environment resonated with the jingle of her light snores attributable to the puffing of her nostrils.

Ramrath was bereft of any iota of sleepiness in his eyes. His raison d'être for not sleeping was neither intense cold nor heavy breathing of Bhagirathi but his been habitual of all of this. The main grounds that he could not snooze off forty winks had been owing to that unique face that repeatedly kept hovering before his eyes. Had his Surju been alive, would not he have looked like him? He felt like giving Bhagirathi a rude shake to wake her up. Why should he suffer this tragedy alone? He felt pity for the old woman. She had suffered a lot in her youth and had continued to be the same for so the last so many years. She must have done away with, pinched off even the vestiges of those memories away from her.

What should Ramrath do? His wakeful vigilant eyes with no trace of sleep made him shiver with icy cold wintry weather than what he would have felt on other occasions.

Every resonating sound gave the impression of the noisier thud than at any other time including Bhagirathi's snuffles and wheezes. Bagirathi was aware that, it was not the rationale for him not fast asleep.

That day, a team of foreign students had come for trekking with some local youths. Shivering with the attack of the severe cold, they had stopped, en route, at Ramrath's shop for a sizzling hot cup of tea. Ramrath's tea had been distinguished in that region for its appetizing decoction of herbal tea with ginger and cinnamon. He had scooped out the same decoction for the group.

A youth stepped out of the group with a hundred-rupee currency note in his hand to slide it unobtrusively in Ramrath's hand and spoke something in language that was beyond Ramnath's comprehension.

"But I have taken the money!" Ramrath was surprised. "Keep it. He says you have made very good tea", an

Indian youth whispered patting Ramrath on his back, while deciphering the crux of his intention.

Ramrath looked carefully at that alien youth. The young man was smiling. Ramrath watched him carefully. His hands started trembling and the hundred-rupee note fell from his hand. His body started shuddering. He felt the chilling effect of the entire snow from the mountains absorbed into and running down his veins.

"Why is this face so familiar?" He started pondering within.

"Sarju." Yes, it is the same nose, that big mole on the chin. How could he forget that?

"Baba, where are you lost? Keep the money. This boy has come from a place that is far away from our country. He is happy to drink your tea."

Ramrath felt like being awakened from deep slumber.

"This boy has come from which country? Where are you guys going?" He somehow managed to ask questions. "Baba, do you know the names of the countries?" He asked a question in return of a question.

"Yes, my son", Ramrath smiled back at him. The student kept thinking about what the tea-seller knew about the name of the countries.

"Baba, he is from the Netherlands. Do you see the hill in front of you? We will trek till that place." He pointed to a hill in front.

The startling likeness between the boy's appearance and his country's name disquieted Ramrath while quiet tears set rolling down his cheeks.

"What happened Baba? Why are there tears in your eyes?"

"Nothing! Just that I remembered someone. Why are you going there in the cold? Now, any day there might be a snowfall." There was a natural concern that had shrouded Ramrath mentally.

"Don't worry. While returning from there, we will again drink tea from your hand."

Those young men in no time became invisible from the Ramrath's sight.

As Ramrath turned around on his side of the bed again, Bhagirathi also woke up.

"Why are you so restless? Can't you sleep?" With half-sleepy drowsy eyes, Bhagirathi rubbernecked at Ramrath. Owing to Ramrath's repeated overturning in his bed, she was feeling cold and could hardly sleep.

"I saw Sarju today." These words emanating from Ramrath's throat had totally fleeced Bhagirathi of her sleep. She got up from her bed and sat down, looking carefully towards Ramrath, assuming that the old man had unquestionably gotten frenetic. Ramrath gazed in the void. Two drops of tears dropped from the core of his eyes.

"Sarju", a name that had given Bhagirathi a lot of happiness for a long time and after a few years, not sure, but he same name had given countless sorrows.

After ten to twelve years of marriage, when Bhagirathi could not produce any children, she renounced the aspiration of becoming pregnant and giving birth to any child. Bhagirathi and Ramrath procured treatment for their childlessness from the *Ayurvedic Vaidyas* in their village and surrounding areas, arranged prayer services to conciliate the benign God. They willingly did whosoever suggested whatsoever remedy but to no avail. They did not possess enough resources to go to the city for the right kind of treatment from a doctor but whenever any hermit or a saint visited the village, Bhagirathi and Ramrath would reach there to bow down in obeisance.

When the marriage had been over fifteen years and they had left the hope of begetting a child, a miracle happened. Bhagirathi became pregnant. At that age, the news of the arrival of a new life generated within them a renewed interest in life. Ramrath had literally gone mad. He pampered Bhagirathi like a queen, and did not allow her to do any household work.

"You stay well. Do not carry any heavy luggage. If you want to eat something, then tell me. I will make it." The unanticipated happiness had made even such a humble imprudent Ramrath an experienced soul.

Bhagirathi would laugh. Ramrath's words would tickle her from within. If she did any household work, he would not like it. They both would indulge lovingly in those little fights.

As time passed, Bhagirathi gave birth to a baby boy.

The whole house was filled with happiness. There was no elderly person in the house, who would have explained the nuances of how the child is raised, but Bhagirathi had such a sweet nature that the elders from all over the village would come and help her. Both affectionately named their son "Suraj", which later deteriorated as "Sarju" in their loving address.

Sarju grew with time. When he was three, he would follow his mother everywhere. Then came that unfortunate day that had deserted their life once again.

After finishing off the day's work, Sarju followed Bhagirathi when she went to the spring to clean utensils and fetch water from the cascade. Anyway, this was not a new thing. Sarju would often cling to his mother.

That day something unique and unexpected happened. As usual, Sarju, who would follow his mother back home every day, did not return home that day. Frantic search for Sarju began everywhere. All searched for Sarju in every house in the village, stream, cascade and spring but Sarju was nowhere to be found.

Ramratha and Bhagirathi were disillusioned. They looked for Sarju even in the rivers. Who knows he might have fallen in them? He was still small. When he could not be found in the village, they inquired about him from the surrounding villages. They made a complaint to the village head. The village head was a good man. He could not tolerate that Ramrath and Bhagirathi suffered yearning for their child. The boy was last traced reportedly with a boy from the next village, when the investigations escalated. The impression of that boy was not good. In the past too, he had been caught in small thieveries After spending a few days in detention center, he absconded from the village to the city. After staying in the city for some time, he returned to the village. After putting a little push on his parents, the investigating agencies ascertained the boy's address from them. By that time, it was too late. The boy was caught in Bombay but he had already sold Sarju for a few thousand bucks.

After a firm hold on the investigation, they further interrogated the boy but who could fight the destiny, the destiny of Ramrath and Bhagirathi acted as per their inscribed providence. The boy had been working for a big gang who would snip children and give them away to foreign couples for adoption for a good deal. In return, they would charge a hefty amount from them. Under the same "modus operandi," Sarju had been also sold to a foreign couple.

The only information they had was that it was some couple from the Netherlands, who had bought and adopted their Sarju. Sarju was not just any article, which they had splashed money out on and procured.

Beyond that point, Bhagirathi and Ramrath had no access. Whatever investigation had happened was also out of their reach. It was the people from their village, who had rallied round for them. Otherwise, they would not have been able to reach that extent for their son.

Sarju could not be found even after so much of an effort. Once again, there had been a spurt of dimness in Ramrath and Bhagirathi's life. At first, they were satisfied that they did not have a child, but afterwards, regardless of having a child, they had been still left starved of the one. Whatever time Sarju had spent with Ramrath and Bhagirathi was just like a delusional fantasy for them.

Their world had never been the same since then and their moments of exhilaration swapped over with lifelong misery. Neither could they survive, nor could their life meet its expiration and their state of anguish had prematurely made both look exceedingly old. Many years had passed since then. Ramrath and Bhagirathi somehow survived the tragedy. However, for both, it was not on the cards conceivable to erase Sarju from their mind, but they had gradually buried their memories inside the thick sediments of time.

After many years, ripping apart through those different seams, the truth about Sarju was staring intently in their eyes.

"Have you gone crazy? Where will Sarju come here now?" Bhagirathi probed, vigorously jolting Ramrath.

"No, I am not crazy. He was Sarju. What do you think twenty-year-old Sarju would look like now? That boy was the same. And then he also told me the name of the country." Ramrath re-counted the entire episode to Bhagirathi.

Bewildered Bhagirathi was absorbed deep in thought. Would that boy, if truth were told, be her Sarju? If it was so, how would she single out and identify him and what would be the proof that he was their son?

"Will they come again?"

"Yes, it is what they said. They were saying that they would definitely come to drink tea from my teastall." Ramrath countered while still lost in his own thoughts.

"In that case, from tomorrow onwards I will also accompany you to be in the shop. The day Sarju comes, I will beseech him with folded hands to put forward my claim that he is my son."

"Are you crazy? He is not acquainted with our language any more. You will not do this stupidity."

There were squabbles between them for a while. Ultimately, Ramrath, overpowered by Bhagirathi's natural feelings, her motherly instincts, consented to her presence in the shop but with the condition that she would not lose her self-control and say anything even after bumping into Sarju.

From the next day, Bhagirathi hurriedly finished her household chores to be with Ramrath in the morning in his teastall. Ramrath was also rendered speechless to see Bhagirathi's energetic crusades. Bhagirathi got up ahead of schedule in the morning when it was still dark with night-shadows, but she remained oblivious, on the spur of the moment prepared breakfast and tied four *chapattis* in a bundle. Her eyes glimmered with the potential possibility of meeting her long-lost son. Her listless body was filled with renewed energy, which all these while had been dead like a living corpse.

Seeing her agile sprightliness, Ramrath was every now and then growing nervous. If that group of students would not come that way, then in all probability Bhagirathi would go uncontrollably panic-stricken mad in the old age.

While sitting in the shop, her eyes were preset with foreordination on that region from where those people were expected to roll up. Repeatedly, she asked Ramrath his expected time of return.

These enquiries, her innocent request for information irritated Ramrath down in the mouth. "What do I know when will they come? Did they tell me?"

Bhagirathi got scared but then she started observing that pathway with twofold enthusiasm but by the time it was evening, she became down in the dumps miserable. It had started becoming colder. There had been heavy snowfall on the higher peaks. Ramrath wanted to close the shop almost immediately. Anyways in the evening, there would be hardly any customers but Bhagirathi did not allow him to put up the shutters of the tea stall. Bhagirathi would often shrink her nose enduring the spiky arrows of icy winds sitting by the side of the measly heat generated by the stove.

Her temperance for waiting in cold weather bore fruitful results. The team of students returned one day and stopped there to slurp their favorite tea concoction. Ramrath had seen them coming from a far-off distance. In a group of ten or twelve boys, he had identified Sarju from a distance but hung around silently. He wanted to corroborate his doubts with Bhagirathi. The boys approached closer to them. Ramrath looked at Bhagirathi from the corner of his eyes. Bhagirathi was staring at the foreign student.

"Baba, make tea. Look, we had said that we would definitely come back." The Indian student, standing near the fireplace, took off his gloves and started enjoying the perceptive heat emanating from the stove.

"Sarju..." the student's attention turned towards Bhagirathi when she whispered in a low voice.

"What is Amma saying?" That student was too talkative.

"Nothing! She is old, she keeps grumbling." Ramrath answered before Bhagirathi could say something.

It appeared as if Bhagirathi had not heard anything. She was staring at Sarju. Same eyes, same face! Mole on the chin! That beautiful expression of smiling diagonally. Bhagirathi thought she would go mad. The tears started flowing from her eyes. "Amma, are you okay?" Another student said when he saw Bhagirathi's condition.

Bhagirathi responded, as if awakened from deep slumber. "No son, I'm fine." She looked at Sarju standing in front of her. Then she looked at herself. There was no match between Sarju and their condition. For three years, they had brought him up and his foster parents in the Netherlands were looking after him. His face was fair, which radiated health and prosperity. Could they have given him such a life? No! Never! If he had been with them, he too would have been sitting with them at this tea stall.

"Son, can you please ask this boy, where has he come from? And what his parents do?" Bhagirathi asked pointing at Sarju.

Ramratha and Bhagirathi both did not understand whatever conversation took place between the two. What he had told them had convinced both Ramrath and Bhagirathi that the foreign student was their son, Sarju.

The young man knew that he was not the biological child of his parents, they had adopted him from the city of Mumbai in India but apart from this, he did not know anything about his biological parents. His father was a good businessperson from the Netherlands and would occasionally come to India in connection with his business. He also accompanied his father on his business trips but had come to this region for the first time.

Bhagirathi went ahead. This gesture of Bhagirathi scared Ramrath from within. He did not know what she would do. He tried to stop her but something from within had put a restraint on him from doing so, moreover, his tongue did not support him.

Bhagirathi came and stood near Sarju and placed her shivering hands on his head. Once again, tears came rolling down her eyes. Her eyes became blurred with tears, but she hurriedly wiped them, so that she could see him narrowly. All the young men, who had come along, were surprised at her gesture and partially upset too. Everyone possessed a query in his mind regarding the good sense for her bizarre behavior.

"Come again, my son." Bhagirathi said in a quivering tenor.

Listening to Bhagirathi, Ramrath sucked in the air of contentment and the Indian student once again get down to discharge his duty as an interpreter.

“I will definitely come.” Saying in his own language, the young man jumped over the narrow paths shaking his hands, and in no time, disappeared from the sight. Bhagirathi was petrified to turn to stone and stood there for some time without moving.

Life once again had moved on to the old pattern, the only difference that had definitely come in Bhagirathi’s life was that she had relentlessly started accompanying her husband to the tea stall. After all, her son had promised to come back again.

□

# 2

# Unknown Relationship

When the horn of the car blazed, his attention automatically turned to the clock. It was half past nine. However, she was already ready but had not taken her breakfast. In a hurry, she punched a toast into her mouth and stepped out with her handbag.

It had been almost a week since she had come to this city, but had not yet organized her stuff and her schedule. Surbhi was working as a Medical Officer in a private company. The company also had an office in that city and they had moved there barely a week before.

At the news of her transfer, Surabhi had felt like leaving the job. At the insistence of Siddhant, she joined her new office. He was also right when he said that when the children were young and they needed us, even then we decided not to quit the job. However, when the children were actively hard at with their lives and Surabhi and Siddhant had been left with nothing out of the ordinary to accomplish on the home front, even then there was no apparent logic for Surabhi to give notice and resign from the job.

Anyway, the company had provided her with a furnished house. There was no problem. The company had provided her with a car for pick and drop in the mornings and evenings. Before her joining there, Siddhant had personally visited this place and satisfied himself. Observe for a few days. Please let me know if you like it. Then I will also apply for the transfer," said Siddhant while leaving her there.

Siddhant was in a government job. He could also be transferred to that city. Anyway, Surabhi also did not wish to be left alone.

Although the city was not very big, the cosmopolitan civilisation was gradually beginning to dominate there as well. The area, in which Surabhi was living, was once isolated from the city. Lovers of solitary bliss had purchased large plots and built houses on them. The cottage houses were surrounded by greenery all around them.

Gradually, the city grew in dimension while the rapid urban development had shredded and wiped out the natural beauty of the region. When land prices swelled up, property dealers grabbed the opportunity of buying the land in that region to divide it into small plots for more profits. Gradually, the area looked like a forest of concrete.

Still some old bungalows stood out as an epitome of the old beauty of the area. One such bungalow was situated next to Surabhi's house. Among the clumps of mango and *lychee* trees, she could see the red-tiled roof of the bungalow. While walking in and out, Surabhi would throw a passing glance at the bungalow many times but hardly could see any creature around.

"How lucky are those people who are enjoying living in this picturesque environment of nature," Surabhi would ruminate over and over again.

It was Sunday. Surabhi possessed more leisurely hours than usual. Woke up late and sat outside on the terrace, sipping her tea. Inadvertently, she looked towards the adjacent house. She saw a middle-aged woman giving some instructions to the gardener. At the same time, she was plucking some flowers from the flowerbeds. She must be plucking those flowers to decorate them in the vase. Surabhi pondered that probably she might be the mistress of the house.

That moment, another person wheeled an old man out on a wheelchair. Probably, he must be the father-in-law of the woman. He can also be her father. Surabhi kept guessing within. For some time, Surabhi kept watching their activities and then went inside.

Sunday was over; Surabhi was again occupied with her work. While moving in and out, she would often look on that side but then could see none.

One day, at nine o'clock in the night, Surabhi was startled with the ringing of the doorbell. Who has arrived at this time? Has some kind of emergency has appeared in the hospital? While she was engulfed with the apprehensive thoughts, Nirmala came there and informed, "Someone has come to meet you."

Nirmala used to live in a nearby colony and during daytime would stay at Surabhi's house doing all her chores. The cook was winding up after preparing dinner for Surabhi when the bell rang. She was preparing to leave. The visitor is a woman. "Nevertheless, who can that be right now?" Surabhi went out tying the belt of her gown.

"Excuse me; we had to trouble you at this odd moment. However, the situation had come to this. My father- in-law's health has suddenly deteriorated and I am all alone right now." Because of being in stress, droplets of sweat had emerged on her forehead.

Surabhi did not ask anything. She asked her to wait and went inside to change clothes. Within five minutes, she was ready with her bag in her hand.

"What would you think that even though we don't know you and still I have disturbed you like that? We live in your neighborhood." At that moment, Surabhi could sense her words and her acute helplessness reflected through them.

"What are you talking about? This is the duty of a doctor." Surabhi tried her best to clear her guilt conscience. " So they are our neighbors and the old man who had appeared with her was her father-in-law, her husband probably stays somewhere out of station, and so do her children' Surabhi contemplated.

Drowned in her thoughts, Surabhi entered their house and headed directly to the bedroom The old man was suffering from high fever. He was lying unconscious, had a wet piece of cloth on his forehead that would dry up as soon as it would be placed on his forehead. A person standing nearby was constantly changing the ice-dipped cloth. The moment both of them reached, he stood on one side.

"Nothing to worry about, it is only viral. He will take two-three days to recover." Surabhi consoled the woman and wrote her prescription.

"You can get these medicines tomorrow morning. The medicine that I have just given will relieve him of his fever and he will be able to sleep peacefully at night," Surabhi told the woman as she walked out.

Surabhi's attention was drawn to the internal decoration of that house. The entire house appeared an antique to her with decorative artistic furniture, wood items and old sculptures. Appreciating the aesthetic sense of the owner, Surabhi came back.

The next day, after about one and a half hours, when Surabhi returned home from office, she again met the owner of the neighboring house who had come to thank her. She had brought a bouquet of fresh flowers from her garden.

"Actually, my father-in-law is suffering from Alzheimer. He has aged as well. That's why I get nervous even at the slightest illness to him."

"What about your husband?"

She bowed her eyes down saying, "He is no longer in this world."

There was absolute silence for a moment. Surabhi did not have enough courage to inquire anything about her children.

In the process of their conversation, she discovered that the woman was Sulakshana and she was a professor of English at the local degree college there.

"Just two years more of my service and after that I will retire."

She sat down for some time but left a clear impression of her personality on Surabhi's psyche.

Next Sunday, she came again and invited Surabhi to come home, which, she found, was an opportunity and did not let this opportunity go waste. Surabhi had no desire of leaving any chance of a new friendship in her neighborhood, while she was alone in an unknown city. At the back of this move was the temptation to see that house closely, which smelled of colorful flowers amidst dense clumps of greenery.

Sulkshana's father-in-law was now perfectly healthy but the chronic Alzheimer condition was practically getting impossible to handle. Moreover, he was above ninety years of age. Surabhi was impressed by this woman's liveliness.

Gradually, her visits to that house increased. There was a sheath between the two, a shell which neither Surabhi nor Sulakshana tried to break.

"You don't feel the desire to talk to me anymore ever since you met your new friend." Siddhant joked while Surabhi blushed.

Siddhants's observations were right. Those days, she would often croon over the phone praising Sulakshana. Surabhi knew that by the end of the next month, Siddhant too would be transferred and then she would get busier. Then, where would she get an opportunity to meet Sulakshana?

As they kept meeting more often, they spoke on more and more issues than one. In that spurt, one day Surabhi asked Sulakshana about her children.

That one question changed the facial expressions of Sulakshana as if dark clouds had suddenly enveloped the blue sky and the tears soaked for years in her eyes started rolling down.

Surabhi was embarrassed at her query. Why did she need to ask those questions? Why did she scour her wounds? It seemed that either she did not have children or she had suffered some other misfortune related to them. After some quiet eerie moments, the answer that Surabhi received was beyond her imagination.

"I am not married, then what about children?"

Surabhi felt as if she had come prostrate on the ground after pinning her ears back to what Sulakshana had said. Then why did she mention her father-in-law, if she was not married? Probably, she must have erroneously perceived something inaccurate.

"Yes Surabhi, this is the truth that I feel like revealing this confidential secret suppressed inside me for years." Sulakshana narrated her story to Surabhi.

Sulakshana's father and Anupam's father were old friends. Both were owners of their respective business houses. When Anupam's father expressed his desire to transform their old friendship into kinship, it garnered a positive response and hailed without any objection from any corner. Although Sulakshana's mother had come out with an excuse and made allowances for her being too young for marriage and she had yet to complete her studies, but her father without more ado assented to her marriage insisting that her in-law's home would be her new home.

Anupam was the only son of Seth Dinanath. When he was three, his mother had died while his father Seth Dinanath was seriously injured in a road accident. Although he soon recovered physically, he could never recuperate from the anguish of the untimely demise of his wife. Dinanath had efficiently played the role of Anupam's mother and father. Since Anupam was young, his well-wishers had advised Dinanath to remarry, but he without demur declined the offer.

When handsome and young Anupam turned twenty-five or twenty-six, he returned home after completing his management degree from abroad and managed his father's business. When Sulakshana's family obtained the marriage proposal of Anupam for her, the entire family was over the moon in a state of high excitement.

Sulakshana had known Anupam since childhood days and promptly discerned the transference in their relationship. Even she was thrilled with the proposal. Their relation had metamorphosed into an extent that Sulakshana, who earlier conversed freely with Anupam with ludicrous humility, hesitated to talk to him.

Their marriage was due within a month. Seth Dinanath was excited. He would almost talk daily to his would-be daughter-in-law Sulakshana. Keeping in mind everyone's likes and dislikes, there was a shopping-spree, moments of exhilaration. Sometimes he would invite Sulakshana over to his place.

"My son is extremely busy and doesn't have time to spare, why don't you help me in the marriage preparation."

Anupam stopped going to the office three days before the wedding, that too, when his father unreservedly expressed his annoyance in public.

However, destiny had other plans. When the dress tailored for Anupam for the wedding ceremony did not fit him, he decided to visit the tailor himself. While he was on his way to return home, but he could never reach home. When Dinanath received a phone call, he immediately rushed to the hospital in a state of dishevelment. However, by then everything was over. He later had the knowhow about that unfortunate incident how a truck laden with vehicles overturned on Anupam's Mercedes in an attempt to save a scooterist.

Severely injured, Anupam was rushed to the hospital with great difficulty. He had died even before reaching the hospital.

How would Sulakshana have endured such a great shock? Why is she with them now? Surabhi's heart was engulfed in a sea of sorrow with the heart-wrenching incident. Sulakshana adhere to a long silence for some time. Perhaps she was trying to wrangle with her tears to hold them back. Surabhi, too, did not utter a word, but after a while, Sulakshana initiated the conversation.

With Anupam's untimely demise, both the families had fallen asunder. Even before Sulakshana's hands could be with customarily applied henna, its auspicious color would have adorned her, cruel destiny had other plans and snatched everything from her at the spur-of-the-moment.

After Sulakshana had overcome her grief, the first thought that came to her was of her father-in-law. She had remained in doubt for few days whether she should visit him or not. Finally, after serious mulling, she mustered her courage and decided to get together with him in the moment of tragedy.

Seth Dinanath had lost his mental balance. He would relentlessly sit in front of the idols of deities in his grand worship room and would stare at them for hours together. He had lost his sense of appetite and sleep. "Why this injustice to him?" Perhaps that is what he must have been soliciting from God.

Sulakshana went directly to the worship room where Seth Dinanath sat looking intently at the holy idols of the deities and for a while, he shifted his gaze towards Sulakshana and looked at her in queerness. He tried his best to identify her, when he could not; he turned his face away from her.

From that day onwards, Sulakshana made it a thumb rule to visit him regularly. Dinanath started recuperating from his illness with minute monitoring by the doctors and dedicated nursing by Sulakshana.

"Daughter, I could not make you my daughter-in-law."

After recognizing Sulakshana, the first sentence uttered by Dinanath, had made both of them, teary eyed.

Deep within, Sulakshana, who was terrified with the accident, was reassured of hope. Dinanath had evolved from his grief and there was no tinge of sorrow and complaint.

Sulakshana was now spending most of her time looking after Dinanath. Gradually, her family members started opposing her visits to Dinanath's house. Sulakshana, however, did not respond to anyone's complaints and continued with her routine.

After losing his wife and son in this city, Dinanath had abandoned his desire to continue to hang around in that city anymore. After winding up his business, he wanted to spend the rest of his life peacefully in a remote quieter place.

After he had persuaded people to buy everything, his

bungalow, his factory at a throwaway price, he was ready to move out from there.

"I will not leave you alone. I'll go with you."

Dinanath was flabbergasted at Sulakshana's implorations. He took a quick look of her face and could fathom her unbending and firm gait. Despite constant protest from her family, Sulakshana had indiscriminately made up her mind to follow Dinanath like a shadow to an unknown city. Once they had been firmly established in their new setup, new set of connections, Dinanath gently enthused Sulakshana to study further.

Sulakshana took admission in a local college and completed her postgraduate and doctorate degree from there. She continued with her education, completed it, acquired one degree after the other and eventually at the continual insistence of Dinanath, she was encouraged to take up an employment in a local college for women.

In an unknown city, since they had not been familiar with many people, hence no one probed them for any answer. Most people they had known possessed the slimmest inkling that Sulakshana was the widowed wife of Dinanath's only son.

Whoever seemed to know them would shower them with praises. While people praised Dinanath for providing his widowed daughter-in-law with an opportunity to read and write, to continue with her education, to pursue her job, to become financially independent, they would praise Sulakshana for sacrificing her life for looking after her father-in-law despite the fact that she was widowed at a young age.

"Almost forty years have passed since then; everyone knows that we are father-in-law and daughter-in-law. No one knows that this relationship has never been accomplished, never reached its absoluteness."

Surabhi was surprised. She did not utter a word anything. Since, it had been too long sitting with Sulakshana, Surabhi came back wrapped up in her own thoughts. Can this happen even in this era of *Kaliyuga*? When people face challenges to sustain their blood relations, Dinanath and Sulakshana had kept alive the relationship that had not been shaped in the first place.

□

# 3

# The Property

At the end, all work in this office was carefully executed. Anyhow, the work of changing ownership of immovable property was risky, especially when the real owner of the property had died. The fraudulent people make a fake document of will, and transfer the ownership of the property making fake death certificates. Many times, an offspring would bring fake death certificates of their own parents.

"It is called abject *Kaliyuga*. The children can't wait for the parents to die, just to grab the property," Bihari Babu said in frustration, while chewing the betel leaves.

"Yes Babuji, this is the matter concerning property. This can even raise the dead from the grave, even prove the living dead and dig him in the grave," Harihar, the peon, responded to him, while rubbing tobacco in his palm.

Many times, these fake papers appear as real and the fate of property worth millions is effortlessly settled either by mistake or by secret collaboration.

There had been an unclaimed piece of land in the city, whose owners had long since left for their heavenly abode. The children had settled overseas. For them, the value of this property was equivalent to worth a penny. The land mafia kept a sharp penetrating eye like a vulture on such properties. There have been many bloodbaths over such plots of land.

The staff working in the property office enjoyed great benefits. At times, they enjoyed monetary benefits for wrongdoing and if the land deal was big, then there would be a possibility of getting a small plot of land. Everyone in that office possessed a habit of taking bribes so much that they would not do even a genuine work without any convenience fees. Any person coming to their office appeared to them like a rooster and the whole office would then unite to slaughter him.

Then something unprecedented occurred in that office. The entire office was inundated one day. It appeared as if there was a deluge, which transformed everything. Till then, the law of 'like king like subjects' operated in the office but eventually with the rise in the complaints against the king of the office, he was eventually changed. Had the king been honest with a slight difference, even then, it would have somehow worked but this was a very different situation.

On his first day in the office, the 'king' gave a long speech on honesty and sensitivity. Most people found this speech boring and thought these values had any relevance probably during Adam's time.

"The ideology of which era was defined by the new Boss?

What if he was the same in reality!" said a junior officer.

"Hey, everyone says the same thing at the beginning, but later turn into the same color. After all, who does not like the crisp green colored currency notes?" said the other officer standing nearby.

Nevertheless, this did not happen. There was no difference between his words and his actions. If a complaint of taking a bribe reached him, he would humiliate that person in front of the entire office and the person would feel ashamed.

At the same time, when the regular inflow of income was stopped for those who led a royal life earlier, they set themselves on the mission to get them transferred from there to another office. Whatever they earned, they would spend a small portion of that for getting the most desirable plum posting.

Similarly, few people in that office were of the same moral attributes as their new officer was. Although, now their number had reduced, irrespective of their reduced number, the officer was happy to have those people in his office.

Now, the official work of the people, who approached the office for work, was accomplished quickly, and those, who approached for illegal and unethical work, could not even step inside the office.

During earlier days, a person claiming to be the only son of a deceased would apply for transfer of property in his name. Whatever had been written and whatever documents he had presented for his claim appeared flawless.

Asking him to come after two or three days, the officer became diligently busy with his official files. Later, when he looked carefully in the registry papers of the house, he saw the name of a woman in it.

Thinking that she must be the mother, he supposed she might have died too. That is why the son had applied for a change of ownership in his name.

"Has your mother also died?" On the fourth day, when the man came to inquire for the progress of his application, the officer fired him with his question.

"No, she lives elsewhere. They are divorced." "When?"

"Yes, it has been twenty-five or thirty years."

"Twenty-five or thirty years. The officer murmured.

Look at the papers of the house. They are only 15 years old. Why would this person buy property in their joint names, twenty-five years after the divorce?" He started pondering. Only this person, who claims to be the son of the deceased, could answer this question.

"But this property has your father's name as well as your mother's name in it." With his eyes fixed on the file, he spoke and then looked at the person sitting in front of him to know the reaction.

"It is impossible. How could this happen?" There were expressions of astonishment on his face.

"See it yourself," he said, while putting the file in front of the person. He wondered whether that person had not seen the registry carefully. Both names were clearly visible on the first page.

"Look here, carefully, 'Sumangala Kumari,'" officer put his finger at the place where that name was mentioned on the file.

"Sumangala Kumari! This is not my mother's name. Her name is Sharda."

"Not your mother! Whosoever she is, she must be definitely from your family and it must be definitely in your knowledge. Action will be taken only when you bring her," saying this he closed the file.

The person returned. Then he did not come back to the office for many days. Probably, he will come with that woman now, or probably he was a fraud. He would not have wanted anyone else to be a partner in his father's property.

Two months passed in this matter. The officer concerned also forgot that any such file had come to his office.

One day, a woman arrived looking for the officer.

"My husband had given a file to change the title of ownership of the house in his name."

"Which file?" He did not remember. He had many such files in his office.

"The one that had the name of another woman as well," she said hesitantly.

"Yes, I remember. However, no one came to inquire for so many days. Have you brought that woman along?" The officer had asked many questions in a single breath.

"Actually, the matter is"....after saying this, the woman looked around and then fell silent.

"Yes, tell me what the matter is?"

"We don't know that woman."

"What kind of reasoning is that? Your father-in-law has written her name in his property papers and you claim not to know her."

After that, the woman narrated the story to the officer and the officer was clueless whether to trust the story as told by the woman or not.

According to the woman, her revered late father-in-law was in a high position in a premier institution in the country. He was famous for his sharpness of intellect and his grasp on the subject but possessed a flaw of rashness in his temperament and could be easily pricked. Whether you call it a sheer coincidence or anything else, he was married to a girl with a similar temperament. She was also a lecturer in an engineering institute and a scholar in her field of knowledge. Neither of them considered themselves inferior. The clash of the ego led to continual verbal spats and eventually both would have lot of days when they barely spoke to each other. Initially, both of them were so busy in fulfilling their ambitions that they hardly thought of bearing a child.

Five years later, when life became a bit stable, they were blessed with a son.

With the entry of a new being into their life, their life revolved around happy moments of emotional upheavals for some time, but after a short time, the ambitions of both became prominent again. There were constant quarrels between them over who would take care of the child. Although, there was an ayah to run errands in the house but the husband wanted the wife to take care of the child herself.

"My job is not less than you, why should only I? I also get tired like you, then why should only I take care of the child, why not you?"

The argument of his wife would often irk the husband that kick started another Mahabharata in the family.

Five years passed by amidst these constant conflicts and the son turned five. They both mutually decided to put their son in a good hostel to testify their duty towards him and walked away from each other towards their own respective paths. The wife got herself transferred to another place with a hope for a better future and the two started living separately.

The son was not keen on joining the hostel nor could he overlook the memories of the everyday quarrels between his parents. He was at the forefront of every fight and a laggard in studies. When he was ten years old, his parents eventually got divorced. They had never cared much about the matrimonial bond that existed between them even before, but after their separation they led an unbridled life. The son remained more in contact with the father but could not study properly. When the son could not do anything until the age of twenty-five years and the father had retired, the father had set up a small business for his son with his retirement money. After three-four years, the son had got married. A year after the son's marriage, the father suffered brain hemorrhage, which made him bodily listless. He neither possessed the power to speak nor walk. When the literate father had to put a thumb impression on all the documents instead of his signatures, he started crying.

"Madam, we looked after him in this condition for ten years. We nursed him for years. It was pitiable to see the condition of an educated and intense man reduced to this condition in old age. The tears would roll out inadvertently. What could we do? The poor person had suffered a lot before dying." She started wiping her tears.

"So you have been married for ten years now." The officer muttered.

"Yes, eleven years."

"And you say that you do not know this woman named Sumangala. After separating from your mother-in-law, he did not marry again?" she expressed her doubts.

"No ma'am. He was with us for the last eleven years. We have never seen or heard of any such thing." She looked completely oblivious of this woman.

"Ask your husband, he would be knowing it."

"If he had known, why would I have come to you? He doesn't know anything."

The story narrated by the woman was not credible and at the same time the ownership of the house could not be changed based on her story. After all, that woman was an equal claimant to the house.

He had explained the nuances of the document to the woman. The woman argued with the officer for a while. Whatever she said at the end of their conversation added to the officer's suspicions.

"See, we do not know that woman, whose name is

mentioned in the registry. Now you help us. We will do whatever you want." The woman came near and said to the officer in an almost whispering voice.

The officer's blood boiled in anger in reaction to what the woman said, but somehow she restrained herself. She now resolved that she would find the underlying cause of the truth of the matter.

She also felt that it was necessary to bring this episode to her senior officer. The officer also felt something suspicious about the whole episode. The value of the property was also reasonably high.

"What if his claim of being his son is also wrong? Otherwise, how is it possible that the son does not know of any woman in whose name the property has been purchased?" The cloud of suspicion surrounded the senior officer in the department.

"I am also thinking the same sir. If you allow, I would like to carry out an inquiry myself in this matter." The woman officer was no longer in the mood to let this person go scot- free.

"Yes, of course. You must find out what the real facts are."

On getting permission from the senior officer, the detective instinct within her emerged. Different conflicting thoughts kept emerging in her mind. Who could be this woman? What could be her relationship with the deceased, and if there was any relation, then why were the son and daughter-in-law not familiar about anything? The next morning, while battling her doubts and queries, she, accompanied by an assistant, reached the place, where the deceased had been staying.

The house was built on a large plot, where large walnuts, cedars, mangoes, litchi trees have been hiding the view of the building. Outside the main gate of the building was written "Aranya Vatika", and the letters had dimmed over the years, but it still seemed to define the uniqueness of the place.

They questioned few people, but all of them were relatively new in this area. Actually, the colony had come into existence just six-seven years back. Earlier, there had been only two houses on large plots.

"We have seen here only an old man and his son and daughter-in-law."

The old man was sick and suffered a lot, as he was paralyzed. He died a few days ago.

"What about his wife!"

"No no. He lived alone with his son and daughter-in-law."

"Is there a family that has been living here for the last fifteen-twenty years?" They asked one person.

"Yes, can you see that house in front of you? They are one of the oldest inhabitants here but they do not stay here. Their security guard stays there. If you want to ask him something, you can ask," one person from the neighborhood told them.

"Sir stays abroad. His son stays in America and sir and *memsahib* also remain there."

"When will they come?"

"Next month. They have a flight on the twenty-fifth."

Determined to inquire, they both came back after twenty-fifth.

"See, we wanted to procure some information about Mr.

Prashant Chaudhary. You are one of the earliest in this neighborhood so...."

Two to three days after their arrival, the officer

again reached there with her assistant. Seeing the robust appearance of the master house owner, at first, they did not have courage to inquire anything, but still they were on duty and had to take some information. They were dependent on these people as they were the only hope.

"His unworthy son is here right now, why don't you ask him?" Hearing his robust voice, they were again stunned.

"We had asked him but he didn't say anything."

They narrated the whole story of name change in the property papers.

"I knew that Prashant's son was undeserving, but I had no idea that he could be a mean fellow." The outlines of being vexed erupted on his visage. After that, he informed them what he knew.

"After divorce, Prashant did not think beyond his research and progress for some time. He was not worried for his son living in either the hostel or what he was doing. However, as he started aging, there was an escalation in the complaints about his son, which alarmed him and he developed a growing desire to share his pain with someone. With the growing complaints of the son, Prashant developed stress and his own work was seriously affected. He developed a serious sense of guilt within. He took the blame of his son's misdemeanor to his heart. Those were his moments of severe depression.

"That was the time when Sumangala entered into his life. Sumangala was a steno in his office. She was an orphan and had sacrificed her life to build a brighter future for her younger siblings. All her siblings later got busy in their respective work and homes. Sumangala, though, was left alone. Sumangala, who had been through almost fifty springs of her life, had even ceased to dream of conjugal bliss for herself.

"Seamlessly, Sumangala and Prashant had tiptoed into each other's lives and soon started complimenting each other. In his married life, Prashant had never known filial love and commitment. The verbal assurance of love from Sumangala naturally attracted Prashant.

"One day, Prashant broke all the social norms and beliefs and brought Sumangala to his house. After all, a new bond of commitment and love had now developed between the two. Some assumed that they were duly married with all the traditional ceremonies in the temple, while others believed both had just started living together.

"Both of them did not care about anyone. Prashant was happy to be with Sumangala but the son did not like the presence of Sumangala at all. She, on her part, tried her best that the son understood and sympathized with his father well but he, anyhow, would try to stay out of the house on one pretext or the other.

"Sumangala and Prashant had invested in this house with profound sincerity with their own deposits. Sumangala would leave no stone unturned in keeping this house organized and decorated.

"After some time, Prashant retired from his job. By then, the son had not settled down in any way whatsoever. Hearing the news of his father's retirement, the son, who till then lived the life of a vagabond, returned home to be with his father. Sumangala was happy. The only son had returned home. She did not know that he had returned for father's retirement benefits.

"The son pleaded with his father to invest in an agency of electronic equipment. Prashant, however, was not in favor of this kind of investment, but, in order to save the harmony of the family, Sumangala managed to convince Prashant. The remaining deposits left with Prashant were spent in getting the agency for the son. Sumangala had already invested her accumulated capital in buying the house. Now he too had taken his remaining capital investment from his fund.

"Although Prashant had refused for making any such investment, Sumangala did not accept.

"He is our only son. Eventually, everything will go to him. If he wants to do something profitable in life, then help him. For our living, our pension will be enough, saying this

Sumangala laughed nonchalantly. There was still some time left for her to retire and she was drawing her full salary.

"All went well for three to four years. The bitterness that existed between Sumangala and Prashant's son, to an extent, had diminished.

"Sumangala started looking for a matrimonial match for her son. Her retirement was due the following year.

"After her retirement, a series of adversities befell on Sumangala and Prashant. The son got married. Jarring discords commenced as soon as the new daughter-in-law has stepped inside the house. The daughter-in-law was so hoarse that she never gave a second thought either to what she was saying or to whom she was saying. Neither she cared for the age nor did she care for the dignity of relationship. She left no stone unturned in twisting the relationship that existed between Prashant and Sumangala as immoral.

"Prashant and Sumangala both somehow swallowed their anguish. Had the son been respectful, then the daughter-in-law would not have gathered enough courage to abuse her in-laws. It is futile to blame the daughters-in-law, when their own son was capricious.

"The daily discords of the son and the daughter-in-law were getting uglier so much so that Prashant suffered a terrible brain stroke one day. He had timely received the treatment; otherwise, the stroke could have been fatal.

Although he could survive, he gradually lost his power to walk and speak. Handicapped Prashant was now bedridden.

"After the retirement of Sumangala, whatever remaining amount was left with her was now spent on the treatment of Prashant.

"After that we went to America on the call of our children. By that time, Prashant neither could speak nor shake his hands." That man was telling the story while the two attentively listened to him. After his side of the story was over, he shook himself from his somnolence. By now, they had understood who Sumangala was but where she had gone was still left to be discovered. Instinctively, they inquired the same thing from them.

"No idea. Last year, when we came back to India, we first went to inquire about Prashant's condition. Sumangala was not there and Prashant's condition had deteriorated. He had quit the idea of survival, hence, how could he get well?"

"You didn't inquire about the whereabouts of Sumangala?"

The female officer could not hide her eagerness.

"No ma'am. I wanted to ask. Why would the son and daughter-in-law explain? Prashant was not in a position to explain. But, yes, Prashant's eyes welled with tears on hearing about Sumangala."

Now they were again in a square one situation. They had reached the same place from where they had started. Where could they now locate Sumangala in a big city like this? The woman officer was upset. At the same time, she was furious with Prashant's son and daughter-in-law. Why this kind of misbehavior had been meted out to a woman, a woman who had sacrificed everything for their father?

"Madam, there is a way to find her."

"What?" Both screamed simultaneously.

Sumangala was in a government service. I can tell you about her office. From there, you should find out from her records, the name of the bank she is drawing her pension from and her recorded address too."

The job was difficult. The assistant refused categorically.

"Leave it, madam. Why are you getting involved in such a long spin? We will not transfer property. If the husband and wife are eager, let them find out for themselves."

The woman residing in the woman officer was shaken out of her slumber by now.

"I will do this work myself. After all, injustice has been done to a woman." Hearing the officer's dry intonated voice, the assistant reluctantly agreed. Finally, this exercise bore fruitful results. In the process of their inquiry, their search finally ended in an old-age home.

There was a marked inquisitiveness in Sumangala's eyes. No one had visited her even once in the last so many years. That unfortunate person did not even know that Prashant was no longer alive in this world.

"He is liberated from the sorrows of this world. He had suffered a lot," saying this; she folded her hands towards the sky in gratitude towards the Almighty for the peaceful salvation of Prashant in death!

"Who are you? How come here?" Sumangala had not yet grasped the secret of the two officers visiting her in an old-age home.

"Your son has actually applied for transferring Prashant's property in his name and ..." and they narrated the entire sequence of events to her.

Sumangala smiled. She called them again the following week.

In the meanwhile, the assistant had made necessary

inquiries from the other people under the circumstances Sumangala had to leave the house.

Most of the people did not know much about them. Although, she did not reveal much, she narrated her story to an old woman residing in an old age home for a long-time that her son and daughter-in-law had literally pushed her out of her house after her husband was completely bedridden.

She went out to her brothers but could not find any support from them as well.

Sumangala, who had spent her saved capital income partially in buying the house first, then in the business of the son and finally in the illness of Prashant, now survived on meager monthly pension. Since then, Sumangala had been living there in the *ashram*. Initially, she even tried to know Prashant's condition once or twice, but Prashant's son and daughter-in-law did not allow her to get inside the house. She never went there after that.

The woman officer was sad. Can anyone do this with an older woman? She was very angry with Prashant's son and daughter-in-law. If they come now, she would tell them that they have not acted appropriately. She kept pondering as to why Sumangala had called them again the next week.

Although, their work was over, they had traced Sumangala alive and the property could not have been transferred without her consent while she was alive, yet they could not avoid the invitation by Sumangala.

When they reached the old-age home, Sumangala handed them an envelope.

"What is this?'

"Now you will not have trouble transferring property in the name of the son."

The officer opened the envelope. It was the gift deed.

Sumangala had gifted her share of the wealth to Prashant's son.

"What have you done? They treated you so badly and you ...?"

She stopped the officer with a hand gesture and started speaking. There was a mixed sense of both perseverance and attachment to her voice.

"He is the son of Prashant and Prashant was everything to me. What Prashant gave me is like nectar in my life. Drenched in that nectar and nostalgia of the memorable time spent with him, I will pass the rest of my life. Everything that belongs to Prashant now belongs to me, by that logic even his son and daughter-in-law are also my own. One gets a lot of satisfaction by giving something to his/her own people, my dear child."

While returning, the words of Sumangala kept echoing in the ears of the female officer and her eyes were moist with tears.

The property was finally transferred in the name of Prashant's son. All the procedures were done legally, according to the paperwork. The senior officer and officer concerned had a feeling of guilt that though everything apparently appeared right, something was seriously amiss. They wished they had not taken their investigation so far!

□

# 4

# Life Changed

It was a nursery school. A school for small kids. A school from nursery to class fifth. Every infant was a greater responsibility. What if they hurt themselves! What if they are naughty and something untoward ensues. Lest they stick a morsel in their esophagus while swallowing, etc. The school management had a colossal accountability. They had employed three to four *ayahs* along with the teachers.

While recruiting *ayahs,* the management was correspondingly vigilant. What, if we recruit a mother? Recruiting the mother, who has her own children to nurture at home, would be a big bargain. It is expected that the mother is naturally affectionate towards all the children with an enormous proficiency to drop behind.

Children unsurprisingly sprint to the swings in school during the mid-meal break, and the likelihood of them tumbling from there and being injured becomes higher. Throughout the mid-meal break, the job of all the *ayahs* was the most exigent. The de rigueur task of guarding the small children from nursery to class second or third during mid-meal break was not only obligatory but also mandatory. On that account, these *ayahs* moved around the children with sheer quickness.

Despite following all the required shields and guards, one day, a child stumbled and fell after the school closed down, while running and hurt his forehead. It started bleeding profusely. One *ayah*, standing far away handling the other children, rushed and snatched the child from the other and lifted him in her lap.

Tears began flowing down her cheeks. She kept crying, while gently rubbing the child's forehead.

"This child is probably her own." thought Rashmi, while waiting for her own child. While witnessing the *ayah* yowl in grief, her heart exuded in compassion. Pitiable poor woman engulfed in this mess for nothing. She quickly gave a passing glance at the woman, ran her eyes on her dress, and presumed her to be a widow.

"It is pitiable; her child fell and got hurt."

This time Rashmi echoed her feelings with the other guardian standing close by and she nodded in agreement.

Probably, she needs my assistance, Rashmi walked towards her, while she thought to herself.

"Is the child terribly hurt?" She asked *ayah*.

"No idea madam", she wiped her tears and continued, "See he is bleeding profusely."

While Rashmi was still engaged in the conversation, a woman came leaping towards her.

"What happened to my child?" She asked, while snatching her son from ayah's lap.

"How did he fall down?" She asked *ayah*.

Rashmi was not concerned with what *ayah* said in a rejoinder as much as she was startled to know that the *ayah* was not his mother.

The woman went away with her child. The tears from *ayah's* cheeks still kept flowing.

"Whose child was he?" Rashmi could not suppress her curiosity.

"Children are the form of God, madam. They belong to everyone," saying this, she wiped her tears while slowly walking out of the school gates.

Rashmi's son came looking for his mother and stood near her. Holding his son's finger, she too walked out of the school with multiple queries trolling her from within.

It is true. Everyone feels the pain of children but Rashmi had witnessed for the first time and had wondered how anyone could feel for the pain of other's child to this extent. A few days later, Rashmi happened to meet her son's class teacher. After a couple of meetings, they had become quite friendly with each other. Rashmi narrated the whole incident of the other day to her.

"You are talking about Fyunli!" said the teacher in quick response.

"Oh! An unfortunate, poor thing!" said she, while narrating her life of suffering and pain to Rashmi.

Her name Fyunli was beautiful, as good as in her attributes. She laughed and giggled all throughout the day. Fyunli, the only child of her parents, lived in a remote hill village. Her father possessed three-four sheep and a small piece of farmland, which were just enough to take care of their bare minimum needs.

When Fyunli turned seventeen, her parents started worrying about her marriage. The easygoing Fyunli was barely out of her adolescence. Fyunli was like a stream of the mountain river flowing ceaselessly down the hills with vigor and velocity. While her mother insisted on her to learn the housework chores, she would not pay attention to the mother's affectionate entreaties.

Fyunli did not learn the housework; still she had to get married. It was not customary in their society to keep girls unmarried for a long time.

Fyunli got married. The groom was the only son of a widowed mother. Like Fyunli's father, his father too raised goats, which was the only source of their livelihood. Sundar was his name. He was handsome in conduct as in name.

A few days after the marriage, when Fyunli was asked to cook, she burnt the lentils and half-cooked the vegetable. The dough became sticky. The experienced mother-in-law understood that the parents had really reared her precariously like "Fyunli".

Neither did she lose her temper nor she did scoff at her, but maintained her composure. She gradually taught everything to Fyunli and within a short time span, Fyunli became a successful homemaker. The melodious life had kicked off. Fyunli, the poor father's daughter, had led a simple life sans any expectations. Nothing could make her sad; she had learnt to regale in the glory of her limited possessions.

One year after marriage, Fyunli gave birth to a daughter and the third year to a son. The family was complete. Everyone was happy. It was cool in itself, but then an incident happened that shook everyone's life.

Fyunli's husband adored his two children and loved playing with them and his goats. Fyunli's son completed a year, and on the same day, a kid goat was born. Sundar loved the baby goat the most and fondly called it Sonu.

Sundar often took the goats for grazing in the nearby jungle and safely herded them back to their shed in a routine. One day, Sundar lost Sonu, while grazing his goats. Exasperated Sundar looked for Sonu at every nook and corner. After frantic searches, he found Sonu in a ditch, comfortably eating leaves from the branches of the tree.

Goat kid Sonu had somehow descended into that abyss but failed to come out of it. Sundar never thought that if his leg slips a little more, he would fall into an abyss. Inevitability in life is sure to come by. In an attempt to recapture Sonu, Sundar tumbled down into a deep ditch and could never get up again.

The life-charm and the vivacity of Fyunli took a one hundred and eighty degree turn. The entire household and its responsibilities including those of two small children and an old mother-in-law plummeted on her shoulders. Fyunli had deliberated of jumping into the abyss at the same point where she lost her husband Sundar to be with him forever. But in that hour of great pain and grief, good sense prevailed upon her and she left the idea of taking the extreme step of ending her life. Fyunli decided to bear her travails for the children. She was solemnly consumed by the obligation of looking after the goats and other members of the family. Slowly, Fyunli took over everything. From a blithe, cheerful teenager, Fyunli metamorphosed into a sagacious woman.

Sundar's mother could no longer endure the angst of his separation and passed away after a year. With her demise, she felt shelter less and without any custodian. Fyunli was left alone in the world with two children to look after.

Slowly, the kids were growing up and so were their needs. Fyunli sent them to school. Fyunli, by then, had realized the significance of education. Sundar and Fyunli had never been to any school and she never wished her kids to meet the same fate. One moment, one accident changed her life forever.

The monsoon was furious that year. It was believed that it had not rained as much in the previous years. Rain showers hopes excessive rain fetches dreads. As it is said "*ati-sarvatra-varjayet*", which is "to abstain from overdoing."

People, who were accustomed to fewer rains over the years, had audaciously built their houses in dried up river drains and canals. The houses atop the hilltops had transformed from traditional to the new style. Stones and clay had paved way for mortar, bricks and gravel. An incessant heavy rain was the harbinger of heavy forfeiture. The roads were broken at many places and the multiple buildings collapsed at others. The plentiful rainy rivers gushed down, breaking embankments.

Fyunli's village was no exception. There was havoc in her village. It had been relentlessly raining the entire night. When the overcast sky cleared for a while in the morning, Fyunli dressed both her children for school before engaging herself in the routine household chores. After a while, unrelenting heavy rain poured, heavy enough to wash away everything. The village school had about fifty children present at that time. The hill cracked breaking the wall of the school, washing it away in its entirety in an avalanche from within.

The older children safely exited the school and somehow saved their lives, the younger children were entombed alive in the rubble there. Someone, around noon, came and broke this news to the villagers. Fyunli was shattered at the break of the devastating news to her. Her children were still very young. They could not run to evacuate from the school. Fyunli was shattered. In the state of shock, she ran towards the school to realize that the spark of her life was smothered. Fyunli was petrified. She did not shed a single drop of tears from her eyes. Fyunli did not respond even when the bodies of her two children, extracted from within the debris, were placed in front of her. She appeared anesthetized.

Her condition worsened and her parents decided to take her with them along. Fyunli had lost her mental composure.

She roamed around the village, partially oblivious of her body and clothes.

Fyunli was young and beautiful. What if something wrong happens to her in a condition like this, was a constant thought that gnawed her parents. In a state of fret and agony, they took a stringent resolve of sending her to an asylum.

Fyunli completed tenure of three-four years in an asylum. Gradually, the remembrances from the past faded and her health started showing visible signs of improvement. Ultimately, when Fyunli expelled her pent- up sentiments and moaned profusely reminiscing about her children and their catastrophic demise, the doctors were convinced that she was cured.

Life is bursting with endless tribulations. One problem leads to another. One such issue was, Where would Fyunli go after leaving the asylum? None had even the faintest of inkling of her parents and their whereabouts. Saddened by the grief of their only daughter, they left their village, leaving no clue whatsoever about their whereabouts.

Parents of all those children killed in the accident were provided financial assistance by the government, which Fyunli could not receive.

"I don't want money, Saab. Get me a job in children's school so that I can secure my two square meals. I will find out a visage of my children amid the innocent children of the school." She pleaded and folded her hands before the officer.

Seeing her pathetic circumstances, her plea was accepted and ultimately she procured a secure job in a school.

Since then Fyunli had become an integral part of the school. Be it a parent or a teacher, she never gave anyone an opportunity to grumble and complain. All the children of the school were like her children. Many parents leave their small children in the school after being thoroughly convinced about her.

Spellbound Rashmi listened to the story of Fyunli. The story of Fyunli is a legend of a young woman, who had lost everything in her life but acquired the whole world.

□

# 5

# The Grain of Wheat

It had been raining incessantly for the last four days. The settlements areas with no metaled roads or well-paved roads of the city had been waterlogged to the brim. Two-wheelers and small cars had fully submerged in water, while buses and trucks were half immersed. The employed people had been on undeclared leave, the children were disgruntled with these holidays. They were confined to home recurrently looking towards the clouded firmament and conjecturing when would the rain stop.

While it had been raining, everything around was closed. Neither milk was in supply nor were the vegetables. The upper and middle classes were not affected much by this confinement. However, they were definitely bored eating the same potatoes, onions and lentils every day.

However, there was a section of people in that area who had to dig well every day to drink water. Those people earned daily wages and then cooked their meals. They mostly dwelled in slums and somehow accomplished their livelihood. The devastating rain had demolished their slums. Their stuff had scattered helter-skelter and drifted away. Residents could barely take refuge in safe harbors.

The government machinery woke up to the entire

situation two days after. By then, not only children but also the grown-up people had started starving.

Cuddled with these groups of refugees, was the family of Vinayak. Four years ago, he had travelled from Kalahandi region of Odisha and had relocated to the city with his family. Apart from him, there were four more members in his family that included his wife and three children in an age gap of one or one and a half years. The eldest son was eight years old, the second, who was a daughter, was seven and the youngest son was five. When they had shifted to the city roughly four years back, the youngest son was just one-year-old infant. Owing to malnutrition and weakness of limbs, he could barely stand firmly on the ground until the age of one and a half years. Later, as he grew up he used to run faster than his mother could grab hold of him.

Vinayak's family had seen so much poverty and hunger in the village that he was not affected by the two-day hunger assault.

Four days later, when the water level started receding, people began returning to their respective homes. The slums had turned into rubble. There were nonetheless some traces of houses left in that pile of rubble. All the families collectively looked for whatever useful was left in that marsh of debris. Their collective efforts had been to locate the items from the debris and had nothing to do with their ownership. Any item found belonged to those, who would lay their hands first on it.

Vinayak and his wife also could successfully pick up some broken utensils, mud-soaked clothes, broken cots, etc.

Gradually, as the water disappeared, more slums cropped up at the same place. Life was returning to normal and more habitable. The government also took stock of the situation for one or two days. Some bread and biscuits were fed to those who had nothing to eat and were wasted with hunger. People swooped down on these packets of food like an eagle. For a single packet, people snarled at each other and in the end, the person in receipt of the small packet of food would be considered lucky. Vinayak, oblivious of his own hungriness, his famishment, underwent that heart wrenching anguish when he caught sight of his children at the end of their tether with hunger. He somehow made his best effort to arrange for their needs. In the end, Vinayak and his wife ate only whatever remained after providing for the children. Thereafter, the glimpse of free food, people ranting for it, and its evidence continued with its perceptible prospect for only some days. Taking food packets in a queue ensured that everyone received their packets whatsoever small, however, the large part of it warmed as well the pockets of the people responsible for micromanaging the system. Overall, there was a fair-like atmosphere in the slum habitation during those days.

The distribution of free food had stopped, the fair-like scenario had also ended. Everyone once again stepped out to start looking for jobs or work for bringing in gross income for their livelihood and survival.

The rain had caused havoc and availability of jobs in the market had subsided. Daily wage laborers living in the slums, either worked with the small businesspersons, or worked for the contractors of big building construction. Excess rain had stalled all the small construction work for the time being. The construction work was expected to resume only if there was continuous sunlight for a few days. These workers were wandering around in search of livelihood thereafter. Vinayak was also one of them. He wandered in search of daily wage here and there.

Vinayak could not find any work for the entire day for

many days. All he could manage was to find work for a few hours here and there. While Vinayak wandered in search for work, his wife would impatiently wait for him in a hope that he would probably walk back home bringing hope and money, only then could his wife cook for the whole family. As a wife, she could easily recognize from his face whether he had found any work or not.

Without food, the children cried while Vinayak and his wife whined. In sheer frustration, he would beat children. Later, they both would regret their grievous act thinking about children and after all what would be their fault. Regardless of their infuriation, frustrations and regrets, beating children had become a routine every other day.

The grocer at the end of the street snubbed them, and refused to hand over anything to them on credit. Vinayak had not been able to settle the payment of the earlier credit amounts as well. Earlier he would often pick up the ration of the entire month from him and would pay for the groceries in the subsequent month. The grocer had however, turned hostile was unwilling to take any risk of providing provisions on credit because of the severe emerging watershed crisis of employment for the daily wagers.

Some women from the slums had opted for their self-employment of picking garbage to earn some revenue. Vinayak's wife would also leave her children at home and had set off doing the job of garbage picking as other women did. Sometimes she would get hold of decent stuffs in the debris. She often wondered at the affluent who would never think twice before throwing valuable and necessary things in garbage. What she did not know was that the bits and pieces, leftover snippets valued to people like her were inoperable for affluent living in the equally affluent houses.

If Vinayak's wife ever went out of the house, it was to

arrange for at least one square meal for her children. The situation was very bad on those days when Vinayak could not get any work for the entire day, while his wife would bring home whatever little she would earn. The self-esteem of the patriarch in Vinayak could not tolerate that his wife had been working on wages to arrange rations for all the members of the house, including him.

The children had been saved from Vinayak's act of violence, but he, in his frustration, would badly thump down his wife. God had given her much staying power and resilience that she would tolerate the atrocities of her husband in silence without uttering a word of revolt. Even after being beaten by Vinayak like anything the previous night, she would still get on to her feet in the morning and leave for work feigning as if not anything untoward had come to pass the previous night.

A month or two had passed like this. The weather too had been turning out to be fine and the market had started picking up. In such a situation, Ramdin, the neighbor of Vinayak, had arranged work for him with a grain trader.

There were many warehouses of the trader and work was spread at many places in the city. There was a constant need for laborers to carry food grains from one warehouse to another and supply them elsewhere.

Initially, Vinayak stared, with wide eyes, when he caught a glimpse of the big warehouse full of grain in the warehouse of Seth. At that moment, he had attached more importance to the grain elevator than the stocked up gold and silver in the stockroom. Looking at the huge warehouses of grain, he summoned up images of the famished people residing in the slum, who were oblivious of the existence of the huge grain warehouses. Vinayak had wished his wife to stop going out for work. "Ever since she has started earning money, she has become arrogant with her mind on the seventh heaven. She has started thinking herself to be a lady." Vinayak continued to think about the situation when his wife stepped out for work while he stayed jobless. The situation when his wife earned and he ate appeared to squeeze the life out of him. He could not do anything.

The merchant, his employer, would not pay him his wages before the end of a week. The merchant maintained a system where he would not pay the workers on daily basis but weekly, which had emerged as a new problem for Vinayak. Infuriated Vinayak, the next day, like a true patriarch, in a tiff with his wife instructed her not to work. His wife, fed up with the daily arguments, neither protested his diktat nor weighed up anything but stopped going to work from the next day onwards.

"Take a little wheat and rice, who will know even if you take out a few drops from this sea? The rest would appear the same here." Ramdin justified.

"But this is a theft." Vinayak was not mentally geared up for any kind of pilfering. When there was no food grain left in the house, the children were crying with hunger, even then this thought never emanated to his mind.

"If the children breathe their last due to hunger, will it not be a sin then? That is far greater moral lapse than stealing. What do you think the merchant has earned this money with hard work and honesty? He is also a big thief. Then where is the moral transgression in stealing from a thief's house?" Ramdin elucidated on a diverse narrative of sin and virtue that Vinayak, however, had failed to figure out.

"Okay, listen; it is only a matter of five-six days, do not ever indulge in that all over again."

Would it be only for five or six days and never after that?

Probably, until he would receive his weekly wages, he would have to feed his famished children who have nothing to eat. On the first day, he appropriated grain worth two fists from the warehouse; his heartbeat was pounding faster than a blower was, his face appeared strained with drops of sweat on his forehead and his condition was strange.

"Oh God! Just a few more days!" He folded his both hands, apologized to God, grabbed a fistful of grain for his starving kids at home but could not a slide a single morsel down the esophagus.

When he received his first salary, he puffed out a heaving sigh of relief and avowed never to do anything wide off the mark erroneous. The vehicle of his life had started rolling on the wheels again.

Later in the week, Vinayak's duty kept shifting between one warehouse to another. The more Vinayak was exposed to the warehouses bursting with food grains, the more he deliberated, "Why do people die of hunger despite having so much of grain in store?"

One day the supervisor sent Vinayak along with other laborer to the other warehouse, which was almost twenty kilometers away from the city to load the sacks of wheat grain from there into the trucks for the factory.

Then, Vinayak was acquainted with an additional truth, a bitter fact that was exceedingly excruciating. The truth that every man jack had to stomach but Vinayak could not digest it.

The rains expose the system during the rainy season. The water had seeped from everywhere around gradually flowing inside the warehouse rotting the wheat sacks due to the seeping water, finally closing the warehouse for three to four months. There was a strange smell of rotten wheat in the entire warehouse.

Wheat was loaded in trucks but some sack bags were rotten and ripped off. They were somehow loaded into trucks. Vinayak was hurt when he saw that. He remembered his native place, Kalahandi and recollected his children suffering there from hunger. He ruminated over the sight of famished bodies turned into skeletons, the memory of the sight kept hovering over him. During the floods and droughts, the human beings were forced to live the dog's life that leapt over every single food packet that would be tossed towards them. Has the merchant or his staff under no circumstances ever noticed or become aware of such people? Perhaps not. That is why they do not suffer when they would come across the human being consuming the rotten grain.

Vinayak vented out his viewpoint to Ramadin and expressed his pain but he could not be anyways placated and calmed down.

"You mind your business. You do not know these big people." Ramdin took a best crack to calm him down. Vinayak, though explicitly gave the impression of being unruffled and poised, however, passed a sleepless night rolling in the bed.

"How has he allowed all his wheat to rot? Now, where are you sending this rotten wheat? This is not fit for consumption by anyone."

When the query had sparked off from within, he could not resist and asked Ramdin the next day.

"Hey, what is that to do with you? Wherever the merchant wishes to send, he will send. Why do you get upset?" Ramdin neither had an answer nor wanted to know.

Vinayak was determined to the core and had wished to find out.

The rotten wheat was no longer edible but, the

breaking news was the government, was distributing a complimentary ration among the poor. The merchant yearned to take home the gross revenue from the rotten grain, so he quietly negotiated with those in the liquor factory before the government order of free distribution was carried out. The liquor factory owners expressed their desire to buy his rotten wheat that could be recycled for brewing the wine.

Vinayak came across another shocking truth that whatever wheat grain government had planned to distribute among the poor, the grain that was not meant for the rich people's consumption, would be redirected to produce alcohol. The rotten wheat would serve the rich, whereas the poor would again remain hungry.

Vinayak laughed aloud. Everyone was shocked to see him laugh. They all looked at him immediately but he nonchalantly kept on laughing for a while and then suddenly started crying. His eyes had become ruddy with constant weeping. In a state of excitement, he rushed towards the supervisor and caught him by his throat.

"You destroy food. When everything is rotten, you intend to make wine out of it. Have you ever seen people dying of hunger? You insult the Food God. You will suffer for wasting food." Vinayak tried to strangle the supervisor. In that, venture his veins puffed-up in resentment.

When the supervisor shouted for help, the laborers went and pulled Vinayak apart. He would disentangle from his grip every time they tried to keep him away from the supervisor, to grab him by the throat.

Police were called. They arrested Vinayak and took him with them. Vinayak was beaten but every time he spoke about the grievous insult of the Food Deity.

Vinayak remained in jail for three-four days but when

he was released, he had lost his mental balance. Some said that probably the police had punched him a lot—that could be the reason why Vinayak had lost his mental balance but Vinayak knew the injury and the cause of his insanity.

People would recount in suppressed tone that when the police were beating him, Vinayak's two fists were closed. In the process of fainting and regaining consciousness, when the police opened his fists, they found rotten wheat grains from the warehouse closed within his fist.

Many days have passed since that incident. Vinayak had turned completely insane. He would blabber to the people that the government would give liquor to the poor as a substitute to food grains. People would turn uncontrollable hysterical would make fun of his misnomers except for few people, as Ramdin who would be au fait with the anguish in Vinayak's words. His wife had once again started picking up the garbage apart from working in one or two houses.

There has been an ongoing debate everywhere regarding the rotten grains, which could never be concluded.

□

# 6

# What Relations

Palak's mind had been disconcerted that morning. The previous evening, her mother had told her about the marriage alliance, the prospective match and his family's visit to see her. She was expected to be ready.

"What should I be ready for? Once again, to be rejected, to be said "no" to." The bitterness of previous matches evidently reflected through her words.

"Keep your mouth shut. You have become arrogant just because you know how to read and write. Look at your friends, everyone has become mothers by now," said her mother, while grumbling and scolding her and then she went away from there.

Palak knew what it was that her mother was grumbling about. Her mother had not been like that earlier. She had been a mother to a son and a daughter and had been always satisfied with her family, her world. Her husband was an officer in a government department and her both children were competent. She had been happy and contented like any homemaker from the middle-class family.

What had that been that she had become so irritable? Why would a mother, who was so pleasant in her conversation with her children, have become so irritable even at the slightest pretext?

Sagar and Swapna had been married for almost forty years. They were blessed with a son and a daughter born respectively after a year and three years of marriage. While Swapna was a firm believer in religious conviction, old beliefs and traditions, Sagar was a champion of modern ideas.

He never discriminated between his son and daughter. Both attended the same school. If Swapna ever restricted Palak from doing anything or curbed her movements, Sagar would immediately interrupt her.

"My daughter is my pride, have you not observed that she is better than your son in her studies? She will not do any household work. She will get a good job and employ domestic help." Sagar was proud of Palak's success, would often boast about it proudly, and further infuriating Swapna.

"What is wrong, if she learns household chores? Whenever you see her, she is busy giggling with friends." Swapna was bound to old beliefs, and was not in favor of allowing her daughter to ape boys.

The days passed by. Both children kept ascending the success ladder. They both had earned their respective degrees in engineering from prestigious institutes of the country. The son thought it relevant to apply in universities abroad for higher education; however, Palak was not willing to study further even though her father tried his best to convince her. She wished to take up a job and be financially independent. Swapna, sometimes felt, that Palak was not interested in self-reliance as much as she wished for freedom. She would often share her thoughts with Sagar, while he would just laugh it out.

Palak was a good student; hence, there was no dearth of jobs for her. She immediately secured a job in an IT firm in Bengaluru with an attractive package.

"Bengaluru?" Swapna chuckled.

"Is there a shortage of jobs in our city? The girl all alone and so far..."

Swapna had not expected it even in her dreams. Palak had been away from home even in the past but then that was when she had joined her college for her higher education studies but it was a college with a hostel for the girls. In Bengaluru, she would be all alone, how would that be possible? Those thoughts would often appallingly disturbed Swapna.

"Mother, don't worry. I have secured a good job, and the company is good. They will provide me with a furnished flat in Bengaluru. You can also come to stay with me," saying this, Palak swung around her mother's shoulders.

Sagar and Swapna had both gone to drop Palak. Bengaluru was far off from their city. It took them two days to reach there.

"Mother, let me receive my first salary, next time I will send you the flight tickets." Palak could not constraint her ecstasy.

Swapna was to a certain extent contented after stayed at her flat. Although it was just a two-room set, but was well furnished and fitted out with essential equipments. It was more than what Palak would have required when she would be alone.

After staying in Bengaluru for a couple of days, Sagar and Swapna returned home. In the initial days, Palak would call them every single day but gradually the frequency of phone calls dropped off and shrunk. Slowly, Palak had resorted to calling her parents once a week. On other days, when Swapna would call her, she would more often than not be engrossed with her official work.

Palak had been in a job for over six months and visited

home. A few days later, she had called to apprise her parents about her company's proposal on an official assignment to send her to the US. Swapna was terrified at the news.

"I don't understand the girl going all alone so far from her home. How will she survive all alone in another far-off country?"

"What do you mean? How will she go? She will go by plane. She is no longer a toddler. She is in a responsible position in such a big company." Sagar retorted irritably.

Palak came home once before going to America. She was oozing with excitement.

"Pulkit is also there. You should go and meet him too." Swapna remembered her son, who had just completed his Masters in Engineering and had procured a job in a company there. Swapna had wished Pulkit to return but he refused.

"Mother, you are saying as if America is like our contry. The city where I have been transferred for company's work is far flung from brother's office. Although, he has promised me that he will come to see me."

Swapna was silenced. Was the agony of the son to sail seven seas to a far off land any less for her that even her daughter has decided to take a trip on the same route to the US. These thoughts had troubled Swapna over and again.

Palak had set off away for her six months' official tenure.

Palak was awestruck by, and exultant to set her eyes on a new country, new world, and new society. When she returned after six-months, she was piled up with more self-confidence

"Mother, I think brother will get married there." She had apprised her mother with an emotional assault.

"Why? Why made you feel like this?" Swapna was nervous. She had even kicked off her mission of seeing girls for Pulkit.

"A girl stays there with him." In a cavalier fashion, Palak had muttered but could not foresee her mother's reaction.

"A girl! With him? How could this be possibly on the cards? How can a girl live with a boy?" It was out of the blue bewildering arrangement for Swapna, brought up in an Indian environment amidst Indian traditions.

"So what is so unusual about this? You know mother that live in relationship has been legalized in India too. Even the court has sanctioned that." Palak had casually retorted.

"My dear, the court though has recognized it, but what about the society? Has the society also recognized it? Regardless of what the court says, it is in this society that we live. What will we do with the legal recognition that the society turns down?" Swapna was shocked to hear what Palak had said but she persistently kept debating it.

"Mother, the law is everything, do you know that people resort to the American law even for the smallest issue. The parents cannot physically manhandle the child, otherwise the child can go to court and the parents can be punished."

"Law can provide justice but not love and belonging. The law cannot forcibly ask parents to love their child nor can it force children to uphold the feelings of the parents." Swapna was perceptibly grief-stricken from within.

She was staggered at everything Palak had said. Swapna wondered about wistfully about the type of country US was and that it could neither boast of any social system nor possess any sense of belongingness. How could its citizens just resort to for everything by the court of law using their legal rights? Even in India, so many laws have been pressed in. The grown up children could be sued if they regress from their sense of duty, their obligatory responsibility towards their parents in their old age. If the boy and a girl wish to stay together, the legal system allows them. Swapna brooded over which court of law could ever beget love for anyone. Could any one repossess and get hold of that civilisation that had a place for everyone and believed in equal distribution of labor? The more Swapna mulled over, the more she got entangled in the maze.

Palak had returned but had provoked Swapna's thoughts to dwell on and kept thinking about.

Two years had passed. Swapna kept asking both Pulkit and Palak for their plans to get married, but none of them fell in with her plan neither acquiesced. Pulkit had come to India once. During one of their conversations, Swapna could deduce that Palak was not wrong in her conjectures. Pulkit wanted to get married to a girl there.

For a long time, Swapna and Sagar could not visit Palak even once. It was she who would visit them. She worked in her office in India and often travelled to other countries for work. Once, Sagar had to go to Mysore for some office work, the two made a plan to go to Bengaluru together.

Palak, who on other occasions would be overwhelmed by the news of her parents' arrival, had not shown any special enthusiasm then.

"She probably is busy with her work." They both thought but continued with their plan to visit Bengaluru to be with Palak.

Swapna had stayed with Palak for four to five days. Palak would be at work all day long despite the fact that Swapna would be alone at home. What would Swapna do in her spare time sitting idle? She could not manage her spare moments without arranging her daughter's house. While spacing out the house, Swapna stumbled on something that was not meant for the consumption of girls. Swapna nervously in trepidation unlocked Palak's closet and was rendered speechless to chance upon male clothing together with Palak's.

"Does anyone else live here with you?" In the evening when Palak returned home, Swapna met her head-on, confronted her with a straightforward point at issue question mark without any dillydallying.

"Yes ... no ... no one else." Palak panicked.

"Do you want to marry him?" Swapna shot the next query without any reservations and without waiting for the response to her first question.

"No mother we are just good friends." In a hurry, Palak had failed to recall that she had just rebuffed the existence of someone being there with her.

"Friend! He stays with you, doesn't he?"

"No mother, he sometimes comes." Palak bowed down her head.

No matter how much she had refused to acknowledge, Swapna had been reinforced and had firmed up her doubts through Palak's corollary reactions and her body language that she had acquired a soft feeling for that boy.

"I want to meet him."

"How do you talk, mother? Do you meet all my friends?

Anyway nowadays, he has gone abroad."

Palak out rightly had rejected the idea of her mother and the visible annoyance had erupted on her face.

Time kept on passing by. Everyone had been busy in their lives in their respective manner. Pulkit had married an American girl. When he visited India with his wife, Sagar and Swapna had arranged a nice reception for them. Palak had also visited then with some of her friends. A few days later, Palak had returned to her responsibilities in her office that had kept her busier. Gradually, frequency of her visits to her parents had dropped. Every time, Swapna would insist that Palak should get married, she would blatantly turn down her mother's plea. As Palak was advancing in years, Sagar and Swapna were getting more and more apprehensive.

One of those days, a friend of Palak gave them a tinkle in a nervous tone of voice beseeching them to arrive at Bengaluru without more ado. Palak had been suffering from downhearted depression and had attempted to commit suicide. Without any further delay, they reserved their air tickets and arrived at Bengaluru. Palak had taken many sleeping pills and had been knocked out unconscious.

"Palak was a very lively girl. What had happened after all that she had to take this step," Sagar and Swapna asked Suvarna, the one who called them at home.

"Aunty, actually Siddharth's marriage is fixed."

"Who Siddhartha?" Swapna had not known any boy with this name.

"You don't know," Suvarna was surprised at the tone. The same expression of phenomenal wonder too was visible on her face and her eyes. Swapna stood there heeding to what she had told about Siddharth and Palak.

Siddharth and Palak had been living together for the past several years. In Suvarna's words, it was "live-in relationship". Everyone whispered allegedly that the two would be married in the near future. A week earlier, Siddharth declared that his marriage had been fixed. Palak and he were just good friends and would continue to be so. He for all time had never experienced affection for Palak and well thought out of her to be his friend.

For some days, Palak kept putting in plain words to make clear to him—recounting to him how she had grown deeply involved with him. She had even expressed to him that if Siddhartha had not been willing to marry her; she was comfortable with it and was inclined to put up with him all his life.

Siddharth declined her proposal, and maintained that

no such understanding had ever been reached between the two. Palak was hemmed in utter downheartedness and in these moments of despair, she popped in many sleeping pills and had let down the contents of the bottle. When Suvarna could not locate Palak, by the grace of God, she reached her house. After continuous ringing of the bell, when Palak did not open the door of the house, she took the duplicate keys of Palak's home from Siddharth, which had been still lying with him.

What had happened after that had become distinctively clear to Swapna. As soon as the physical condition of Palak had improved, Swapna and Sagar brought her along. They did not take into account nor found it appropriate to bump into Siddharth on the matter. The person, who could not understand their daughter despite staying with her for so many years, would he have understood them?

It took some time for Palak to return to normal life. Swapna and Sagar gave her their full support with the exception of Swapna, who would sometimes get irritated out of sorts. Her mind, culturally ingrained, could never give a positive response to what her daughter had done. Even though court had declared 'live-in relationship' legal, Swapna would never resign herself to the court's verdict.

Palak was slowly but surely turning out to be normal. After two or three months, she had been adamant on going back to her job but Sagar had refused her plea outright.

"Get your accounts cleared from there. I'll go along with you. We will arrange for your job here only." Both Palak and Swapna had felt the firmness in Sagar's voice.

Palak had started working in her city in full swing. The company was not as large as the Bengaluru-based company was, but it was not too small either. Palak had no objection to working in her city.

Swapna had been on a lookout tower for a matrimonial alliance for Palak, but as they say, the skeletons from Palak's past had ceased to leave her. Bengaluru was far away but the news flew the coop like thin air.

Just a few days back, she had crashed into Mrs Mathur in the market. With the proper gesture of hands and eyes, she chattered about Mrs. Sharma's daughter. When she had finished communicating about her, she did not fail to remember inquiring about Palak.

"Why did you ask Palak to leave her job? She was in a very good company there."

"No, no, we did not ask her to leave; she rather wanted to come back to her own city... That is why," Swapna, despite not wanting to, completed her sentence while stuttering.

"This is also fine. Mrs. Verma, who lives in your neighborhood, has something else to say. I also protested that this was not possible. A girl from such a cultured family cannot do this." Mrs. Mathur tried to read Swapna's face carefully.

Swapna pretending to be in a hurry, left Mrs. Mathur but her eyes kept following her for a long time. After coming home, Swapna vented her anger on Palak. "This girl has not left us with a face to show."

In the darkness of the night, Swapna clasped to Sagar's chest and cried bitterly.

Sagar gently stroked her head and kept giving reasons. He reminded her that how after many attempts Palak had returned to normal. Any such situation should not occur where Palak would again resort to any wrong step. It was the combined responsibility of both to look after her.

Sagar possessed the twofold responsibility of looking bearing in mind both Swapna and Palak. He would every now and then put his reasoning in plain words to Swapna and sometimes to Palak. Even Palak in a state of distress would approach Sagar.

"Will mother carry on with this all her life? Neither she herself will not rest in peace nor will she let me be ever peaceful."

Sagar often explained to her that her mother had been brought up in traditional Indian values. The relationship between a man and a woman to her is limited to a relation of a father, or a husband or a brother. Apart from this, no other relationship between a man and a woman ever existed. Therefore, he expected Palak should cotton on with her mother.

Only he knew how much Palak could grasp and to what extent but Sagar never missed any opportunity of squaring off the relationship between the mother and the daughter.

Swapna's whopping concern was to settle Palak in her life. She started receiving matrimonial alliance for Palak but none of those alliances could materialize. At every failure to materialize her alliance, Swapna would become razor-sharp with her remarks while pointing the finger at Palak for her earlier mistake.

Palak would get upset at the idea of any pretensions, but Sagar would persuade her to listen to her mother, rustle up her mind and reach a decision for another relationship. Despite her mother's insistence that day to stay at home and not visit office, she still went to the office. In the evening, when she returned tired, she did not get an adequate amount of time to sponge her face. The prospective boy had arrived with his parents in a short time.

As and how Palak had been, she went and sat in front of them. When she glanced at the boy, she was shocked beyond her comprehension. Siddharth, with his parents, was sitting in front of her. When Siddharth saw her, he was also shocked.

Palak could not endure taking the weight off her feet for even two minutes. She knew that her mother would be angry but she still got up and left. As soon as she entered her room, she piled up in her bed. "Siddharth's marriage was fixed, then this marriage? Did he know that he was coming to see me?" Many questions emerged up and cast doubt on her mind.

She did not come out even after continuously been importuned by her mother. Swapna blurted out at her after their departure.

"What do you think of yourself? The family of the boys had liked you but..."

"But I don't like him." Palak had raised her a bit.

"But why? After all, what is wrong with that boy? He lost his first wife barely after one year of marriage and the boy is also almost your age."

"Oh! So, this is the real reason," Palak thought. Siddharth's wife had departed from this life. He was planning his second marriage. Palak had the idea of what to do. By sending Siddharth to her doorstep, God has again provided her the opportune moment to pronounce justice. She possessed the firm power of the eternal providence of God. It was Palak's turn to say 'NO'.

□

# 7

# Endless

Jhumki woke up with the chirping of the humming birds. It was time to get up. Her every body part was aching. She wished to sleep for some more time but could not possess the nerve. She staggeringly got up to her feet and proceeded straight to the kitchen to be in charge. She could take notice of her husband's snores even from the next room.

Those snoring sounds had augmented greater than before inadvertently accelerating her heartbeat and her steps. Simultaneously, her pain deepened. It was not that she had suffered the pain for the first time. Even before her marriage, her drunkard father many times would beat her black and blue without a reason. Her father's drinking habit, his behavior, thereafter, would often upset her mother, and she would even vent her wrath on her.

Jhumki was the eldest of four siblings. She lived with her parents in a slum, settled along the railway line. Her father worked as a laborer and whatever he would earn during the day, in the evening would squander his earnings in his drinks. The onus of nurturing her four children almost fell on her mother's shoulders. She was a domestic help in four to five houses and could earn enough to cater to her family's hungriness and save them from starvation.

Gradually, her father's drinking habit had catapulted from bad to worse. Apart from scattering his money away to comply with his liquor addiction, he surreptitiously monitored their mother's earnings as well. Whenever their mother refused to give money to their father and would abuse him, he would beat her mercilessly in return. The children would often get aghast hearing the earsplitting laments of their mother. They would also scream at the top of your voice in support of the mother in an effort to match up their screeching laments with those of their mother.

Jhumki had turned fifteen years. Jhumki was growing up fast and had seasoned before age, and could figure out the anguish of her mother. In order to save her younger and innocent siblings from the wrath of her drunken father, she would take them in her lap and put them to sleep.

None of the four siblings had ever been to school. When Jhumki was small, her mother worked in relatively few houses but as she grew up and her family grew in number, the overall expenses of the household also escalated.

Owing to the addiction of the father, the burden of household expenses fell on the mother's shoulders and that of handling the brothers and sisters fell on the Jhumki's shoulders. Although people living in the colony belonged to the similar economic background and family circumstances, even then some people from the neighborhood could afford to send their children to the nearby government school. Jhumki used to watch them go to school with keenness in her eyes. She wished if she could also read and write.

Her friends from her locality often would share stories about their school with her. The famished Jhumki would often drool at the idea that her friends from her locality would also get food in the school along with education. Had she been to school, who would have handled her younger siblings? She had no option but to sulk.

At the corner of the slum was Lala's shop and also his pucca house. At the exit of the slum, the first concrete building belonged to Lala. The people living in that slum would buy necessary goods from him and if needed, would borrow money from him on interest.

The people were poor and their requirements meager. Sometimes their children and sometimes they themselves would fall ill. Sometimes they needed money to celebrate festivals and sometimes perform the rites of birth and death but whatever they earned was not enough for meeting the expenses of the house. In those moments of need, Lala would be their immediate savior. While lending the money, he would lend them principal amount only after deducting the first installment of interest.

The illiterate workers possessed no familiarity with the calculation of interest nor would they query anyone about it. Lala was like God, their savior to them, otherwise, who would have given them such a large amount? It was a different matter that when they could not repay the money their wives and children had to repay their loan by serving Lala. People had often seen, several times in the morning, the wives and daughters of the defaulter coming out of Lala's house.

Lala had a big family. Lala's wife, after giving birth to their four daughters, was down in the dumps disheartened and felt under the weather. Lala would continually hurl abuses at his wife after the birth of the daughters, which would be further depressing for her.

Lala had married off his two daughters and had been blissfully exultant in their respective homes. Their younger daughters were fifteen and ten respectively and attended to their ailing mother. Lala did not even observe his wife and had adamantly maintained his room away from his wife's room. Because his room had been away at a distant, no one came to know about Lala's misdeeds. Lala's wife was further suffocated with her husband's misdeeds especially when she had her young daughters in the house.

"Oh God! I cannot bear it now anymore. Take me up there with you." She would repeatedly say her prayers with tears streaming down from her eyes while she would raise her disabled hands in prayers.

God listened to her ardent prayer. Lala and his wife both got liberated from the pain of life when she left for her heavenly abode. Lala observed the ritual of the thirteenth day with fanfare to bring peace to his wife's soul. He believed that by satisfying the poor people's appetite would probably might earn him the divine grace of the Almighty; thus, Lala invited the people from the slum too on the thirteenth day.

In the lure of good food, Jhumki also reached the ground in front of Lala's house. Lala and his servants were themselves asking people about their wellbeing and feeding them personally.

"Your wife will directly go to heaven, Lala," Ramdin had said while gulping hot *halwa* down his throat. Lala's chest had puffed up with pride since he had become rich because of those poor people in the slum. He was enjoying his present status because of them. He could afford to observe the ritual of thirteenth day of his wife's demise with such a fanfare. Otherwise, what had been his financial condition when he had to run away from his village to come to this city?

Before coming to the city, owing to the outbreak of famine in his village Lala did not have a single grain to eat in his house. There had been a mass migration among the youth who were migrating to cities since then from their respective villages in search of work. Sixteen-year-old Sukhram was also among them. "Sukhram," yes, this was his name. People had become familiar with favorably addressing him as 'Lala' while Lala had blanked over his bona fide given name.

After he had reached city, Lala struggled to try his fate at many things but even after the lapse of few days, he could not secure any piece of work for the self. Since he did not possess a single penny, he had to satisfy his appetite from the littered trash. When he secured some work, he started getting daily wages. Once ready money from his daily wages started pouring in, Sukhram developed mental activeness. He started his business, with *paan* kiosks in a slum, which later progressed to its present shape.

Seeing him earn a substantially decent amount, his parents arranged his marriage to a girl from a nearby village and as Sukhram's business continued to grow, so did his family.

Jhumki had never eaten such delicious food before. In rapt attention, she licked yogurt from her leaf plate. She had not only finished yogurt but also every single trace of yogurt on her plate, which though had dissolved in Jhumki's abdomen, but she had still been dissatisfied. She looked with lustful eyes for Lala's servants who were serving food. If ever someone approached towards her side, she had decided that she would definitely ask for yogurt from him.

Although Jhumki was only fifteen years old, God had blessed her with a stature that made her look two or three years older than her age. When the children from the slum suffered malnutrition, and their body formation made them look much younger to their actual age, Jhumki possessed an envious body structure and facial glow.

When Lala's gaze shifted towards her and remained fixed at her for a moment. "Haven't seen her before. From whose family she could be?" He thought to himself and when he could not suppress his desire to know more about her, he slowly walked towards her and stood in front.

"Want anything else?"

"No ... No ..." replied startled Jhumki at his voice.

The leaf plate had slipped from her hand. For a moment, she kept staring at the leaf plate that had fallen from her hand on the ground. Probably, she was looking for whether anything had been still left in it.

"Where do you live?" was Lala's next question. "Here in the slum."

"In the township?" I have never seen her before. How did she escape from my eyes? Lala thought in his mind.

"Whose daughter are you? What is your father's name?" "Lubhaya Ram."

"Lubhaya Ram!" Lala was shocked hearing his name.

How could such a clumsy house have such a beautiful daughter! Her ever drunken father would never have paid attention to the children. How many times both husband and wife have been to his shop, borrowing a petty advance on interest. They would take their household goods from his shop on monthly credit. Lubhaya was infirm and tempted towards addiction while his wife had been diligent and determined. Whenever she would visit Lala's shop, she knew how to respond strongly to Lala's stupid things.

As soon as he emerged out of his thoughts, Lala looked around for Jhumki but he could not trace her anywhere.

The thirteenth day ritual of his wife was over. Everyone openly praised Lala's generosity. With the feast, probably his wife's soul might have rested peacefully, but Lala's peace of mind had been certainly disturbed and his restlessness had increased. He could not sleep despite running around with his business activities and exhausting himself every day. His wife had been in the bed for the last eight-ten years had been non-existent to him, but after her death, she had ceased to exist.

The idea of being left alone when both his teenage

daughters would get married would irritate him or was he in the hunt for an alleged reason to get married again.

When there had been no one to run this lineage after him, then for whom was he earning then? His mind resonated with valid reasoning.

"I should get married the second time." When that idea emerged in his mind, it would emerge with the picture of Jhumki licking yogurt from a leaf bowl.

"How much debt is left of Lubhaya Ram?" The next day, he got his accounts checked by his accountant. "Every strand of his hair is dipped in debt."

"Call him and his wife today itself in the evening," said Lala with a distinct sparkle in his eyes.

His accountant understood that Lala is eyeing elsewhere otherwise, he would not have called Lubhaya and his wife. Although he still could not understand, how far Lala had sighted and what had been going on in his mind.

Trembling with unearthly fear, Lubhaya's wife took him to Lala. Lubhaya was already drunk and not in his senses.

"You can't get any more debt now. For the past few months, you have not even paid interest amount in full. Tell me now what is it that you can give me", Lala asked, while looking into the ledger book.

Lubhaya could not bear his own weight, what could he say but his wife folded her hands.

"You are our godfather; our expenses have been increasing for the last several months. Sometimes our child is ill, sometimes I myself."

"If you are sick, have you reduced your spend on alcohol, see how he is rolling. You have enough money for your drinks but not enough to return the borrowed money. I have said, you will not get the loan now", Lala stood up taking the ledger book in his hand.

"Lala, have mercy on us. Our children will die of hunger.

Lala, I beg you please don't do it." Lubhaya's wife cried.

"Why are you crying now? You should have sense to return the money." Lala started moving inside, leaving the dazzled wife and husband outside gaping for mercy. "There must be some solution Lala."

Hearing this, Lala stopped. He wanted to suggest a solution to Lubhaya and his wife. He, however, was not in a hurry. He called Lubhaya the next day.

Deliberately, he called Lubaya alone. He knew that it would be easy for him to entice him and explain.

The next day, super excited Lubhaya returned after meeting Lala. He was partially happy and partially intoxicated. However, he could not lay his feet on the ground. "What did Lala say?" Wife asked him as soon as he arrived.

"Hey! Don't ask what he says? Made my heart happy. My daughter will rule there and all my debts will be forgiven." I could only say that much with his faltering tongue that was unclear to his wife.

The whole night Lubhaya had been drinking. The next morning when he regained consciousness, he apprised his wife about Lala's proposal.

"He wants to marry Jhumki and in return he will clear all our debt."

"Why Jhumki? She is only fifteen years old now. Lala's daughters too..." Lubhaya's wife did not understand this proposal.

"So what happened? We have to marry her. Where can I find a better groom than this?" Lubhaya had said yes to Lala.

After many deliberations, it was Jhumki, who became a bridge to clear all the debt. She became his wife after taking ritualistic seven rounds with Lala around the holy fire in a temple. The life of Lubhaya had also changed.

Jhumki though had become rich she was too young.

There was an open atmosphere in her house but in Lala's house there had been lot of restrictions. Moreover, Lala was suspicious by nature. If she stepped outside the house, Lala would signal her with his eyes to stay indoors.

Lala's both daughters were also of her age. Seeing them play, Jhumki wished to play with them. How could she? She was, nevertheless, scared of Lala. His mature but inhuman display of love would repeatedly hurt her tender heart.

One day Lala went to the market to get goods from the shop, and then Jhumki got a chance to play in the courtyard outside with both his daughters. As luck would have it, Lala arrived early that day. He grabbed her by her hair, dragged her inside and started beating her. That day, Lala had raised her hand on Jhumki for the first time.

It slowly became a daily routine. Now even if she laughed a little louder, Lala's body would get furious to the core.

It had just happened the previous day when Lala's eldest daughter had visited them with her husband and children. Her husband was a jovial person. Although, he was much older than Jhumki, but his joviality with her had infuriated Lala. After they left, Lala took a stick and started caning her and simultaneously abusing her.

"You are oozing with youth and young energy. You are not ashamed of joking with an alien man." He blurted out many more cheap allegations against Jhumki. Lala got tired of hitting but she did not utter a single word. Lala got tired, threw his stick aside and started with vulgar abuses. Jhumki heard something and ignored. Whatever she heard, she ignored all that.

Jhumki had now gradually learnt to ignore Lala. On many occasions, she would intentionally do those things, which Lala hated or asked her not to do. Sometimes she would suddenly look depressed, as if she had lost everything.

Sometimes she would laugh loudly for no apparent reason, and, on other occasions, she would cry loudly. These reactions of Jhumki would infuriate Lala further.

Four months had passed by when Jhumki came to know that she would soon be a mother. Rest five months had been even worse. Jhumki, who had lost her childhood and who was married to a man much older than her father, was now losing her mental balance. At this stage, Jhumki gave birth to a son. Lala was happy. After all, Jhumki had given him an heir but what about Jhumki! She could not even understand what happened to her. After all, what was her age? She had not even completed seventeen years.

Gradually, Jhumki's mental balance deteriorated so much that she did not have any feelings for her son as if he was not her own child. Only Lala's daughters looked after the child. Lala got worried. He had the heir but who will look after him? The daughters will get married and go to their respective homes. At the most, they will stay with him only for the next four-five years.

If Jhumki's condition would not improve, Lala would be left alone. Lala was anxious to have foreseen a situation where he would be left alone with a crazy wife and a four or five-year-old son.

In this mental state, the cunning Lala had been once again on the lookout for another victim. He wanted to marry another young girl, whose family had been heavily indebted to him. The condition of Jhumki was getting worse day-by-day and the debt burden on Lubhaya was increasing with the same pace.

□

# 8
# Strangulation

Tying the end of her *dhoti* on her forehead, Kunti sweltered in the scorching summer and mowed the fields. Even with the sickle in her hand, she would be repeatedly covered with sweat. Soil had glued to her towel meant for wiping her sweat. It was incomprehensible to figure out the actual color of the *dhoti* she had been wearing. Her dhoti had been knotted all over. Kunti had tied wherever her old *'dhoti'* had been torn. She had only two or three old *dhotis* out of which she had kept one of her *dhotis* aside for marriages or other occasions.

Ever since her husband Mangsiru had been to Delhi, her life had also transformed a bit. He had brought two-three *sarees* for her. Kunti could not wear those *sarees,* while working in the fields.

Oh! It had been extremely hot that day, and it had appeared as if the sky had rained fire. Kunti's throat had dried up, parched. There were small terrace fields without any traces of trees in the vicinity. Kunti felt like sitting in the shade of the trees for a while to drink two sips of water. Since, there had been no trees in close proximity in the area; Kunti's plastic bottle filled with water had been figuratively steaming. Last month, Mangsiru had brought the plastic bottle for her. He had told her how in the cities the water was sold in the plastic bottles. When Kunti heard about it, she had exploded into torrential laughter. "Water! Is it meant to be sold?"

"Hey! What do you know what happens in cities?" His eyes had flashed when he had expressed that. It had not been clear why the glow in his eyes had scared Kunti. What if, Mangsiru would get wedged in the city's glare!

Kunti dampened her tongue and throat with two sips of water and started reaping the wheat harvest. That year the harvest had been comparatively better than the previous years. Had Mangsiru been here, he would have taken two to four fields on lease. No one knew from where the idea of going away to the city for an employment in a huge bungalow had propelled within him. When Mangsiru was in the village, he and Kunti would take on lease the entire fields of not one but two families to plough.

Kunti had been hardly fifteen years when she had entered Mangsiru's family fold after her marriage to him. In addition to her husband, she had a father-in-law and two younger brothers-in-law in the family. Her mother-in-law had died long ago. Her father-in-law had two daughters, who were married. As there had been no woman in the house, his father had planned Mangsiru's marriage to Kunti. He was at that moment twenty years old.

Although, most of the families in Sumerpur were from the *Thakur* community, but at one end of the village, there was a cluster of houses meant for lower castes. In the name of ownership of land, these people hardly possessed any land of their own and hence, they worked in the fields owned by the people from the *Thakur* community.

From the perspective of the mountainous villages, Sumerpur was well-thought-out a big village. The village had around forty or fifty families of the *Thakur* community and ten to fifteen families of the low caste. The village, overall, would always burst with energy. The emergence of a new migration trends in the last few years had left the entire village high and dry. The village had assumed an abandoned look. The inheritors from the rich households had migrated to the city on the alleged reason of attaining higher education but then never returned to the village. When their elderly parents would become helpless, they too would renounce their village for the cities to be with their children. If ever these people would return, they would return for few days on the pretext of holidays. Although, they would profess their quick visit as picnic, but their visit would be predominantly for putting their fields on tenancy and settle the accounts.

Academically bright children from the lower caste had secured jobs for themselves with their conscientiousness efforts and the financial assistance from the government. There had been few families, who could not afford to send their children for higher education beyond a certain class, due to poverty. The possibility of securing the job for them did not arise. Those people, whose children had been employed in the cities, could survive in the hills on money order economy and had stopped working in the fields. However, at times the expenses of poor landless families had been sustained with great difficulty. The situation had changed, as there had been more farms and fewer laborers.

The progenies of the families, after the death of their elders who had been residing in the villages, had mostly not returned even for their fields. They hardly cared even if their fields had been left barren. Then there had been those families where the elders had still been alive and their attachment to their fields had not diminished. They possessed single desire that their fields should not remain barren and should yield some crop or the other. Kunti had taken up the labour work in one such field.

She had taken a crack at her best to convince Mangsiru to abandon and walk out on the intention of going away from the village, as there had been many farms in the village to cultivate and produce grains. Kunti and Mangsiru together could have produced a lot of grain with their hard work. It would have been enough where they could have kept some produce for their family's consumption and put on the market for sale the rest. Kunti had awakened to the emerging market pressure for the local ragi and millet produce that had been a staple food for the people in the hills had kicked off its retailing trade in the cities too.

A number of institutions, at the block level, would buy those crops from them.

It had been ten years since Kunti had been married. Meanwhile, many things had apparently transpired. She herself had become a mother of two children, her father-in-law died and the eldest of her two brothers-in-law had been married. His wife was so quarrelsome that she could not live with Kunti even for two days. Dejected Kunti had taken the bold decision of separating the kitchen and its responsibilities. They had kept alive two blazing flames in the same house. The younger of her two brothers-in-law had left the house, lured in by the enticing city, had been exerting him in a hotel there. He would come whenever he yearned to return home. In one of those days, while he would warm up to set off his business with a small hotel, Kunti had lined up her strategy to get him settled into matrimony. He had already been twenty-five years old but had not yet married. The anxiety of getting his younger brother-in-law married had been constantly gnawing Kunti. Had Mangsiru been there, he would have been her reinforced support.

Mangsiru had never been conscious about his earnings earlier. While living in the village, he would be satisfied with whatever income he would earn. Had both Kunti and Mangsiru worked laboriously together, they would have stilll earned a decent living that would have been enough for their survival. Both of them had been hard working in their own right. They would have taken many cultivable farms on lease, and with an escalating scenario of migration, they would have been the sole owner of the entire produce. Kunti had not been on her guard when Kundan had lured Mangsiru with enticements that he reached an agreement to go to Delhi. Kundan had been working as a security guard in a bungalow. When the owner of the bungalow had retired from the Indian army, he had got his bungalow constructed with great enthusiasm. He had two children who had shifted abroad. Two years after the colonel's demise, his wife had also shifted to America with her son. Kundan had been taking care of the bungalow since then. There had been many such bungalows where security guards had been employed to keep a watch.

Kundan had extended his larger than life castle in the air beyond to Mangsiru, where most of them had been beyond his imagination.

"Hey man, what are you doing here? Come with me, I will get you work. Hey, there you will know what life is! There is nothing here."

While Kundan narrated, with his eyes brightened up the charms of the city life, it had a cascading effect on Mangsiru brightening his eyes too in appreciation of Kundan's flight of fancy prognostications.

For the next few days, after Mangsiru had blown hot and cold indecisively between a series of affirmations and negations, at the end of the day had migrated to Delhi, leaving

Kunti single-handedly to tend to two children. Although her brothers-in-law and sister-in-law lived in the same village, she hardly possessed their espousal. Kunti never hankered after her husband to depart for the city, while she would be left forlorn in the village. It had been three years since then when her eldest son Chunnu and younger daughter Muniya had been merely four years and two and a half years old respectively.

Two months after moving to Delhi, frightened Mangsiru had returned to the village.

"I have told everyone there that my name is Mangal Singh. Don't know why I was named Mangasiru?" As soon as he came, he had blurted out in front of Kunti.

"Why? What is wrong with this name?"

"It appears to be an old name, Mangsiru...as if we were calling out the name of a month."

There was nothing wrong with what Mangsiru said. Earlier, it used to be the customary trend with nomenclature. The child born in the particular month was named after the month. Mangsiru had been named as such owing to his birth in the month of *Marghsheesh* (*Agrahanyana*) the Hindu calendar month that falls in November and December.

The owner of the bungalow, in which Mangsiru had secured the job of a security guard, had his own business in many cities. His wife had died and his two married daughters had been residing in the US. The owner himself lived out of Delhi, mostly for work.

"It will be impossible for me to frequently come home. It's a new job now. After a few days, once I know what my income is, I will take you as well. My Chunnu and Muniya will study in English school."

"Why? Hasn't your boss told you what salary will you expectedly receive?"

Kunti felt strange at whatever Mangsiru had said.

"Hey, what is a salary?" Kundan was saying that there is more earning than that.

"More earning?"

"You will not understand now. You will understand when I will bring back a lot of things for you." Mangsiru's eyes were shining in anticipation.

After that, Mangsiru had again returned six months later. Yes, in the meantime his family had been receiving a letter and money orders of one or two thousand rupees. For the first time, when the postman had kept two thousand rupees in her hand, she got exceedingly confused. Where would she keep so much money and what would she do with it? She did not even know how to count. She had seen a storehouse of grain, but not the currency notes. She used to buy everything for herself in exchange for the grain only.

Six months later, when Mangsiru had returned, he had been a completely changed person. He wore pants, a shirt, had black glasses on his eyes, wore expensive shoes on his feet, moreover, his entire demeanor had been one of its kind and unique. Kunti sat in front of him, wearing dirty clothes and blowing the stove.

"Why do you live like this? You should live a little gracefully. Dress well; put a little cream-powder. See how girls live tip-top in cities." Mangasiru took out a nice *saree* and some make-up items from his bag and kept them in her hand.

"Why do you talk like this? After applying cream-powder and a good *saree,* can I go to work in the field?"

Kunti said, while taking the *saree* and other accessories from him.

"Who is asking you to work in the fields? I will earn and you eat and enjoy in leisure. It is only a matter of time. Then you can also come along with me to the city."

"When I have to come with you to the city, I will come. Right now, the work that I have at home has to be done. One should not easily leave his roots." Frustration was clearly visible in Kunti's voice. To her, her husband appeared distant and an alien.

After that, every time Mangsiru would come home, Kunti found him more distant from her than that before. Mangsiru, on the other hand, could never get over the parties in his Sahib's bungalow from time to time. There would be many visitors for the party, most of them belonging to the higher echelons of society. Variety of dishes would be prepared and served with exotic liquors.

"Kunti, had you been there, you would have seen how girls dress nowadays and how much money people have. People enjoy it."

Even in the darkness of the night, Kunti could see the sparkle in her husband's eyes.

"If you were there, you would have seen it." Mangsiru would often wish to pronounce those words but somehow ceased to utter "I will take you there too". The initial desire to teach his children in English school had somehow become desolate in comparison to the initial twinkle in his eyes. The fact is that whenever he would visit his home, he would definitely carry a lot of clothes and toys for his children. He loved his children a lot and they would wait impatiently for him to return soon once he would leave.

"*Bhabhi* where are you? Unexpectedly, I have been looking for you for long." It was her brother-in-law Bisesar, who stood there near Kunti in panic, bathed in sweat. Kunti's heart almost stopped. Fearing the bickering by his wife, Bisesar would never speak directly to Kunti. It had been three years since his brother had left for the city, but

Bisesar had never directly inquired about her welfare. Then, what had happened that day that had made him appear so nervous?

"What happened, *devarji*? Why are you sweating?" "*Bhabhiji*, I went to the neighboring village."

"So?"

After listening carefully to what Bisesar had told her, it was enough to blow her mind away.

There had been electricity in that village prompting rich enough people to buy television sets. Someone from the village had seen Mangasiru on the television screen being escorted by the police officers but surprisingly, he had identified himself as Mangal Singh. The villager had not been wide of the mark with his appearance, his visage that had been similar to Mangsiru.

"What an old name is Mangsiru? It looks like it is the name of some month. I am now Mangal Singh." Kunti instantaneously recollected those words of her husband, which had been resonating in her ears.

"But what has he done? Why were the police officers taking him away?" Kunti was shocked.

"I don't know much but it seems to be a case of murder." Bisesar had said fearfully.

"Murder! How can a man like Mangasiru kill anyone?

There is definitely some misunderstanding." Kunti's eyes were filled with tears.

"How can I tell with surety, *Bhabhiji*, I haven't seen TV myself? I have just listened to what people said and told me." Kunti somehow had managed herself, and returned home.

There had been anxieties and lot of apprehensions raging within.

On one hand, she had tried to convince herself that

whatever Bisesar had told her might not have been true, on the other, she had become confused as to why would the people of the surrounding village fail to identify him?

The series of events that had occurred in the next few days had been nothing short of a nightmare for Kunti. Within a few days, the news of Mangsiru's arrest had spread like wildfire across that region.

Mangasiru and his master had been caught in a disgusting crime. Their crime had been so hateful that even its narration had been nauseating and would have raised hair on ends in utter hatred. They had been accused of killing young girls after having molesting them.

There was a slum just a little away from the bungalow, in which Mangsiru had been working. The children from the slum area could not go to school for their education, so they would roam hither and thither. Some of those children would do garbage picking. Somehow, the girls from that slum had started disappearing one by one.

When one of the slum-dweller, whose daughter had been reported missing, he tried to report the matter to the police. Initially, the police would not register their complaint; but would rather haul them over the coals. When people from the slum would point a finger at the owner of that large bungalow, the police would beat them instead. After all, how could they tolerate those disgusting allegations against the rich and powerful? Those owners of the big bungalows, who were supposedly big-hearted, hosted feasts, attended by the elite and high-ranking people of the city. Everyone in the area knew the hospitality and the reach, of the owners of those big bungalows. The police officers would also take favors with them, as they too had attended the parties many times hosted by them. The sin pot was bound to erupt one day, so it erupted.

The carcasses of many dead children had been found in the adjacent drain. Among them had been the skeletons of some young girls, who would visit the big bungalow to entertain the guests from time to time.

Although both the owner and the servant were caught, the entire blame befell on the servant. Supported by the police officers, the owner had clearly stated that he had not been aware of what had been happening in his bungalow in his absence.

The police visited Mangsiru's village for some more clues. They questioned Kunti. Since no one had anything appalling to say about Mangasiru's past, so they refrained from saying anything. Most of the villagers had not known when Mangsiru, a laborer in the fields, went to the city and became Mangal Singh.

"He can't do that, sir! He loves his children very much, so how can he do this to the children of others?" said Kunti with her blurred eyes.

When everything had been against Mangsiru, in that scenario who would have pay attention to her? The police came and went back without any substantial proof against Mangsiru. He was tried for rape and murder along with his boss acquitting the owner of all the crimes one by one.

It had been two years since then when Kunti and her children had become untouchables for the villagers. Those villagers who had given their fields to Kunti on lease had taken their fields back from her. Nobody had given her work on daily wages, as if she had been a criminal.

Kunti had admitted the elder son to a big school as per their ambitious plans about their children but soon the school authorities had removed him from the school. Chunnu was taunted not only his classmates but also the teachers. In the class, he was made to sit separately. After coming home, Chunnu would cry and ask his mother multiple questions.

"Has my father killed the children and eaten their flesh?"

Chunnu would often ask.

Such questions would perforate their mother's chest. How would the innocent child tolerate such allegations? Mangsiru had been alleged to perpetrate those crimes, which he had not committed. After losing her ground, dejected Kunti had withdrawn Chunnu from the school. Moreover, it had been becoming very difficult for her to feed her children, so how could she afford to educate them? She had not seen Mangasiru in the span of two years.

Although she wished to see him, and had known the truth, but was not sure whether he had really done the untoward or had been simply paying for his master's deeds. She had just one question to depend on Mangsiru for an answer. She had been resolute to forgiving him, provided he would have negated all the allegations. No matter what punishment would have been given to him by the court, she was determined to apply to the higher court for justice. Before that, she had first desired to meet him. Mangsiru had been kept in the biggest jail in Delhi.

She pleaded with many people in her village to take her to Delhi just once. She also pleaded with her brother-in- law, but to no avail. Her younger brother-in-law had stopped visiting the village after that incident.

The greatest challenge for Kunti had been the crisis of feeding her children that had deepened after the incident. When the food stored in the house had started depleting, she had folded her hands before the village head for assistance.

"My children will die of hunger. Why punish my children for what my husband did?" Tears had rolled down her cheeks.

The headman of the village had shown him a soft corner on her plea. Kunti had breathed a sigh of relief when he helped her get a few days' wages under the government scheme.

One day, she received the horrific news about the court that had pronounced its verdict. Since there had been no available evidence against the owner, he was duly released while Mangsiru was sentenced death penalty.

Kunti had received the news two days later. The day of the execution was determined after some time. The news had increased Kunti's discomfort. Once again, she possessed a deep desire to meet her husband. But, how could she?

Kunti and her children had not been willing to step out of the house anymore. Wherever they went, they faced hatred or apathy. Kunti had started feeling as if he had not been her husband, who had committed the crime, but it was she who could be held responsible for the crime.

If Mangsiru had committed the crime, he was punished, but no one had been ready to understand why innocent Kunti and her children had been punished, and Kunti kept suffering every moment all her remaining life.

□

# 9

# Threshold

That day, Anuradha had been happier than ever. It had appeared as if sunny days had returned for some time. The happy moments for Anuradha and her family had reverted suddenly. She had been pleased with a high level of energy surging through her body. It had been 2.00 P.M., and her home was at a four-hour journey from the city. If she boarded the bus scheduled for 3.00 P.M., she would reach her house probably by 7.00 P.M.

"Yes, that would be fine." She pondered and waved to call a passing by auto-rickshaw. The auto-rickshaw raced towards the interstate bus stand.

There were skyscrapers on both sides of the road, large showrooms, and gleaming indigenous and foreign luxury vehicles parked outside them. All those buildings seemed to be left behind with the speed of the racing auto-rickshaw. The buildings, the trees, and the showrooms all appeared to have been running at an equally fast pace along with the speeding auto-rickshaw.

Delhi is such a city. Everyone visibly seems to have been fast on the trot. No one yearns to stop, even for a moment. People are apprehensive of the impending danger of lagging in the rat race of life if they ever stop. Anuradha, too had pervaded with the restlessness of the city by the time she reached the bus stand. However, to no avail, as she arrived at the bus stand, there had been no bus scheduled for her city. However, she did not have to hang around for long. Barely fifteen minutes after, she saw a roadways bus inward-bound the bus stand. Anuradha breathed a sigh of relief. Had the bus not appeared, she would have to stay at the house of some friend or relatives. It had been beyond her physical capacity to roam around in a city like Delhi for long hours, and her lungs could not bear the effect of the bad air emitted by vehicles in the city.

Anuradha sat on the bus. In a short while, the bus had left Delhi behind, but the concrete forest had chased their bus for a long distance. Anuradha's nostalgic memories had hovered over her and had harmonized with the speediness of the bus.

Anuradha recollected the day when she had participated in the annual function of college during the final year of her graduation. Her dance and music teacher had helped her when she observed her keen passion for dance inherent in her since her childhood. Anuradha had been born in a lower-middle-class family and was one of the five siblings begotten to her parents. Anuradha, the fourth child among the five siblings, was exceedingly beautiful. Anuradha enjoyed the total share of beauty. She was endowed with beauty, which could have been divided among the other four siblings as well. Anuradha would have looked like a princess had she not grown up wearing the old clothes of her elder siblings. As Anuradha was growing up, she had begun to realize how beautiful she had been. This realization made her complete with a feeling of pride.

She was extremely fond of dancing since her childhood days. When she was in school, any cultural program in the school would be incomplete without her participation. With the recognition of her innate talent, an idea emerged to provide her with the formal classical dance education in the school. Still, Anuradha's parents had not consented to that. After her parents' refusal, the teacher, on her own accord, had started giving her private classical dance education without charging any fees. Any dance form that Anuradha had learned would come alive every time with her brilliant gestures and facial expressions.

The trend that had started in the school had been carried over to the college. With the growing beauty, Anuradha became more beautiful with age, and with constant practice and effort, her talent for dancing also developed further.

In one such ceremony, Anukul saw her and was mesmerized by her beauty and talent alike. Anukul's father was among the dignitaries of the city. He was invited as the chief guest for the anniversary function of the college. After completing his education, Anukul had joined hands with his father in his business. He had accompanied his father to attend the college function. That day Anuradha participated in *Saraswati Vandana* in folk dance and displayed dance drama, etc.

In *Saraswati Vandana*, she had captured the dance floor to the beats of *Vara de Veena Vadini.* In the dance drama, she had assayed the role of 'Radha' wooing 'Krishna' with her charming sentiments, whereas in a Rajasthani dance, the green-colored stole had a multiplier effect on her beauty.

Anuradha's beauty, her talent for dance, and her gestures enchanted Anukul. After Anukul saw Anuradha, he remained fixed to the seat. He often forgot to clap. After every presentation of Anuradha, only the crescendo of thunderous applause for her performance would shake him out of his swoon.

“Papa, I want to marry that girl,” Anukul could not resist expressing his desire to his father as soon as he reached home.

“Which girl?” The father deliberately pretended ignorance, though he knew the girl Anukul was referring to.

“One who participated in *Saraswati Vandana*.” “Who is that girl?”

“I do not know. I saw her for the first time today.”

“If you don’t know, then find out. Will you marry her?

Without knowing this?”

Anukul jumped with joy. After knowing the family background and financial status of Anuradha, Anukul's happiness was shredded to pieces when his father outrightly refused to accord his permission for this alliance. “Are you against my matrimonial interest with Anuradha because she is poor? Can’t fulfill your dowry demands?”

The father was shocked by the question.

“I said, this marriage is not possible. We also have some status in the society.”

“Then you keep your status with you. I will stay apart after marrying Anuradha. I will manage my livelihood by doing a job somewhere.”

The father felt dejected with his pulse going down. He had not expected an answer like this from his son. He understood his anger could spoil things. He tried his best to make his son realize the societal norms. He clamored for his community, respect, and honor. Anukul, however, did not budge from his decision.

The father could not resist for long and, after some time, agreed to his son's insistence. He, however, could not agree within. He had married both his elder sons into status families. Anukul was the youngest among his siblings and had enjoyed all his mother's attention throughout, making him a stubborn person.

Anuradha's parents became shell shocked when they received the alliance proposal from a reputed family in the city. There was no place in their house where they could have accommodated such guests. Anukul's father got frustrated after seeing the condition of Anuradha's house. How will they arrange marriage following their reputation? However, they had to find a solution to the problem as well. They willingly bore all the expenses of the family of the bride. Anuradha's dreams were like a flight of solid wings. A proud smile settled on her face. She developed a myth in her mind that she was the best among all in her family.

In an auspicious time, Anuradha became Anukul's companion and came to her in-law's house. Witnessing the grandeur of the marriage ceremony, Anuradha's family could not believe it. The glare of pomp and show made them so nervous that they remained seated in neglect in one corner of the venue.

On the auspicious day of the marriage, Anuradha looked like a fairy tale princess, who had just descended from the sky, disguised as a bride. Dressed with gold jewelry and brocade garments, Anuradha would not consider herself inferior to a princess.

Anuradha reached her in-law's house. Elated Anukul, with his fulfilled desires, poured out his whole heart before Anuradha. Anuradha, overwhelmed by the expression of his love, found a speck of hesitancy stuck to a corner of her mind. Anukul lived in a joint family. His mother and two sisters-in-law hailed from prosperous families similar to his. His sisters were married off in the family's equivalent in stature and reputation. Neither of the two sisters-in-law liked Anuradha, for they were partially jealous and partially due to their temperament.

Anuradha, who was proud of her beauty and had always

enjoyed being in the center of everyone's attention, was deeply hurt by this neglect. Not only this, she was subjected to acute bickering by Anukul's family when rituals of the marriage were being performed.

"What do you know about big houses and their customs? Probably all these rich customs don't take place in your house." Anuradha felt terrible and stopped talking in disgust when her husband's elder sister said this one day. Because of all these petty matters, tension often prevailed in the house. Even Anukul's parents defended the elder sisters-in-law, as they had not been thrilled with his marriage to Anuradha.

"I can no longer be with these people," Anuradha announced one day. She was confident that Anukul would not afford to ignore her plea.

Anukul spoke to his father. Although Anukul's father was initially shocked to hear what his son had proposed, he too was fed up with the daily squabbles. He thought it reasonable to divide his property among his sons. Anuradha was happy now that meant she would have the sole proprietary on her husband and be the unchallenged queen of her house.

Seven to eight years had passed. Anuradha was now a mother of two children. Her physical beauty had not faded. Anukul doted on her to the extent that he would provide her with whatever she wanted. Anuradha, always surrounded by the chain of servants, did not wish to visit even her parents' house. Now, their house was devoid of such luxurious amenities as were available to her in her own house. Even Anuradha's parents and siblings did not appreciate her arrogance, but they could not do anything.

Destiny had other plans and not all this could continue for long. Anukul managed to survive in a road accident, but he sustained the worst kind of impact of internal head injuries.

His memory began to fade. Wherever he would go, he would get dizzy and sometimes faint. Anukul had lost his father long back, and both his brothers were busy with their families and business. There was no one to help him at this moment of crisis.

The impact of Anukul's deteriorating health had a visible adverse effect on his business as well. Their family and business could survive for a few months on whatever investments Anukul had made. However, as time passed, the responsibilities and the expenditure skyrocketed. A lot of money was being spent on Anukul's medicare without any visible signs of improvement.

Anuradha, who was pampered and had become habitual to the luxuries and comforts of life and enjoyed accessibility to anything and everything, had to become an unbridled spendthrift. With this accident, Anukul suffered a considerable setback. She was, until then, not accustomed to facing difficulties. Anukul's illness had made him irritable, while even Anuradha could not tolerate the responsibility of both parent's situation. The irritable temperament of both parents had a profound impact on their children. The otherwise cool and calm had started becoming tense.

At this moment, if anyone came to extend his support to the family, it was Abhishek, Anukul's friend. Abhishek was a childhood friend of Anukul. Abhishek belonged to an equally wealthy and prosperous family like Anukul and was many steps ahead of Ankul in intellect. After completing his education, he chose to own a business instead of opting for the job. He possessed a charming persona and tact of getting his work done from any office, and none had the guts to oppose him. Owing to this magical streak in him, he had established his own business properly within a short period.

It was a time for Abhishek to manage his business by using his credentials and simultaneously handle the shattering business of Anukul. He knew that for Anukul to run his company was no longer possible, and in this way, he took Anuradha with him.

"*Bhabhiji*, you are an educated and a sensible lady; why don't you help Anukul?" One day he said to Anuradha, waking up her latent capabilities.

She remembered her talent for dancing and all those people who surrounded her in appreciation of her dance. Had she wished, she could have earned name and fame for herself. She was married at a young age and lost her budding career and her interest in her passion. Anukul treated her like a queen; what about her own identity and individuality? What about her talent? She had now become a typical homemaker.

She had forgotten her dance capability for so many years, but now she must prove herself by taking over the responsibility of her husband's business. This idea occurred to her many times now.

Anukul had never thought of Anuradha in such a situation. He wished that Anuradha should discharge her duty looking after her home and raising her children. Even Anuradha could not guess whether she was ever unhappy with her life and its arrangements. The question now was whether he would give her permission to take over the business.

After Abhishek's prompted her, Anuradha became interested in it. She pleaded with Anukul and finally took his permission.

Anuradha stepped out of her homely threshold.

Abhishek and Anukul both assisted her with her business work. Even after persistent labor and hard work, the business work could not proceed in any direction. Anuradha was gradually getting frustrated.

One of those days, Abhishek suggested a new business partnership to them.

"Why don't we do export business?"

"But what exports business? Which product can be exported?"

"Handicraft products from here. You have seen how women from the surrounding villages make beautiful products from cane, etc. You have to give them a little encouragement for improving their art, and our products are ready. Handicrafts are in great demand abroad." Abhishek was excited.

"*Bhabhiji,* you are a woman, and since you are an artist too, you know what art is. You can fill in the colors of your imagination in those products and see how successful we are."

Anuradha enjoyed this work. Following her interest, Abhishek presented a brighter prospect of their business in the future, which Anuradha could not resist.

For this purpose, Anuradha had come to Delhi with Abhishek to procure the necessary license of the export business. Anukul was expected to accompany them to Delhi but could not because of his ill health.

One day Anuradha found Abhishek's conduct strange in the office when he pushed her forward for official negotiations. Although she was Abhishek's partner in the business and her presence was required to complete all the official formalities, but she felt that Abhishek should not have pushed her forward.

She then thought that Abhishek probably was training her for the nuances of business.

Lost in all these thoughts, Anuradha came back to her home in no time. Anukul was also happy in Anuradha's sense of happiness and achievement. After a long time, there was a moment of joy in the house. "May God bless Anuradha with success?" He secretly prayed to God for his divine blessings. Anyway, after the physical deterioration, God left him with faith only in the holy gifts

This business flourished, proving Abhishek's prediction true. As the company grew with more assignments and contract orders, Anuradha became unusually occupied with the new business, and Anukul started feeling neglected.

Anuradha would spend most of her time managing her business. Her meetings with Abhishek grew. She often had to stay out of the house for business commitments.

Initially, Anukul did not say anything, but he started protesting when he saw his children being neglected. But Anuradha was addicted to her success.

Her travels within India and abroad increased every month. While meeting new people for business, Anuradha was on cloud nine. How could she hear what Anukul said? She could listen to only the compliments that Abhishek showered on her. She could hear the words of colleagues and friends, who were showering praises on her.

"*Bhabhiji*, you have a Midas touch. Like a touchstone, everything that you touch turns to gold," one day, Abhishek took Anuradha by her hand.

"Whatever work you intend to accomplish, and whomsoever you meet, believe me, that work flourishes. Do you know how lucky you are for me?"

He would croon many such words to her, enough to overwhelm Anuradha. Her pride was her conceit now, and she would puff her shoulders and stretch out her neck.

Two to three years went very fast as if they had wings.

When businesses expanded, they became prosperous. Anuradha never inquired Abhishek for an account, nor did she has any interest in it. She would blindly sign the cheques wherever he said.

As Anukul raised his complaints about her negligent approach towards children, Anuradha shifted her children to a hostel. The ill-health of Anukul was hand in glove with his frustration, which made the situation even worse. The freedom of Anuradha was now disturbing him. Sometimes he would suspect Abhishek too, wondering whether he was taking undue advantage of Anuradha.

Anukul would often be lost in thoughts. Abhishek was his childhood friend, but how he had set up such a big business made Anukul doubt his actions.

Abhishek and Anuradha would often go out together. Initially, Anukul was happy as long as he thought it was the need of the business for Anuradha to step out of the house, but then he realized that Anuradha often sought excuses to stay out. Her face would glow as soon as she heard any proposal of going out with Abhishek.

Her eyes would brighten up. These petty movements would irritate Anukul nonetheless, and all illogical thoughts would surround him. Something like an unknown and invisible fear had started settling in his mind. Are Anuradha and Abhishek getting close to each other? Abhishek is an intelligent player. Anuradha is impressed by his words. She is not ready to hear anything against him.

"Anuradha, do you know how much profit your business is making?" Anukul asked Anuradha perceiving apparent happiness.

"No, this account is maintained by Abhishek. I only know that business is doing well," Anuradha oozed with enthusiasm.

"But you should also check the accounts." "Why? I have full faith in Abhishek."

"Following someone blindly with open eyes is not good.

Abhishek is a very clever person. You must be careful."

"I am not clear. What problem do you have with me? You are sitting idle at home and unnecessarily get upset like this."

Finally, this debate ended in a quarrel. Anuradha, in a fury, stumped her feet on the ground and left her house.

Whenever Anukul said anything against Abhishek, he would see similar reactions from Anuradha. By now, Anuradha had developed a steadfast trust in Abhishek.

Two or three years had passed. Anuradha would enter her own house like a guest, or it could be said, she rarely wished to come home. People generally try to find an excuse to stay at home; she would look for a reason to stay out of the house. Abhishek had now sent his family to Delhi. He had winded up his entire business from here. He had just one paternal house in which his elder brother lived with his family. Their parents also lived with his elder brother.

"Why don't we also leave this place and go to Delhi?" One day Anuradha told Anukul about her wish. Hearing this, Anukul felt terrible about her but still preferred to keep his mouth shut. He peacefully refused to shift his base to Delhi. "Why? If we go there, we can focus all our attention on business. Every time I have to rush to Delhi for every small work, while I feel worried about home."

"You feel worried about home!" Anukul had a strange smile.

"You don't care about the house even when you live here."

Anuradha was infuriated once again. Her home visits were now less frequent. Perhaps she had bought a flat in Delhi.

Abhishek was now in the process of starting a new business. Some new people had joined him now. Anuradha was now feeling neglected, but by now, she had become so dependent on Abhishek that she could hardly do her work independently.

Finally, one day Abhishek closed down the old business, and whatever he had saved from that business, he invested it in starting a new business. Anuradha was apprised that the two new partners had joined their company besides them. Anuradha's heart was filled with pride while signing on lots of papers. Anuradha, who blindly followed Abhishek, without any iota of suspicion, signed all the documents.

The old office had felt as small, so they took a big office at the new place. Work was going on in the office. Until then, Anuradha came to spend time with Anukul.

"Heard you have started a new business?"

"Yes, there was not much profit in the old business now."

"Abhishek must have said that?"

"Again, you have started this. Why are you so stirred up at the slightest mention of Abhishek?"

"Leave it, tell me how many partners are there in the new firm?"

"I do not know? Abhishek had prepared all the papers."

"Then God is the master."

"Again, you have started."

It was the only conversation between the two, and that too ended with arguments and wrangling.

After the initial bouts of frustrations, Anukul had started recovering. When his mother and brothers saw his condition, at first, no one intervened for fear of Anuradha, but, later, when they saw Anukul being so neglected, everyone extended his help. Anukul, who was suffering from Anuradha's apparent misbehavior, found a ray of hope in his mother and brothers.

With the moral and financial support of the brothers, he again passionately attempted to revive his business. He deliberately did not mention it to Anuradha. He knew that Anuradha, a big dreamer, would not like this small effort by him. It seemed practically impossible for Anuradha to return from the path she had selected for herself and the journey she had undertaken.

The human mind is relentlessly covetous. There was a time when Anuradha had nothing. She was born in a family that could barely afford two square meals. Her destiny took a massive turn, and she entered a family, which was prosperous. Anukul, too, fulfilled all her desires and never lacked either in amenities or in luxuries. However, Anuradha turned her back on her doting husband, Anukul. She had forgotten, or she was intentionally ignoring the time she had spent with Anukul. She was at the height of success because of Anukul, whom she now considered inferior and a worthless person.

Anukul's sisters-in-law and mother cursed Anuradha, but he would ask them to keep the peace.

"She tried to help me run the business. In this endeavor, if she has gone too far and is successful, what is her fault? Her work has spread so much that she is left with no spare time now." Anukul would answer his charged-up mother in a peaceful tone.

"Anukul, what kind of person are you? She is giving you so much grief, and you are still favoring her. You seem to have forgiven her, but God will never. Remember, my son; divine justice doles out without any prediction." She raised both her hands upwards towards heaven as if she was asking for divine intervention.

Anukul was fully aware of his agitated mother's restlessness and pain within her. Wasn't he also suffering within from the same turmoil? Wasn't he burning in his fire? It was so, but the fond memories of his children made Anukul yearn for peace. He had regrets for Anuradha. He worried about her. Many a time, he expressed his sincere concern for Anuradha without any visible effect on her.

He had a firm hope that Anuradha would return to him one day, which proved to be true. Anuradha returned but under what condition?

This time Anuradha went to Delhi but returned very soon. She had a fake smile and appeared restless. Anukul did not find it proper to ask anything from Anuradha at that time.

Anuradha wanted Anukul to ask her while he waited for Anuradha to burst out. He knew that it would be difficult for Anuradha to remain reticent for a long time.

Anuradha was shocked and upset. Anukul was silent. Anukul's incredible patience to say anything to Anuradha was disturbing her.

Almost a week had passed. Neither said anything. Ultimately, Anuradha burst out and shared the matter with Anukul after fruitlessly waiting for long.

"I was thinking of getting the children back from the hostel."

"But who will keep them here? You will go back in a few days." Anukul looked at Anuradha from the corner of his eyes and could guess that she wanted to say much more.

"I won't go anywhere now," Anuradha said from the deepest corner of her throat. There was a deep note of despair in her voice.

"But why?"

Then, what Anuradha told her was beyond the expectations of Anukul.

After leaving her house, when Anuradha reached Delhi, the new office was ready, but there was no room for her in it. When Anuradha asked Abhishek about it, he just smiled. His smile was not usual. There were expressions of crookedness on his face.

"You don't need to come here anymore."

"You are kidding, Abhishek. Aren't you?" said Anuradha in a faltering voice.

"No sister-in-law! Not kidding. You are no longer a partner in this business."

Anuradha felt as if she had heard something wrong. The whole office turned around before her eyes. She almost fainted when she caught hold of the chair lying nearby to support her.

Abhishek no longer needed Anuradha. He had taken advantage of Anuradha, her beauty, her talent, and Anukul's reputation as much as he could. He abandoned Anuradha and threw her away like a fly from the milk pot when he had new companions. Anuradha, in her ignorance and blind faith, had signed all the documents. Even if she contemplated legal action, it wouldn't have served any purpose or proved anything.

Anuradha cried, even threatened, but did not affect Abhishek. It was his well-thought-out move. Finally, Anuradha returned after losing all her battles. After years of devotion to her business, that entire she possessed was a flat in Delhi and nothing else.

Telling all this, Anuradha wept bitterly. Her entire body shook with intermittent hiccups. Anukul did not attempt to silence her.

Anuradha kept crying and sobbing. When tired, she became quiet. Anukul was also silent. At this time, he did not wish to poke her for anything. Nor did he want to remind her of all those moments when he tried to warn her about Abhishek. How often had he wanted to remind her that he wanted her to be strong and move ahead? Nevertheless, not at the cost of family.

It was not that Anuradha did not make any mistakes. When Abhishek was with her, she did not pay any attention to Anukul even once. Her guilt feeling was so strong that she could not see straight into Anukul's eyes.

When Anukul's mother and sisters-in-law heard the news of Anuradha's return, they also reached Anukul's house to console him.

"Why has she come here now? Don't you remember she mistreated and abandoned you in your illness?"

Anukul kept quiet. He did not utter a single word. Had he spoken, it would have given rise to an ugly situation. Anukul remembered Anuradha's love post-marriage and her struggle to save the house when he was ill.

If she had wandered for some time in the desire to achieve success, should she not be forgiven for this mistake?

Anuradha heard their conversation. What would Anukul do now? The pictures from her past life passed through her eyes like a reel of a film. She realized how much Anukul loved her. Could he ever wish anything wrong for her? The dreams of flying high had now left her cripple. What would she do? Where would she go?

A few more days passed. Anuradha was waiting for Anukul's decision. He had not said anything regarding bringing their children back from the hostel. Perhaps he does not want to get them back. Who knows, he may even send her back to her maternal home.

The weather had suddenly turned bad on that evening. Clouds and lightning caused a harsh noise in the entire atmosphere. Anukul had left since morning and had not yet returned home, while Anuradha walked around in restlessness. The outside storm was in tandem with the battery within her. Although Anukul appeared calm from outside, what was going on in his mind was that Anuradha was utterly ignorant.

When the car outside came to a screeching halt, Anuradha jumped out of bed and opened the door. She saw Anukul together with their two children. Anuradha, for a moment, was clueless.

"I wanted to surprise both you and the children. Otherwise, how could I see such happiness on your face?"

Anuradha's eyes welled with tears at what Anukul had said.

"You have also learned to do business now. You will have to do double work now. Take care of the children too and take care of my work as well," infatuated Anukul looked at Anuradha.

Anuradha was happy. While hugging both her children, she burst into tears. She had suffered punishment for crossing her limits and ignoring family for business.

The clouds were beginning to clear, and the moon peeping through them was spreading its light. A beam of such light was ready once again to shine in Anuradha's life as well.

□

# 10

# How Alive Again

Sunil's heart skipped out of his mouth, whenever the roadways bus moved up on the hills or went gliding downhill on the bumpy uneven hilly road. When he peeped out of the window of the bus, he could see the long serpentine river flowing between the two hills. The road was so narrow at places that it seemed as if one wheel of the bus was off the road. Sunil closed his eyes in utter despair as soon as this idea appeared to him that even the slightest negligence of the driver could have rolled the bus through the valley into the deep river gorge.

His own head had started swaying with the circular roads of the hills. Deep within the self, he repented his idea, and started cursing his decision. How had he decided to come to an unknown and unsolicited place indiscreetly without much thought? He wished to jump off the bus somewhere en route the journey in the middle and board the return vehicle, but he had no idea whether any vehicle would be available for his return at all at that time.

The bus had been moving slowly up the hill, its engine had been making a lot of sound. This place was about two hundred kilometers away from his city. In cities, it hardly would have taken four-five hours to cover a distance of two hundred kilometers but the same distance in the mountains could be covered in about seven to eight hours on the circular mountainous routes. At any of the turns, if any passenger would gesture at the bus to stop, the driver would stop it. Unlike in the cities, vehicles are not available in the hills after every short interval. If one bus would leave any place, then one would have to wait for hours for another bus. In such a situation, passengers would not like to leave any bus available at any time. There was a time when an equal number of passengers sat on the rooftop of the bus as those inside it that made Sunil more apprehensive. How will the driver balance the bus? Once the bus would reach safely, he would never try to return home in the hills.

Anyways, who had been left in his house that would have waited for him? Many years ago, his great grandfather had left his ancestral village and had settled in Dehradun searching for greener pastures. As long as his grandfather had been alive, he would sometimes visit the village for marriages, weddings, etc. However, the contact had ended there. When Sunil's father had died, he was only ten years of age. His father had been in a government job and his mother had managed the household expenses with a pension drawn by his father. They had provided education to their two daughters and one son. They had married both the daughters. Other members of his family had also shifted long ago to Dehradun, so they had also never seen their ancestral village. Sunil had known his village was somewhere in Tehri Garhwal. He had not known the name of the village. If he had seen anything in the name of the mountains, it was Mussoorie.

After completing his graduation, when Sunil could not get hold of a job for himself, he had tried his luck as a contractor, as per the advice of some of his friends. He could achieve only a little success. He had worked with a class contractor of PWD. He had been living alone after passing away of his mother last year. He did not wish to live in the city. When he got a contract to build a road in a remote village of Pauri, he had considered it an opportunity to connect with his roots. As a result, he had been sitting in that bus.

If Sunil left Dehradun at eight in the morning he had to change two or three buses to reach his destination by six in the evening. Once he would reach his destination, he would view the vast spread of panoramic scenery and would forget all the fatigue of the long hazardous journey. The milky snow- clad peaks seemed so close that they could be touched. Although it was summer, there was a sensation of mild cold in the winds here.

Sunil spent his first night in a guesthouse in PWD. Harilal, the security guard in PWD, was a very cheerful person. Sunil had heard that Harilal was from a nearby village. Harilal had lost his wife after leaving a toddler baby girl with him. The girl had turned eighteen years.

"If there is a slight delay in reaching home, she will scold me a lot." Harilal had said with a smile. He made a gesture pretending as if his daughter had been standing in front of him.

"For how long will your job be here son?" Harilal had asked Sunil.

"I will be here for a long time, uncle. A road has to be built by me so that vehicles could go on it. It will take a long time to make it."

"You will not be able to stay in this guest house for so long."

"No uncle. I will stay here for just two to four days, and then I will go to the city and bring my luggage. Till then, you can find a room for me here and make arrangements for food and drink somewhere around."

Harilal did exactly as Sunil had asked him to. On returning from home, Sunil realized that Harilal had arranged a room for him in his own house.

"Son, this is a poor man's hut. Stay here. People in this village do not rent out there houses, so I thought we shall manage with you in our house."

From that day onwards, Sunil started living at Harilal's house. There he met Bindiya. She was the daughter of Harilal. She had a round *bindi* on the forehead. She had red cheeks like the red mountain apple. Bindiya would flutter like a carefree mountain waterfall and come to his room. Neither she was shy nor hesitant. She was so guileless that she would consider others also as guileless.

Harilal would have his breakfast in the morning. For his lunch, he would take four *chappatis* with him. As the guesthouse had been situated at the end of the road, the movement of people in it was very low. However, for Harilal, duty had always been a duty.

Sunil would also leave for the site in the morning. While coming from Dehradun, Sunil had brought a lot of juice and biscuits with him. In the morning, Harilal gave him tea filled in a steel glass. Sunil ate two rusks soaked in the tea in the morning and that was his only breakfast.

Although Sunil had brought a stove with him, he did not know how to cook.

Owing to hesitation, he could not tell this to Harilal. He had not eaten properly for two-three days and felt weak and exhausted. Exhausted after a day's long work, Sunil would often hit the cramped cot lying in his room as soon as he had reached home in the evening.

Harilal had given the cot to Sunil. This cot, woven of

coconut ropes, seemed to be more like a cradle and less like a cot.

Just like any other day, Sunil had been lying on his bed that night. During the day, he ate rice and lentils cooked by other laborers at the same site. After three to four days when he had eaten food made at the site for him, he felt full satisfaction. On those days, he had no desire to eat rusks and biscuits.

"If I could get a glass of tea, then I would feel good." He thought lying in the bed.

Bindiya had appeared like an angel beating loudly at the door chain. Sunil had taught her how to beat at the door chain; otherwise, every now and then she would appear like a storm.

"Babuji is asking whether you are cooking." She asked while shaking her skirt pleat with one hand.

"No."

"So what are you eating?" "Nothing."

"Then, how are you alive?" Saying this, her big eyes grew bigger in utter surprise. "If I don't get to eat a meal of cooked lentil and rice in the morning, I would die." When she found that Sunil was quietly listening to her, she continued with her talk.

"My father eats *chappatis* during the day, but I cook lentils and rice for myself in the morning." Sunil listened silently while Bindiya was talking.

"Bindiya ..." Harilal was calling her up.

"Oh! My God! My father is calling. I came here and got involved in the talks." She hit her forehead with a palm. In this attempt, the scarf that she had tied on her head had fallen on the ground. While lifting the scarf from the ground, her two long knotted plaits had almost hit the ground. The red colored floral silken threads attached to the end of the knotted plaits dipped on the floor had covered with mud and dung. Sunil's eyes had rested on the charm of her face exposed it without a scarf.

The issue of Sunil's daily meals had been solved, on that fateful day. His day would usually begin and end with Bindiya.

Every day, before he would leave for the site, Bindiya would place four *chappatis* and vegetables before him.

"What is this?" "*Kalyo* (Breakfast)."

"So much!" Sunil was surprised at the quantity of breakfast.

"Is this heavy? It is not so. Here, people eat like this. Okay, tell me what have you been eating in the morning for the last four or five days?"

"This." Sunil had placed the packet of rusks before her.

"Now you take it." Sunil handed over the packet to Bindiya when he saw her glancing at that packet. He later learned that Bindiya had consumed the entire packet at a single go.

Gradually, Bindiya had become Sunil's habit and his life. One day, he proposed to Bindiya in front of Harilal.

Hearing that, Harilal was so shocked as if he had touched a burning coal.

"Sir, there is so much difference of status between you and me? How is it possible?"

"Why? Are you not human?"

"Sir, that is fine but our caste."

"I don't believe in caste system." Sunil's voice was firm.

"What would the villagers say? How will I stay in the village after this marriage?" Harilal was more worried about what people would say than her daughter's future.

"Don't you like me? Am I not a worthy groom for your daughter?"

"No such thing, son. You deserve so much. My daughter will be very happy with you. But..."

"Then what? Why are you bent on spoiling the happiness of your daughter for the sake of the villagers?"

"What about your family?"

"My parents are not in this world. I have two married sisters. They would not oppose me." Sunil said confidently. In the midst of many doubts and apprehensions, Harilal had finally said yes. After that, Bindiya had undergone a perceptible change. Bindiya who would earlier laugh and giggle at the slightest innuendo had covered herself in a garb of diffidence. She would rarely enter his room whenever Sunil would be around.

She somehow maintained a distance from Sunil. As soon as she came to know about her prospective matrimonial alliance with Sunil, she felt as if she had overnight grown up into a woman. She had witnessed how some of her friends had left the house of their parents after marriage and had gone with an unknown stranger. After their marriage, whenever they would visit their village, they would come back to their parents like a guest.

Does she also have to leave her father? Her father would be left alone. Who would take care of him? Who would cook food for him? Those wandering questions would often haunt her to make her sad.

One day she clarified all her doubts from her father.

"Baba, do I have to leave you alone and go away from you?"

Harilal was shocked a bit and looked at his daughter. He thought perhaps that she was not happy with her marriage. On the other hand, was she just scared of the prospect of leaving her father?

"Where are you going Bindiya? You will be here only."

Harilal had convinced her in a shaking voice.

"Baba, after marriage, all girls leave their village. Savita, Nirmala, Lakshmi and many girls."

"Your husband has to live here and work here, where are you going?"

When his project would be completed, then he would leave, thought Harilal. He felt a lump in his throat, his eyes had been filled with tears and he had bowed his head down to hide his tears.

The questions of his daughter had made Harilal to ponder. Bindiya had been right in her statement. Even Sunil would not stay there forever. After five to six months, his work would be over. Then Bindiya would have to leave and Harilal would be left alone. Thinking about that prospect, his mind shivered. How would he send the part of his soul to a far-off place? He had never been acquainted with the prospective groom. Harilal had believed what he had told him.

All his apprehensions proved to be baseless when Sunil had introduced his two sisters to him on the wedding day.

"Our brother's choice is very good. His choice and his happiness is our happiness. He has never made us feel that we have neither our mother nor our father alive," His elder sister's eyes had become moist while she said that.

Bindiya was married to Sunil in a typical but simple custom of the hills without any show-off. When turmeric was applied on Bindiya's face during *Haldi* ritual, her enchanting beauty had enhanced manifold. Her face shone with a rare aura. When Sunil looked at her, he could not take his eyes off her. The face has shone so much with just a little makeup. Sunil was elated at the mere imagination of Bindiya's beauty when she would come to the city and dress like a city woman.

Shortly after the wedding, all the guests had left and life had returned to normal.

"I am thinking of selling these goats now. Who will take care of them after Bindiya?" Bindiya almost broke down when Harilal had said it.

She thought if she had become an alien to her father that she could not even take care of his four goats. She wanted to say something but Sunil spoke in between.

"What are you talking about? Bindiya will handle the house the same way she used to handle earlier. Now the three of us are a family. Why did you think Bindiya and I are different? What will she do all day long?"

Bindiya appreciated her husband when she heard him speak. She was attached with the goats as much as her heart would beat for them. She had looked after them since they were small lambs. She missed her heartbeat at the mere idea of her goats being sold.

After a month of marriage, Sunil got a job in a big project to build a road in the same area. After securing a job in a major project, Sunil started considering Bindiya as his lucky charm. He thought of increasing his work by staying at the project site.

Seven to eight years passed in no time. Meanwhile, Bindiya had become mother of three children and Sunil had become an A class contractor. Goddess Lakshmi was very kind to him. He had forced Harilal to give up his job. He constructed a *pucca* house of six rooms in place of the *kutcha* house. Children as well as grown-ups would wait by the side of the road when Sunil rode on his bullet to go to his project side and its sound would reverberate all over the hills. Sunil's work was now spread to many places. He had sold his ancestral house in Dehradun to buy land there in the city itself. He wished to build a house for his family to stay in Dehradun so that his children could get the best of education there.

When the house was ready to shift in, Sunil had brought his family to Dehradun. Harilal had refused to come. After spending all his life in the village, his traditional thinking did not allow him to shift with her daughter and stay with her family. Bindiya felt, for the first time, that she was married. She had to renounce her ancestral home, while Harilal too endured the pain of separation from his daughter.

Bindiya had come to the city, a large city. In fact, she had come to Dehradun with her husband earlier, but not for more than two or three days. Then they had stayed in the old residence. The new house was much bigger and more convenient than the old one.

It had taken Bindiya and the children several days to understand the nuances of their new house. Bindiya would often wonder how the water kept in a tank would get heated as soon as she pressed an electric button. Besides, many other things in the city and in their new house had simply seemed wonderful to her. After coming to Dehradun, Bindiya had been occupied with her family and Sunil neck deep into work. Gradually, Sunil had started changing. He had developed the lust for earning more money, for which he was willing to do anything. He would come home late in the night. Sunil had started drinking and would often rebuke Bindiya at everything.

Shortly after coming to the city, Bindiya had noticed that there had been a lot of empty space in front of the house. After putting in a little effort, she had planted some vegetables there. For a long time, Sunil hardly noticed anything. One morning Sunil's attention had shifted to the sprouting seeds when they ripped open through the earth crust and started breathing through the open air.

"What have you sown here?"

"I had brought some vegetable seeds from home. I have sown the seeds right there." Bindiya excitedly told him. She thought that Sunil would be happy, but his face had turned red with anger.

"Oh, you are rustic. Don't you know that vegetables are not sown in front of the house?"

Bindiya was horrified to see the anger on Sunil's face. After all, what had been wrong with that? She could not understand. In the village too, she had been sowing vegetables on the land in front of her house. Then why could she not do it in Dehradun? She could not hold back her tears when Sunil rebuked her for this. She continued to stand there silently with her head bowed down.

Sunil had softened down a little when he saw her in that pitiable condition. He had immediately toned down and gently told her that he had a plan of making a lawn by planting grass there. Most of the houses in cities had been designed with that objective.

Bindiya could not understand how grass could be better than the vegetables. She could not dare ask him anything.

From that day onwards, Bindiya had stopped taking initiative of any work on her own. Even if she had to shift the chair from one corner to another, she would ask Sunil, which made him more annoyed and he would quarrel with her more. The constant recurrence of such incidences would make Bindiya misty-eyed. Life had been going on in that manner.

As Sunil's work kept progressing, the number of his friends also increased in proportion. Every day, there would be parties at home. Alcohol would be served to the guests and intoxicated guests would create a lot of ruckus. Bindiya had decided to keep quiet and hold her tongue, as her children were growing up. Had she opposed him, he would have called her uncivilized and ignorant. "This is what happens in business. What do you know how hard you have to work to earn money? I am doing everything for you and the children," Sunil would say it very often.

Bindiya never understood how throwing a liquor party to friends earned him money.

Children were growing up, so was the daily influx of money into the house. Sunil had bought land at many places. The increase in money and amenities had increased Bindiya's suffocation in the same proportion. She had increasingly felt that her husband was not with her anymore and that she had lost him. Sunil would enter home drunk late in the evening. Although Bindiya had protested a couple of times in the beginning, she could gain nothing out of it except abuses and physical assaults. Bindiya thought it appropriate to keep quiet thinking that otherwise their quarrel would have an adverse effect on the children. She was left with no hope of happiness in her life. She had a big house, and all the luxurious amenities, but Bindiya longed for the freedom of the village. She had been extremely cheerful there. Bindiya and Sunil had been so much in love with each other then and so were the children. In Dehradun, Bindiya felt like a caged bird in a golden cage. In the village, she would roam freely like a mountain deer but she felt imprisoned in the city. She would have been happy even in the confines of her home prison but what about her husband! She wished to get his support.

Time was passing by. Day by day, Bindiya had been reduced to the structure of bones. Sunil was busy with his work and his elder daughter had started going to the college. The younger daughter and son were in twelfth and tenth respectively. The daughters had been more attached to the mother. Seeing their mother's wretched condition, they would feel like gnashing their teeth at their father. They would bring all kinds of clothes, jewelry, food and drink for their mother, but Bindiya had been, by now, devoid of all enthusiasm for clothes and accessories and had lost her appetite for food. Sometimes, she would possess a strong desperation to end her life. For the sake of her daughters, she could not garner enough courage to commit suicide. She was not much worried about her son. Her son possessed sharp intellect and abhorred his father's habits.

Some more time had passed. Within four and five years, Sunil married off both his daughters. The day their younger daughter got married, Bindiya felt free from all her responsibilities. By then, her son had been off to the most prestigious engineering college.

Sunil had wished that his son complete his engineering degree with distinction in civil, so that he would later help him, but his son rejected his suggestion and did his engineering in information technology. Sunil had been furious with his son ever since then and had been shocked at his disobedience, but then, he again got busy in his life.

Bindiya had been left with nothing exciting in her life. Their daughters had gone to their respective homes. Their son had also shifted to another city for further studies. The husband and the wife were left in the house and throughout the day, she would see her husband for the namesake. By the time he would come home and meet her, he would be so much inebriated that he would lose all his senses.

The presence of daughters at home would earlier prevent Sunil not to bring his friends home for the drink party, but after their marriage, frequent drink parties had become a routine feature. Until late at night, congregation of Sunil's friends had continued to make a ruckus in the house and they would demand different mouth-watering delicacies. They would ask for fried dumplings, chicken and sometimes mutton. Even after providing all the food items to them, Sunil would still rebuke her. He would use the words like uncivilized and illiterate for Bindiya and would scold her in front of his friends, while they would unscrupulously laugh at it.

"Why don't you die? I will be free from your rustic presence, while you too would be liberated." Sunil blurted out one day in a state of inebriation, while Bindiya had felt the pain of being dejected and wept bitterly. At the same time, she also liked his comments. What was the purpose of her being alive? She had been a burden on her husband, and one day, when her husband had left, she consumed poison.

After a little turbulence, everything had become quiet. Bindiya had felt liberated, flying like the clouds in sky and felt that Sunil had reappeared before her much like the old lover-boy before they had married. Bindiya was elated and her body trembled with ecstatic emotions. After all, she was entering her old world with a cheer. Everything was quiet and serene.

Sunil returned late in the evening and was shocked to see his house in the grip of pitch darkness. His house appeared ghostly that evening. He knocked at the door but could not get any response from inside. It was almost 11 P.M. The entire surroundings seemed clueless.

Sunil thought Bindiya might have already gone to sleep that infuriated him and left the house in anger. He spent that night with a friend. In the morning, he had started walking towards his house. The nagging hangover of the previous evening had still hovered on his head. He tried to break open the door and went inside.

Seeing the inside view, all his hangover dissipated into

thin air. He found Bindiya's lifeless body lying on the floor. The mouth oozed lather, which had dried up and had left a white streak from the corner of Bindiya's lips.

Sunil got scared when he saw Bindiya's condition. Within a short time, people from neighborhood had gathered there and someone from there had reported the matter to the police. After sometime, the police team had also reached there. Sunil had good acquaintance with some of the police officers neither Bindiya had blamed anyone for her death either.

"Papa, you have killed my mother. Now, I do not have any desire to come home," said his son to Sunil that had shocked Sunil. He looked towards his daughters for support but they also turned their backs towards him in utter disgust.

What has happened to the children? What had he not done for them? He had provided them with good education, good lifestyle, had never let them feel short of anything. What did he achieve by all this? Sunil could effortlessly puzzle out the hatred of their children, the ocular expression of hatred in their eyes that he could not tolerate. At that moment, he felt as if his three children had been the most ungrateful species upon earth. It would have been better had he left them in the village to grow up into boorish characters.

The memories of how he recklessly treated Bindiya had been disturbing to him. What happiness could he give to her after they had come to the city? He had become quarrelsome and abusive to her. His humiliating and abusive nature had made Bindiya to end her life prematurely. The flood of memories was too much for him to handle and that would easily make him upset.

The daughters went back to their homes and got busy. Sunil was completely left alone in the house. The four walls of the empty house were frightening for him. His house ceased to be a home anymore and appeared like a haunted one.

Sunil had taken refuge from the hollowness of his existence in drinks. He had been left with none, who could have stopped him from drinking. In his arrogance and misconception that he had a lot of wealth, he lost everything including his wife and children. Even his friends deserted him after looting his wealth and money.

His son straightaway refused to carry on his work and did a job instead.

To help him in his old age when he lost his health and money and all friends too, he kept a boy at the house, who would cook also for him. Sunil, sometimes in his sleep, would be of the opinion that it was he, who had killed his wife.

People from his neighborhood would say that Sunil was unable to bear the pain of his loneliness. The wife's sudden death had driven him insane.

□

# 11
# Ramkali

Ramkali took a deep breath when she stood in the long queue in the big hospital. A small hospital in her village was far better than the big one in the city. There was at least no crowd in that hospital. It is a different matter that visits of the doctor were rare in that village hospital. For the treatment of any illness of the villagers, the compounder, who was appointed there, would do the job. More than eulogizing the doctors, the village people considered the compounder their God.

However, the compounder, who at other moments was like a God, would simply apologize at his incompetency to treat when a disease appeared beyond his capacity. "Now when the doctor will come, only will he be able to tell you what has happened," the compounder would say helplessly. "Is he a bigger doctor than you? You are the big doctor for us." The innocent people usually would not understand why they were saying that. For days, the doctor would not visit the village, in that condition, the compounder would direct them to the big hospital in the city.

He did the same with Ramkali. Ramkali did not understand what ailment she suffered from and since it was a serious one, he had recommended her to the city hospital.

"I am recommending you to the doctor in the city. Take this paper and go to him. He will do a thorough medical check-up."

Ramkali was overwhelmed. The doctor had taken good care of her despite the fact that she was an ordinary person and a wife of a truck driver.

Ramkali lost both her parents to an epidemic outbreak in her village, when she was barely five years old and her younger brother was only two.

Because of the societal pressures and expectations, their father's younger brother and his wife had raised Ramkali and her younger brother. However, Ramkali's brother could not bear the separation from his parents and after a year, he too had passed away. Ramkali was left with no one whom she could take into consideration as her own.

When she was fifteen years old, her uncle and aunt wished to get rid of her responsibility and married her off. Her husband Sumeru was a truck driver. He too had no relatives, so he could not get any marriage proposal until the time he had turned thirty. He often remained out of the house because of his profession. When someone told Ramakali's uncle about Sumeru, he immediately agreed for matrimonial alliance of Ramkali with him.

When marriage of Ramkali and Sumeru took place, her uncle took lot of money from Sumeru, as compensation for raising Ramkali agreeing for her marriage with Sumeru. Sumeru, at that moment, was more concerned about settling into matrimony and he, in that case, accepted every precondition set by Ramkali's uncle.

Fifteen-year-old Ramkali did not understand the significance of husband and in-laws. She, however, knew the household chores well and was in a habit of working.

Since he had been alone, without any commitment and

had earned a lot of money, Sumeru hardly paid attention to his house. Whatever he had earned was extravagantly spent on food and drinks. Ramkali, after her arrival had transformed Sumeru's dilapidated hut and hadmade it hygienic. After marriage, Sumeru had stayed at home for fifteen days, and Ramkali, who had been aspiring for love and affection since her childhood, found the love of her life and had enjoyed her marital bliss.

After one year of marriage, Ramkali gave birth to a child when she was sixteen. Sumeru was elated, rather highly excited. His life has been organized after he had a wife and a child of his own. Sumeru looked for opportunities to stay at home. Sometimes, the profession of being a truck driver would irritate him a lot. He would take his truck from one city to another and that would sometimes keep him away from home for months. Sumeru would feel overjoyed when on rare occasions he got an order to deliver goods to the places closer to his village.

At other times, he wondered why he had got married in the first place! Life before had been good. He could go and stay wherever he sought after. Nobody will disturb you and ask any questions. A person with a professional commitment like him should not get married.

Ramkali could reveal his pregnancy to him only after the second trimester had been over. Until then, Ramkali had alone encountered the changes that occurred within her during those early six months. At times, she would be lying listless, oblivious of her surroundings when she would feel like neither eating nor working. When the elderly women of the village looked at her, they understood her condition and caringly explained it to her. It was then that Ramkali realized what had happened to her. She was filled with excitement when she fondly remembered her husband.

How and when would she disclose the good news of her pregnancy to him? When would she eagerly proclaim her pregnancy to her husband? Sumeru had not been around but when he arrived, she had lost her enthusiasm.

Ramkali panicked as the date of her delivery was approaching near.

"Can't you stay here for a few more days?" She had nervously requested Sumeru.

"For some days, means how many days?" "Till the time the child is born."

"There is still some time left. What has the midwife told you?"

"Any time after fifteen days."

"Fifteen days! Are you crazy? How can I stay here for so many days? The owner has asked us to go after two days to Kolkata with the goods."

Sumeru could not stop even though he wished to and returned when his child had already turned one month old.

As time passed, Ramkali had become used to Sumeru's erratic professional commitments. For Sumeru who was by now a family person, staying away from home was no less than a punishment. The forced separation from family, especially Ramkali had made him go astray. He would visit the roadside eating joints on the never-ending long highways. There had been many more things available in these joints apart from food and drink.

A few more years had elapsed without any obvious changes in their life cycle. Ramkali had been by now the mother of two children and had reconciled with her life. However, for the last few days, Ramkali had been noticing that Sumeru had been physically fading out.

The sanguine face of handsome young Sumeru had started turning pale, the obvious radiance of his visage had been disappearing. Even after the hard day labor as a truck driver, the happy-go-lucky Sumeru had been careful about what he ate and drank. Hence, there was never any adverse effect on his health. Could it be possible that he could not take care of himself? Was it simply because he could not maintain his expenses as he was spending a large portion of his earnings at home? Or, was it something else?

When had Sumeru visited home the last time, he had been suffering from high fever and could not eat anything because he suffered an intense pain in his throat. Owing to his constant fever, his precious ten days of his work had been wasted. Although he had temporarily recovered with medication given by the village compounder, but his weakness persisted for a long time.

At that time, Ramkali had realized the upsurge of new life within her. Owing to the propagation of government health schemes, rural women had been taking adequate care and enough precautions of pregnant women during their pregnancy. With this all-round awareness, Ramkali would often visit health center two or three times for her calcium and iron tablets. She was completely healthy but when Sumeru had come lately, his condition had deteriorated. His pitched cheeks, sunken eyes, persistent mild fever, sore throat and then, a few days later, a rash had emerged on his body upsetting Ramkali. What had happened to her husband? Immediately she took him to the village hospital. When the compounder saw Sumeru, even he could not diagnose his ailment immediately.

"Sumeru, you go to the big hospital. They will test your blood. Only then will we know what has happened to you?"

"But Doctor, personally check him and see how much fever does he have. His entire body is burning. Just see those blisters on his body."

Even then, while conducting his clinical examination, the compounder desisted from coming into physical contact with Sumeru. Ramakali, on the other hand, detested compounder's expression of disgust. Ramkali and Sumeru had returned with some colorful tablets and medical tincture. While they were leaving the hospital, the compounder had counseled them to consult bigger hospital for better treatment.

After taking the medicine for three to four days, Sumeru's condition improved a bit. Ramkali reminded him to visit a big hospital for a blood test.

"This time I would be going to Delhi with goods. I will get myself examined in the big hospital right there." Sumeru went away, but he could not get free time for months together.

In the meanwhile, when Ramkali went to the hospital for her medicines, the compounder asked her to visit for her treatment to a big hospital situated in the town at a short distance away from her village.

"Take all your old slips and take a letter of reference from me. It would be easy."

"But what is the matter, Doctor, and why I have been referred to a big hospital. Everything appears fine."

"Are you a doctor or me? I have a feeling that something is wrong, so I am asking you. Consult a doctor and get yourself tested further. Yes, did you receive any news of Sumeru? How is he now?"

"No, no news."

Following the advice of his doctor, Ramkali visited a big hospital in the town that had been about fifteen kms away from the village. The old jalopy buses had been plying on the road. Most people in those buses traveled with their foot on the footstep, while others sat on steps on the rear door. Those buses would be mostly full to capacity from inside. She had breathed a sigh of relief when a young man had vacated the seat for Ramkali. She had been in the eighth month of her pregnancy.

When she reached the city hospital, she was horrified to see the crowd in the hospital. She felt better when she saw a woman from her village that had been to this hospital earlier and had been familiar with its functioning.

Ramkali got her outpatient slip and deposited it in the doctor's room, for calling out her name at her turn.

"When your name will be called out from inside, only then can you go inside," the woman who had accompanied her had said in an authoritative tone.

Two benches had been placed outside the doctor's room, but the patients had occupied both. Some patients who could not get any place to sit had been standing; others had been walking, while those, who had no physical strength or had been too weak, sat on the verandah floor. Ramkali had been sitting in once corner of the verandah, while she awaited her turn.

Many people had been shuttling in and out of the doctor's cabin, but Ramkali patiently waited for her turn. She could see that some out patients who had just entered the hospital had gone directly inside the doctor's cabin, while there had been others in the corridor who had been waiting since morning, still they had been kept waiting. There had been a lot of clamor about the obvious discrimination in the doctor's call. While waiting for their turn, people would lose patience, burst into accusations, verbal spat before everything would be peaceable again.

Ramkali's name had been called after almost one and a half hours. She produced her old medical slips before the doctor as soon as she went inside the doctor's room.

"What's wrong?" The doctor asked.

"I do not have any problem, the doctor in the village said that I must consult a doctor in the city. And yes, he has also given a reference letter addressed to you." Saying that, Ramkali opened the knot at one corner of her *'dhoti'*, took out a folded paper, and handed it over to the doctor. The doctor read it and then looked at Ramkali. She could observe her changing facial expressions.

"What work does your husband do?"

"He is a truck driver."

"Is he sick?"

Whatever Ramkali knew, she had told the doctor. She could not understand why the doctor had been asking more about her husband when she had come to the doctor for her medical examination.

"You have to get your blood examined. We will take your blood sample and will send it to another city for further investigation. It will take fifteen or twenty days for the report to come. Send someone here with this slip to get the report."

Ramkali returned after giving samples of her blood. She was surprised that she probably had been suffering from a disease, and its investigation could be possible done only in the city.

When she had reached home, a new problem had been waiting for Ramkali. Sumeru's friend, who was also a truck driver like him, passed by from his village and delivered a message to Ramkali. Sumeru had been seriously ill for fifteen days and had been hospitalized.

"What has happened to him?"

"The doctor has told me about a bad disease. I do not even remember the name of the disease properly." He had become sad. What should Ramkali do now? Take care of the children, handle her affairs to the other people in the village or go to the city to take care of the husband. Even if she would have gone to the city, she could not understand where to go and to whom. Then she thought about her children and her own condition. Tears of helplessness had come rolling down from her eyes. She remembered what the doctor had said when Sumeru had come home. He had then asked Ramkali to get Sumeru examined by a doctor in a big city hospital.

"Brother, you please take care of him. You people are a big support. Once he gets home after complete treatment, I will not let him go again," Ramkali wiped her tears from the ends of her *dhoti*.

Sumeru could never come back. After a month, the family received the news of his death. He was suffering from a very bad disease. When the news of his death had reached the village, many people had started gossiping about it.

"I came to know that Sumeru was suffering from a contagious disease."

"Yes and this disease do not affect to morally upright people."

"What does that mean? Which types of people are infected by this disease?"

"Those who visit bad women."

Similar gossips had been doing round everywhere among women too, who would abruptly stop when Ramkali would reach the village well for fetching water.

Looking at Ramkali, everyone would pick up their pitchers to leave that place in a hurry.

Ramkali could not grasp the disease Sumeru had suffered from and the reason for them to avoid her.

Whether Ramkali understood anything or not, the circumstances had been becoming odd for her.

The news that Sumeru suffered from AIDS and died of it had been spreading like fire in the entire village and surrounding areas and Ramkali could be a probable victim of that disease.

Illiterate, uneducated villagers maintained safe distance from Ramkali. In those unprecedented situations, Ramkali had not remembered that she too had given her blood sample for the test.

She had forgotten about it, but one day, all of a sudden, it struck the village hospital compounder to collect the blood test report the day he went to a big hospital in the town for some official work. Ramkali's condition had deteriorated by then.

As the sun started to set in the evening, Ramkali's labor pains went up. Groaning Ramkali started walking towards the hospital.

The compounder was shocked to receive Ramkali's blood report. "What is this! Has her husband given her his own disease? Even she is HIV positive." Nobody knew how her child was?

The compounder reached the village hospital at that moment to discover Ramkali shrouded in utter pain piled up in one corner of the verandah of the hospital.

Her face had turned pale with acute pain. The compounder had been utterly confused with the report of Ramkali fluttering in his hand.

"Can somebody ask her to leave the compound? She is walking freely around with a deadly disease." Listening to his voice, the rest of the hospital staff had also come there. They had forced Ramkali out of the hospital premises. The truth was that everyone had been cautious and had taken utmost care that she did not touch them. Ramkali had come on the road in that precarious condition.

It was a night of thickening darkness for the helpless woman, who, in the dead of the night, had given birth to a dead child in absence of the medical care. A large hoarding of the Health Department erected outside the hospital appeared in stark "AIDS does not spread by touching. HIV-infected people need your support."

Ramkali's illiteracy had become a bane for her at that moment. Had she been able to read what had been written, her pain had become more acute than the labor pain, what she had been going through.

It was a pity that even the educated hospital staff did not understand its real cause, remedy and precautions and had abandoned Ramkali to her fate.

□

# 12

# Juhi

Juhi had been crushed. Juhi had been suppressed. There had been hundreds of wounds all over her mind and body. It had appeared as if spiky cactuses had grown all over her, and she was intermittently, injured by its thorns.

Juhi, who had suffered that day, had been the happiest person until the previous day, just like the excited flowering buds of Jasmine. The buds of Jasmine had blossomed. Similarly, Juhi had blossomed into a flower with the sheer freshness of its smell tossing delight all around. It was the most beautiful flower with a unique combination of freshness and joy.

Juhi was born in a very poor family and oozed with loads of beauty since her childhood. When she was a child, she looked like a doll with her pink lips, black and big eyes and sharp nose. Her father used to work as a laborer with a trader and lived in one of the huts in the illegal slums in one corner of the city. He had come from the border region of Bengal in search of work to a far away in a city in Punjab. When he had got married, he brought his wife to the city.

They soon became parents of a daughter barely after one year of marriage. They had named her Juhi. Although neither of the two had literally known the meaning of the word, still they had named their beautiful daughter Juhi after the name of the female protagonist of a hit film that had released in those days.

By the time Juhi was six, she had three more siblings. It had been becoming very difficult for them to meet the family expenses from the meager earnings of her father. Despite that, he had sent Juhi to school. When the six-year-old Juhi had gone to school on the first day, the parents' chest had swelled with pride. Neither of them had ever been to the school.

Juhi was not only possessor of a radiant physical beauty, but had also been razor-sharp intelligent. When she returned home from school, she would never get a chance of studying at home. Juhi would take care of her siblings so that her mother could handle household chores. Even then, Juhi would come first in class. Her parents apparently had nothing to do with her studies, in spite of that; Juhi had carved a niche for herself in the hearts of her teachers.

By the time Juhi had reached the fourth grade, her two younger brothers had also entered the school. Her mother would be at home with her younger sister. Her parents were illiterate but they wanted their children to get proper education. In order to fulfill their dream, they had started working hard. Her father would work overtime for extra income until late at night and mother had started working in some houses. When her three children would go to school, her mother would take the younger daughter in her lap and go to work. Juhi had passed fifth standard. Both her younger brothers had been studying in fourth and second standard respectively. However, how would Juhi study further? Her younger sister, too, had been coming of age and had started going to school. Her parents had loads of expectations for their daughter Juhi, who possessed the potential to learn and had been virtuous, but they could not afford to continue her education.

However, they often thought that their daughter would study well and would secure a reputed job somewhere. They had envisioned a dream that one day a beautiful prince would drop in and would take her with him to a fascinating world. However, their dream had shattered.

Juhi's aspiration of studying had got a new push when she had secured scholarship in her school and a teacher had abetted her in her pursuit.

Juhi had reached Intermediate school, which had been meant for providing education to girls. There she had seen a new horizon for the fulfillment of her aspirations. The onward journey had been much tougher than expected. Her parents had somehow managed the expenditure of the school education of their four children. Both of them labored hard day and night so that the future of their children could be secured. On seeing her parents' sacrifice and hard work, Juhi would become upset. However, Juhi had decided to help her parents. After completing her eighth grades, she had taken up home tuitions of some children at her home in the evening. Even then, she could not help much. In the slum area, where she lived, how could the people afford for their children's tuition fees when they failed to arrange enough to either eat or cover them?

"Mother, I will also go to work with you in the evening." In desperation, she had confided her pain in her mother one day. Her mother had been shocked at what her daughter had said.

Her eyes had filled up with tears at the sheer imagination of her daughter washing dishes, or sweeping floors in the houses of others. As Juhi had turned fourteen, her beauty had been radiating like a precious stone with her growing age. While gazing at her innocent face, her mother would pulsate with her unknown apprehensions. Would she work in somebody's house? She had not been sure whose evil eye had swallowed her up. She had been working in many homes for many years; she could barely protect her reputation from the covetous gaze of men. Would their innocent daughter Juhi be able to save herself? Her apprehension and her fallacies had given her goose bumps. She had hooked Juhi close to her chest. She wanted to protect her and cocoon her in her motherly warmth but Juhi had become taller than the safe haven of her lap. Her efforts had seemed wasted.

"As long as our hands and feet are moving, you don't need to do anything." That is all she could say.

However, their hands and feet, their physical strength could not remain integral for long. One day, while loading heavy goods into their tempo, the tempo had toppled on Juhi's father. Although, he had survived, however, due to lack of timely medical help, he had gradually started losing the strength of both his legs. At that time, Juhi had been a student of tenth grade. Juhi's father had become bed-ridden augmenting the grouchiness of her mother. She would knock down, verbally abuse and would use foul language against their children on trivial matters had become a daily practice.

Juhi had understood that she had enough of education and had decided to look for some work instead. She had somehow appeared for her high school exams and had desperately started looking for some work.

Nirmala had been Juhi's classmate in the school. Although, Nirmala's family was not as poor as Juhi's family, the monetary situation of her family had not been very good either. One of Nirmala's acquaintances had been

Nimmo Aunty who had employed girls in her house for making of pickles, papad, and dried lentil dumplings, etc. that she could sell later in the market. Some girls had been employed for sewing work as well. These girls in return for their work would receive respectable remuneration in accordance with their performance.

"You take me along to her. I badly need to work." Juhi had held Nirmala's hand to assort well with her.

"Mother, I will do the job." Juhi had told her mother all her conversations that had taken place with Nirmala.

Her mother had neither argued to further her offer, nor possessed any options. Her husband had been handicapped and had taken to bed. Their three children had been on the verge of missing school and their elder daughter had been idly sitting at home after passing her tenth grade.

It had not been long ago when she had wished to protect Juhi from the prying eyes of the people. They had been making all efforts to protect their precious, diamond-like daughter from bad omen. However, the situation had not been under their control anymore. Her parents had given their approval for her to work and had derived big satisfaction that their daughter had secured a job for herself with a woman.

Juhi started going to Nimmo aunt's house. Many girls had been coming to work there, but amongst all, Juhi came from the family background that had the worst economic condition.

After the completion of the month, Aunt Nimmo held out three notes of five hundred each and gave them to Juhi.

Juhi would sometimes stare at those notes and sometimes towards Aunty. She had clenched the notes tightly in her fist. Juhi had grown up amidst acute poverty, and had remained bereft of basic amenities. She had never seen so many currency notes worth their value all together but then she had earned them with her hard work.

For the fear of spoiling her currency notes, she had handled them carefully, had tied them to her handkerchief for fear of spoiling them with anxious perspiring hands.

On her way back home, she had remained extra cautious and had conscientiously surveyed all the people sauntering around her for fear of sneaking thieves. She experienced strangeness in her state of mind with mixed expressions of happiness and apprehensions that she had undergone.

She had taken great care while reaching home and had unfastened her handkerchief's knot to deposit her first income in her mother's hand. Her handicapped father would be reclining in one corner of the small house of one room. Their eyes would well up with tears when they comprehended their daughter's intelligence. Juhi had been the same daughter for whom they had possessed splendid ambitions, had desired to provide her with the best education. Their destiny had a number of other plans and Juhi had to set off for her work at a young age. However, Juhi's happiness could not last long. She had thought that when she would start earning, there would be happiness and peace in the house, and with extra income, she would provide proper education to her younger siblings. She herself could not study beyond her tenth standard. The discontinuity with her education had literally smashed her dreams. She had pledged to herself that she would not allow it to happen with her siblings.

Like every other unfulfilled dream, their dream too had remained just a dream. Her meager earning of bare fifteen hundred rupees had proved to be much less than what had been needed. Her siblings had dropped out of their school. Her brothers would play with the children of the slums all day and the younger sister would share their mother's labors with her household chores. Throughout the day, her father would rebuke her, slap her on the wrist, and her mother would hurl verbal abuses.

Juhi had been working. Had she been happy? Gradually, Juhi started withering. The continual mental stress had its direct toll on her work. Everyone felt it including her Nimmo aunty. "What's the matter, Juhi? You are generally sad now days. I have noticed that you are not wholeheartedly engrossed in your work," inquired Nimmo aunt one day at the most opportune moment in time.

How could she spill the beans about her family matters to the outsiders? Hesitant Juhi contemplated within. Her Nimmo aunt had been precociously intelligent and clever. She forced her to speak the truth. She had been au fait with Juhi requirement for more money, so that she could bring her dream of providing her siblings education and making them independent to fruition.

Juhi had sought more work as well but it had all been in vain. The fate of her family and her had been destined to remain unchanged.

Customers would visit Nimmo aunt's house for the goods prepared and packed there. Aunt Nimmo, often in an impulse, would take a crack at her consumers to seek out monetary help for Juhi. Although, she would be hesitant to part with an assiduously hardworking and honest girl like Juhi, but her misery had been too big for Nimmo aunt to put up with and endure.

Sumit, a young handsome youth of thirty-two years, had been one of Aunt Nimmo's consumers. He had good business and possessed good connections. Sumit enjoyed a social viability and great reputation among who's-who of the city and often helped the people with their businesses.

"Son, can you please help her. She is very disturbed." Aunt Nimmo thought it appropriate to talk to Sumit. He carefully observed Juhi whereas, she, in compliance with his gaze, instantaneously looked down.

"Till which class has you studied?"

"Tenth."

"Do you know how to do the typing work?"

"No." Juhi nodded her head in negation.

Although Sumit resounded with assurance to lend a helping hand, for Juhi there had been hardly any ray of hope in his words.

Sumit arrived almost after two months. He told her about the job opportunity, available job vacancy and an interview with the strong possibility. He took her along with him.

The first interview failure had been followed by a succession of interviews lined up one after the other. Whichever office she would visit, they would make inquiries about her computer knowledge. Few more months had passed while rushing from one office to another in search of a job. The monetary condition of the house had been deteriorating fast, whereas Sumit had been proportionately getting more sympathetic towards Juhi. He would sometimes extend her financial help from his own pocket. Although, Juhi would not appreciate such kind of favors, but the picture of her sick father's slackened face and her idle and listlessly wandering brothers would impede her from resisting any act of kindness extended towards her.

"You do one thing. Come to my office and learn computers, once you are free from Aunt's work", Sumit had suggested when Juhi did not get a job even after several interviews.

Juhi was hesitant and had felt nervous. Sumit been acquainted with Juhi's financial condition and that it would not have allowed her to visit small institutes to learn computers and type on it. Should Juhi accept his proposal? Once again, the image of a listless father laying on the bed, the half-naked brothers running aimlessly in the streets of the slum and a sister who had been the victim of the mother's wrath without any reason, passed through her eyes like a slide. In such distressing financial condition, accepting Sumit's suggestion had been the only sensible option available to her.

The next day's morning sunrise, the new break of day had filled her with renewed energy and had brought a ray of hope, a likelihood and possibility for Juhi. From the next day onwards, she had started going to Sumit's office for her evening computer practices. Sumit had an office in just a small room, conveniently partitioned from the middle of the room into two. Sumit had occupied a small cabin for himself while his two employees huddled in another slightly bigger cabin. Juhi would leave her Aunt's office at around four in the evening and would reach Sumit's office, walking a distance of fifteen to twenty minutes crossing through the narrow streets of the city. Sumit had assigned a job to a boy from his office to impart the computer knowledge to Juhi. Whenever Sumit had a chance, he would personally monitor her progress.

Juhi had been happy, rather exceedingly contented. While moving her fingers on the keyboard, she could feel the rhythm and the supple softness of the velvet. Watching the letter tumbling out on the computer screen whenever she would press it on the keyboard had been similar to watching a beautiful drama on the silver screen in awe and wonder. With the twinkling of the eye, she would be filled with reverence for Sumit. For her, Sumit had been no less than the manifestation of the divine *Avatar* of the God.

Two months had passed. Juhi had become familiar with the hang of both Hindi and English typing.

"I would have retained you in my office but I already have employed two people. It is not right to expel any of them." Two days later, Sumit opened up about his further assistance, while informing her about her forthcoming interview.

Juhi had been filled with gratitude towards Sumit. Whatever he had done for her had been no less. After everything, he himself had made an effort to procure a job for her.

On the day of her interview, Juhi had been excited since morning. It had been her first job interview ever since she had learnt to operate computers. She had been expecting a proposal of a monthly salary of no less than four to five thousand. Would she succeed? She prayed to God, had prayed that she could succeed, so that she could afford treatment for her handicapped father, her younger siblings could go to school and her small house could once again become heaven for the entire family.

She pulled out her best suit, which she had very diligently folded and kept under the pillow for hard press, and got ready with baited breath. Once again, she bowed down in ritualistic obeisance in front of the picture of God and stepped out of the house with great confidence.

She had barely walked a few steps outside her house when she saw two cats had emerged in front of her and had started fighting and muttering. Juhi backed up in pulsating apprehension. Although, she had never been superstitious and had never suffered from the impending omen, but the sound of the roaring cats had left her with a pounding heartbeat. She had felt at that moment that those two cats would pounce on her. Her legs started trembling her heart was shocked. She could breathe a sigh of relief only when the cats had run away a little farther from her. She started walking towards her destination.

As soon as she stepped out of her slum, Sumit had been waiting for her in his car.

"You look good." Sumit had said, while courteously opening the car door for her.

Juhi had shared a smile with him while sitting in the car. The car had started racing through the streets of the city. After some time, Juhi had felt as if the car had been racing out of the city. Tall flats and office buildings had been left behind somewhere. She eyeballed Sumit from the corner of her eyes to review his intention. He appeared super elated, occupied in his thoughts hummed the famous lines of a film song.

"This office is a little far away." She felt in her bones whether Sumit had read her mind.

After a while, their vehicle had entered a huge green compound with many small buildings within. Juhi felt a bit strange for she had not known anything beyond Sumit's office.

Sumit brought her to a room, a room that could be anything but not an office, even Juhi possessed the sagacity that something had not been viable in that room. The room had two chairs and a table huddled at one corner and a big bed in the middle.

He seized terrified Juhi by her shoulders and pushed her down on the chair and everything that happened after that had been nothing short of a nightmare for her. Juhi's dream of making it big came crashing down. She had been left with some currency notes in her fist. Sumit had been muttering something to her, but she could decipher only a few words spoken by her, while some had been incomprehensible to her. Even during the day, he had said something incomprehensible to her. The words spoken at both the moments had muddled and jumbled up within her psyche mentally confusing her. Why should Juhi trust Sumit?

"I like you very much. Since the day I have seen your hard work, your honesty and truth, I have loved it. I have loved the feeling of doing something for your family, for your home."

Listless Juhi could partially hear his words and nothing more than that. She had been lost in thoughts why he had committed this gross sin with her? Why would someone mess with the person whom one feels secure with?

"You looked very beautiful today. I could not stop myself. Whatever punishment you wish to give is acceptable to me." Sumit bowed down his head.

There was obsessive silence in the room for some time. Sumit's head appeared tilted in shame for the crime that he had committed, while Juhi's head was bent down in disgust of the crime he had committed on her.

"You get ready. Let's go for the interview now. "

Juhi entered inside the bathroom. She opened the tap and wept bitterly with the sound of the flowing water. She stayed inside the shower for a long time, and desperately tried to run the dirt down her body along with water. Surprisingly, Sumit was not inside the room when she stepped out of the shower. After a while, the door of the room opened but the person who stepped inside the room was not Sumit.

After two or three hours when she stepped out of that

house with Sumit, she had by now discovered his new face and a new aspect of his character.

"What can you do? What is your status? Are you very educated? Those with postgraduate degrees are stumbling for jobs. In comparison to them, you are just nothing. What are you, just high school pass? Still, you have guts to dream big. You wish to get the best treatment for your father, educate your brothers and sisters. What do you think? You will fulfill your dream with fifteen hundred rupees that you get from Aunty?"

Open your fist and see how much money you have in your hand. This is your one-day's earnings. Calculate how much you can earn in a month when you have earned so much in one day. All the sins of your family will be washed away. Otherwise, you and your family will rot in the gutter like insects and pests."

The emotions on Juhi's face kept emerging and receding. Few moments before, Sumit had sneaked some rupees in her hand. Were those currency notes the value of her body? Sumit had used her for carnal pleasures and...?

Disgusting! She felt nauseatingly disgusting. However, what had been that greed that had not let her loosen her grip. He stared at Sumit with her fiery eyes.

"Why are you looking like this? See, you will get nothing by being emotional. You are beautiful, and young. You have this ability. Take advantage of it. Erase the poverty of your family."

"How much money would it be?" Juhi thought.

An eagerness had aroused in her mind to quietly open the fist, to know the total amount of money she had at the moment. She could guess they were the currency notes of five hundred each. For the last several months Juhi had been taking three notes of five hundred each from aunty.

She was aware of its thickness. The thickness of the notes that she held in her fist at that moment had been much more than that.

What would be the total amount? Would it be two thousand, two and a half thousand, yes maybe, only this much. If it had been two and a half thousand in a day, then how many would it be in a month? The calculation had been far ahead of her imagination that she could never even had it in a dream.

Her father could have been treated with that amount, her mother could get rid of the job of a house sweeper and her three siblings could go to school. They could have moved out of the house and could have shifted to a *pucca* house elsewhere. They could have led a life like that of a respectful man.

What about her own honor? What about that? One day, her parents, siblings would have found out where that money had been coming from. Could she face them that day? Could she tell them that to remove them from the swamp of dirt, she herself had been trapped in the mud?

Juhi felt the emotional quiver. Like a clever player, Sumit had been trying to read her expressions. He was aware of the condition of Juhi's house and the state of her mind. Like a clever fowler, he had been watching the bird fluttering in his trap. It was regardless of how many birds had he trapped in his net and had calmed them down. In comparison to those, she was a zilch.

"Don't think too much about it. Just think now that your family's condition is improving because of you. You are doing such a sacramental job of saving the lives of five people in your house."

What, sacramental! Juhi liked this word. She could not decipher the difference between the definition of sins and virtues, but what she could understand was that she was saving five lives by sacrificing her everything.

"You are doing this work in compulsion, but these girls from big families; they do this for their comfort. You would not feel it is a sin, while doing this. Many poor girls like you are helping their parents in this way. A lot of girls are coming to Nimmo aunt too..."

"Nimmo aunt!" Juhi was shocked to hear her name. had she also been involved? Had she with Sumit planned the trap for her?

"But you don't think aunt did it. She doesn't even know that the girls working with her had been involved in the flesh trade too. She is a very tough woman; she is ready to die for the sake of helping someone." Sumit revealed the reality of aunt making Juhi was satisfied that her trust had been restored.

"Let me leave you home."

Sumit said. Juhi stood up while pressing the mechanized notes tightly in her fist.

"Rain Basera Hotel & Resort", as soon as she came out, she had noticed the board out there. Hotel and resort does not mean office at all, was all she had understood.

All along the way back, the words of Sumit and her own engrossing thoughts within had been overlapping and confusing her. Sometimes, she would look at her fist with sweaty notes, and sometimes she looked at the condition of her house. She was doing this, would her parents, siblings never come to know? She felt as if they had come to know everything and all of them had been looking at her in sheer hatred.

"I know how I had protected you from the evil eyes till now, but you! Why did you do this, Juhi?" She imagined her mother crying, while her brothers and sister gazing at her with utter abhorrence in their eyes.

Juhi was shocked. Her dream, which she had seen clearly with open eyes, could possibly turn into reality. "Leave me here. I have to buy something from the market." She got off Sumit's car shortly before the slum area.

Sumit smiled like a cruel fowler.

"I will wait outside the colony tomorrow," he said and moved the car forward.

Juhi stood there for a while and then slowly walked towards her colony. Many doubts emerged like a cloud of thick fog. While she had decided to listen to Sumit and proceed with the proposal of sin to create a paradise of material wealth for her family members and loved ones.

However, on the other hand, she was not ready to accept it. Despite being from a poor household, she did not have the courage to turn her back to the moral impressions that her parents had given to her since childhood.

While Juhi slowly kept moving each step, lost in her own thoughts, she heard the loud shouting voice of a man. She was standing in front of an unfenced building. Many laborers were working there. A woman laborer, with her half-torn *dhoti*, somehow managed to cover her body and her honor, was up to feed her child crying out of hunger, when the manager employed by the contractor shouted.

"You need a complete salary but don't want to do any work. When you tell them anything, they try to make an excuse for a small child to avoid work. Sometimes it is on a pretext of feeding the child and at other times and excuse of the child being sick."

The man on the pretext of scolding the half-naked laborer was staring at her naked body with the lewd expression in his eyes.

That incident, where the laborer women could spook

his eyes and spat on him with hatred, reminded Juhi of the entire incident that had happened to her that day.

"You bloody bastard." The laborer woman abused him in a shouting manner.

"If I give him everything, then he will give me my salary even without any work. When I did not come to this, he did not allow me to feed my own hungry child even after so much hard work." She weaned the child from her breast and lifted the vessel.

When Juhi heard this conversation, the clouds of doubts started fading and she overcame her dilemma. She was an illiterate laborer, whose husband probably might also be working somewhere in the same construction site. Where could she have complained about any injustice happening to her? At the site, she was resolute to protect her honor from the prying eyes of the contractor and had refused to tolerate his excesses.

Had she wanted, she could have lived a life of comfort by fulfilling the wishes of the contractor. In that case, she would not have to do any work and would have properly raised her child. However, she had not chosen that path. Despite being from the very lower and resource less section of the society, she still possessed the courage to save her honor. Despite working on wages, she could maintain the life of uprightness without any scar, any guilt feeling. Then why could not she do it? Juhi had been educated until class tenth. She had also been doing a respectable job at aunt's place. At least, Sumit had already taught her to operate her fingers on the computer. She could now work harder. She would pick up typing work at some office. She would do anything but certainly would not resort to what Sumit had desired from her.

All the illusions that she had within herself had

disappeared. Although, it was dusk, Juhi's life had brightened up with a renewed light like the fresh morning rays. She put the entire money in the hand of that laborer woman and quickly got out of there.

Instead of going home, she moved towards Nimmo Aunt's house. She had to go to the police station with her to teach Sumit a lesson, so that he would not dare crush any other Juhi ever.